Language Policy

Although we may not be aware of it, the way we use language in our daily lives is regulated by both overt and covert means. *Language Policy* delves into the hidden agendas which operate behind language policy, examining the decisions surrounding language use and emphasizing the effects of these decisions and potential constraints on different groups within society.

Drawing on examples from language policies in the United States, Israel, and United Kingdom, Elana Shohamy introduces a broad view of language policy, from explicit use by governments, educational bodies and the media, to implicit and covert uses. The book reveals and examines the specific mechanisms used to create language policy such as language laws, educational policies, language tests, citizenship requirements, propaganda and even educational material.

This critical exploration of language policy concludes with arguments for a more democratic and open approach to language policy and planning, suggesting strategies for resistance, activism and ways to protect the linguistic rights of individuals and groups.

Language Policy will be of interest to students from a variety of disciplines including linguistics, education, sociology, political science, philosophy and communication studies.

Elana Shohamy is a professor of Language Education, Tel Aviv University. Her previous publications include *The Power of Tests*, 2001.

Language Policy

Hidden agendas and new approaches

Elana Shohamy

Routledge
Taylor & Francis Group

LONDON AND NEW YORK

First published 2006
by Routledge
2 Park Square, Milton Park, Abingdon, Oxon OX14 4RN

Simultaneously published in the USA and Canada
by Routledge
270 Madison Ave, New York, NY 10016

Routledge is an imprint of the Taylor & Francis Group

© 2006 Elana Shohamy

Typeset in Sabon by RefineCatch Ltd, Bungay, Suffolk

British Library Cataloguing in Publication Data
A catalogue record for this book is available from the British Library

Library of Congress Cataloging in Publication Data
Shohamy, Elana Goldberg.
   Language policy : hidden agendas and new approaches / Elana
Shohamy.
      p. cm.
1. Language policy.   2. Language and education.   3. Language
awareness.   I. Title.
P119.3.S5   2005
306.44'9—dc22   2005007298

ISBN10: 0–415–32864–0 (hbk)
ISBN10: 0–415–32865–9 (pbk)

ISBN13: 9–78–0–415–32864–7 (hbk)
ISBN13: 9–78–0–415–32865–4 (pbk)

. . . so Ima, why don't you just call it the hidden agendas of language policy?

(Orlee Shohamy, September 3, 2000)

Orlee, this book is for you.
It is through "languaging",
in all its forms, that you live.
It is through "languaging"
that our deep connection and profound love continue,
beyond time, space and even death.

(March 2005)

Contents

Epilogue: Language as a free commodity   167

Figures and tables

Figures

Tables

Dedication to Orlee

Languaging with Orlee

The book is dedicated to Orlee, who has been an observer, an expresser and a user of language in all its forms – words, gestures, body, rhythm, pace, dance, expressions, books, stories and . . . endless conversations.

Orlee grew up in languages; she was born into English, immersed in Hebrew and languaged in multi-codes. She was schooled in English until the age of six, acquired Hebrew in grade 1, and was convinced she had lost all her English. Some labelled her "semi-lingual" and studied her "language attrition", but, in fact, she was "multi-coding": Hebrew, English and much more. On her return to Israel, having spent a year in Toronto, she was convinced she had lost all her Hebrew, but she continued to "multi-code", using language in all its forms. When she became a writer, closely observing, feeling, touching and weaving through the lives of young people in New York City, she did it via English, but also through multi-coding. Orlee lived in languages, through languages and with languages – words, worlds, music, dance, stories, books, jokes, rollerblading, laughter, observations and . . . talk, talk, talk.

It happened on January 11, 2001; Orlee was born on September 3, 1975. What is so amazing (Orlee's favorite word) is how Orlee continues to "language", to "multi-code" through laughter, tears, happiness, memories, longing, experiences, cries, observations, conversation and her own writings. We continue to language, never stopping, through objects we see, people we observe, interpretations we make, episodes we laugh about, books we read, injustices we protest against, scenery we view, ideas we challenge, pictures we take, routes we ride along, thoughts we share, opinions we express, issues we argue about, people we love, food we eat, events we celebrate and mourn, songs we hear, places where we continue to bike and rollerblade.

Our language has no "fixed words", no full sentences, no pragmatic rules, but it does have the most beautiful melody; it is a true dialogue (and a trilogue when Daphna is around). It is deep, profound and meaningful. It is a new language we are inventing as we go along in this continuous, infinite journey; we are learning it right now as we go along to new places, new experiences, new feelings, new energies, new sorrows, new pain, new laughter, new emotions, new ideas, new memories, new dreams and even a new future. It is dynamic and energetic, and it takes us to places we have never been before; sometimes it is in death, other times it is in life, but most often it is in both. It is our world, a free and private world, with no boundaries, a new world that only we understand. We continue to shape it as we ride along, together, in this deepest connection of past, present, future and everything in between.

Preface

This book had a very difficult, almost impossible birth. I was sure I would never be able to write or think again, sitting in front of the computer immersed in sadness, pain and the feeling of "an end". It was *through* Orlee and the beautiful people around me that I was able to continue. Daphna (Shohamy) and Yoram (Shohamy); Yair (Avgar), Merrill (Swain), Tim (McNamara), Ayala, Yaakov, Sara (Sussman), Hana (Kendel), Tamar (Levin), Dubi (Pekelman), Alastair (Pennycook), Bernard (Spolsky), Ellen (Bialystok), Benny (Hary), David (Nevo), Andrew (Cohen), Martin (Wein), Jim (Lantolf), Mirjam (Hadar), Ofra (Inbar), Dotan (Leshem), Navit (Nave), Smadar (Donitsa-Schmidt), Jonathan (Mozes), Louisa (Semlyen), each in their own way, provided the best friendship, care, support, understanding, tolerance and just good, happy and lively company in very sad times. I truly and sincerely owe these people my life, for providing endless love, a place to share pain, to open up, not to escape but to face reality head-on and to realize that there are still many reasons to continue.

Special thanks and love to you, Daphna; we have walked together, hand in hand, heart in heart in this awful experience of sorrow and pain, but also along with Orlee, in this continual struggle to try to make a life again as we still keep asking: "Did it really happen or is it just a bad dream?" You, Daphna, know so very well what it means to try to focus, concentrate, write, read, work, research and seek happy moments in this dark world of desperately seeking Orlee, our symbiotic "other". Thanks for your warmth, intimacy and understanding, and for sharing the battles of living with sadness and appreciating beauty, energy and meaning, at the same time.

And thanks to my students, the best rewards in the academic world, eager to learn, discuss, argue, challenge and provide the most valuable fountains of knowledge. The students of the Language Policy class of Winter 2001, on the first day I returned to work, insisted I tell them about Orlee, who she was, what she did, how she looked, what she dreamed about and hoped for. The opportunity to connect with students on an open and equal basis is unique. Special thanks to the students of the Critical Language Pedagogy class of Fall 2003, where we shared our deepest identities, each one of us being "the other" in a different way, whether a language victim or a language "winner", marginalized or advantaged, in the context of a struggle against imposing policies, discrimination, rights, fear, equality, voice, identity, connections, boundaries, recognition, injustices, protests, stereotypes and barriers. It was about experiencing critical theories in real life – with Russian immigrants, Orthodox Jews, Muslim women, and "the powerful majority", where we learned what it is all about. Revealing these issues in the Israeli context, a society where all factors interact but also divide along every imagined variable – language, gender, ethnicity, religion, politics, left, right, natives, immigrants, loyalty, the military, patriotism, territories, occupation, nationalism and peace, all embedded in a context of rage, fear, tension, discrimination and protest. But there is also the possibility of conversation, discussion, and dialogue. The visit of Judith Butler to Tel Aviv University in December of that year provided validation of many of the issues discussed in class. It was in this class that the following conversations took place: an Arab student said: "What I hate most is when people who talk to me discover after ten minutes that I have Arabic accent in my Hebrew and then they ask: 'Are you an Arab?', 'Are you really an Arab?', 'Are you sure you are an Arab?' . . . and it is then that the conversation stops and they walk away. My accent gives me away." Another Arab student (in response to the above said): "This is why I cover my head. Like these people who talk to me know from the beginning who I am; yes, I am an Arab, I don't have to wait for my accent to reveal it, I am performing it right away, yes, I am an Arab, and a proud Arab." Or the student from the former USSR who has been living in Israel for ten years, and always gets the following reaction to her response to "Where are you from?" and when she answers: "Israel", it is followed by: "But where are you *really* from?" Or this from another student: "Now I will be honest with you all; here in this class we say all these nice things about tolerance, equality, protest, co-existence." Then, turning to one of the Arab students in the class, he said "But I will be honest, I am afraid of you, I see you committing suicide on my TV in my own living room, how can I not be afraid of you? I am overridden by fear".

In this class, thoughts and emotions were free, open and ready to be challenged; we each learned about language stereotypes and discrimination, but most of all we learned "to wear the glasses", that enabled us "to see" language discrimination, language identities, language marginalization and to critique it and protest against it head-on.

Finally, a reflection about writing after a tragedy: writing a book after the terrible event of the death of a daughter should be impossible. It makes no sense. How is it possible to focus on a single issue, on a topic, while dealing with such meaningful things as life and death? I could easily identify with the main character in Paul Auster's *The Book of Illusion* (2002), trying to find a meaning to life after the death of his wife and two children in an airplane crash: "My outward purpose was to study and master the films of Hector Mann, but the truth was that I was teaching myself how to concentrate, training myself how to think about one thing and one thing only. It was the life of a monomaniac, but it was the only way I could live now without crumbling to pieces" (p. 27).

There was just too big a gap between life and language; bridging it was not possible, it did not make sense. But it was at this very point that I began to see the connection between the two: when it comes to language one can see language in every life and life in every language. Life and language; language and life. It is "languaging" through writing and writing through language that has given me a way out of the "monomania". Language is just everywhere; its connections and effects are universal. I see all things through language and within language, the world, society and my personal life. I began to see again, an ability to see in the way expressed by Italo Calvino (1985) (whose words appear throughout the book): "it is enough to wait for one of those lucky coincidences to occur when the world wants to look and be looked at in the same instant and Mr. Palomar happens to be going by. Or, rather, Mr. Palomar does not even have to wait, because these things happen only when you are not awaiting them" (p. 115).

Introduction

While language is dynamic, personal, free and energetic, with no defined boundaries, there have always been those groups and individuals who want to control and manipulate it in order to promote political, social, economic and personal ideologies. Thus, language is used to create group membership ("us/them"), to demonstrate inclusion or exclusion, to determine loyalty or patriotism, to show economic status ("haves/have nots") and classification of people and personal identities. Further, language is used as a form of control, by imposing the use of certain languages in certain ways (correct, pure, native-like, grammatical, etc.) or even governing the right to use it.

Language policy falls in the midst of these manipulations and battles, between language ideology and practice. It is through a variety of overt and covert *mechanisms*, used mostly (but not exclusively) by those in authority, that languages are being manipulated and controlled so as to affect, create and perpetuate "de facto" language policies, i.e., language practices. These mechanisms are used overtly and covertly in conversations and negotiations as well as in fierce battles in order to exercise control over the language space. Thus, in order to obtain meaningful understanding of the "real" language policy, there is a need to deduce it through the languages that are created as consequences of these mechanisms. The mechanisms, it is argued, are in fact language policy tools. The effects and consequences of these mechanisms can often lead to violations of democratic processes and personal/language rights. It is the existence of these very mechanisms and their effects on covertly creating actual language policy that make up hidden agendas, unknown to the public. It will be shown how a naïve mechanism such as a street sign, a school language test, a school language policy or a citizenship test create the actual practices, often with no official declarations. Once awareness of this process is evident, there is a need to engage in linguistic activism and resistance via these mechanisms, whereby language policy, in this expanded view, is negotiated and discussed. Language policy, therefore, needs to be understood in a broader perspective that includes mechanisms, policies and practices as well as the set of negotiations, conversations and battles that take place among them. Yet, it is of special importance to note the power of governments and large corporations who have direct access to power structures of society such as educational systems, laws, sanctions taxes and penalties and can therefore manipulate language policies through the mechanisms more easily. It will also be shown how awareness of the expanded perspective and the mechanisms can offer a channel of negotiation and protection of rights.

This book begins with an expanded view of language, arguing that it is personal, open, free, dynamic, creative and constantly evolving. This concept of language does not have the boundaries of language x or language y, since it spreads beyond words and is manifested through a variety of multi-modal representations and different forms of "languaging". Yet, in spite of such views, language is commonly perceived as closed, stagnated and rule-bound. Language is manipulated, as it is used as a symbol for unity, loyalty, patriotism, inclusion and legitimacy, especially by various collective groups. Language policy (LP) falls in the midst of major ideological debates about uniformity and diversity, purity and variations, nativity and "foreign-ness" as manifested in policy documents stating "officiality", language laws, standards, etc., in an effort to affect actual language practices in accordance with these ideological agendas. It is argued here for the need to examine and interpret LPs in broader ways than just policies as it is shown how these language policies need to be interpreted through a variety of mechanisms that are used by all groups, but especially by those in authority, to impose, perpetuate and create language policies, far beyond those that are declared in official policies. Thus, the study of LP should not be limited to formal, declared and official policies but rather to the study of the powerful mechanisms that are used in most societies nowadays to create and perpetuate "de facto" language policies and practices. The mechanisms discussed in this book include language education policies, language tests and language in the public space; it is through these policy devices that "real" policies are created. Evidence from a number of studies (e.g., academic achievements of immigrants, the imposition of unrealistic views of language correctness and monolingualism, various types of accommodations, types of language tests, linguistic landscapes) is used to demonstrate these effects. The main claim is that the real LP of a political and social entity should not be observed only through declared policy statements, but rather through a variety of devices that are used to perpetuate language practices, often in covert and implicit ways. Moreover, these devices, which on the surface may not be viewed as policy devices, are strongly affecting the actual policies, given their direct effects on language practice. Thus, it is only through the observations of the effects of these very devices that the real language policy of an entity can be understood and interpreted. It is proposed that a new and expanded view of language policy be adopted to incorporate these policy tools as, implicitly and covertly, they contribute to actual policies and language realities. It will be shown how such mechanisms are used by all members of society, from individuals to social and political groups. Yet, it is especially those in authority who have access to power and sanctions and therefore tend to use these mechanisms as a powerful way of manipulating state ideologies. It calls for a critical view of language policy to show how it leads to actual practices promoting political ideologies of the nation-state that perpetuate language purity, create language hierarchies, marginalize and exclude groups, and thus lead to the violation of personal rights and undemocratic practices. Finally, it is shown how the mechanisms can in fact be used in constructive ways as part of a dynamic process of multiple discourses for negotiations and battling existing language policies. Such views could lead to the creation of inclusive policies, which are open and dynamic, and where policy and practice closely interact and contribute to a democracy of inclusion, the protection of personal rights, along with strategies of language awareness and activism.

This book begins by viewing language in broader terms as an open, free, dynamic, creative and constantly evolving process with no defined boundaries, involving multi-modal representations and different forms of "languaging" (Chapter 1). Yet, language is still view as a closed, stagnated and rule-bound entity. This is because language is used in manipulative, oppressive and imposing ways, especially in nation-states where language has become a tool for creating, imposing and perpetuating collective identities, homogenous and hegemonic ideologies, unified standards and categories of inclusion and exclusion. Thus, the use of certain languages, in specific manners, with specific accents, becomes a marker of group membership, categorization, loyalty, rejection and acceptance. Such uses of language have obtained the support of linguists who replaced language descriptions with language prescriptions, i.e., how languages *should* be used. Terms such as native language, native accent, language correctness, mother tongue, grammar rules, standard spelling and foreign languages were all used to enforce differentiation and categorization. It is especially in the new nation-state, which recognizes the existence of diverse groups of immigrants, indigenous, global, transnational and others, that language continues to play a major role in the midst of battles between authoritative groups seeking to sustain homogeneity, hegemony and monolingualism for the sake of national identity and the power of other groups demanding recognition of their language and cultural diversity, representation, participation, a voice and rights (Chapter 2).

Given these battles, language policy (LP) plays a key role in perpetuating language behaviors and ensuring that ideologies turn into practice. Yet, LP as defined in the book is not limited to official and declared documents which often pay lip service to inclusive ideologies, but incorporates a variety of mechanisms, some overt, others covert and hidden, that serve as major devices that affect and create de facto language policies. It is through the manifestations of these mechanisms that the actual and real language policies can be revealed as they are used to create real policies. The real LP, then, needs to be examined broadly, through the effects of the different mechanisms (Chapter 3).

Part II discusses the mechanisms that are used to perpetuate language ideology and practice and shows how they affect practices using a variety of data. It specifically addresses declared policies: language education policies, language tests and language in the public space including ideology, myths, propaganda and coercion. Each of these mechanisms is discussed, and its effect on actual policy is examined as well as the impact on democratic principles and personal rights (Chapters 4–7).

Part III examines the consequences of the mechanisms on LP in terms of democratic principles and personal rights associated with languages (Chapters 8 and 9). It shows how too often LP, along with these mechanisms, violates democratic principles and personal rights, in the form of impositions and exclusions that prevent people from having full participation in and the benefit of a democratic society. It then argues for the use of democracy of inclusion as a principle that can be followed in multilingual and multicultural societies, consisting of mutual understandings and negotiations claiming that the different languages and people contribute to the wealth of democratic societies (Taylor, 1998). It suggests ways of applying critical views that examine the definitions of language and their consequence in terms of democratic practices and personal rights. It also shows how the mechanisms can play a major role in negotiating policies and practices and where policy and practice can affect each other so that language is viewed in more open ways and where policies are negotiated and discussed. The mechanisms, then, can serve as arenas and tools in this multiple discourse of negotiating language policies and promoting democracy of inclusion and personal rights through awareness and activism.

The Epilogue discusses the unique traits of "language" as a free commodity that can be used and shaped by all. Unlike other biological markers, language represents freedom of speech, choices and uses with unlimited resources that need to be protected from impositions as part of personal freedom and democratic choice.

The sub-title of the book, *Hidden agendas and new approaches*, has a number of meanings. It refers to the way that language, with its open, dynamic and fluid nature, is manipulated for political and ideological agendas, turning it into a closed, fixed, stagnated, pure, hegemonic, standard and oppressive system. This phenomenon is not known to the public, who have been indoctrinated into perceiving language as a closed, correct, standard and pure system, an agenda moved by politicians, linguists and educationalists. But the term "hidden" also refers to affecting and perpetuating language policies through the variety of mechanisms discussed in this book. It is the effects and consequences of the mechanisms on practice, on personal rights and democratic practices, that are considered the "hidden agendas". It is the effect of a mechanism such as a street sign or a language test that delivers a direct message as to the real language policy, beyond declared statements.

There is no awareness as to the effect of these mechanisms (i.e., language tests) on language policies as they are not perceived as policy devices that have strong effects on these policies. Yet, they manage to affect policy in very powerful ways as those affected have no choice but to comply.

The case of Israel is used throughout the book to illustrate and support many of the arguments. Beyond my own familiarity with this language context, my having spent most of my academic life there, Israel offers a unique language context. Hebrew, a language that was not used as a vernacular for centuries, was "revived" at the end of the nineteenth century and throughout the twentieth century. It has become the main language of the Jews in Palestine, then Israel. Hebrew is now used in all domains of public life, a phenomenon that receives attention and admiration from ideologues, politicians but especially from linguistic communities eager to go through a similar process for their own languages (e.g., Irish, Welsh, Catalan, Maori, etc.). Yet, a major component of my own work in the past few years has been devoted to criticizing the manner in which the revival was carried out, focusing on the cost of this policy to other languages as well as the discrimination, coercion, exclusion, impositions and violation of rights, in the name of unity and cohesion. The efforts of sustaining "the miracle" continue today with similar impositions, as is described in various places in the book. The second reason is the political reality of Israel being a "classic" nation-state with aspirations for common ideology, history, culture, religion, solidarity, unity, patriotism and loyalty of Jews "returning to their homeland"; a situation that is reinforced by "the Arab-Israeli conflict". Israel thus provides a context where battles, contradiction and negotiations between aspired homogenous and hegemonic ideologies and the multi-ethnic and diverse realities as well as a strong urge for globalization are all happening simultaneously. This situation offers a special opportunity to study language policy in a very complex reality.

Part I

Language, manipulations, policy

Language policy (LP) is viewed in this book in a broad way, beyond statements about policy but rather through a variety of mechanisms that create de facto language policies and practices. Yet, an expanded view of LP requires also a broader view of language itself, from a closed and finite system to a living organism, which is personal, dynamic, open, energetic and creative, spreading beyond fixed boundaries towards freedom of expression. Language is commonly viewed by policy makers as a closed and finite system, as it is often used as a symbolic tool for the manipulation of political, social, educational and economic agendas, especially in the context of political entities such as the nation-state. It is in these contexts that languages are used for categorizing people, creating group memberships, identities, hierarchies and a variety of other forms of imposition.

Chapter 1 expands the notion of language from a narrow and closed entity to one that is open, personal, free, constantly evolving, taking different colours, shapes and forms by its different users, in a variety of situations, locations and points in time. Accordingly, language has no fixed boundaries as "language x" or "language y", since it spreads beyond words and other linguistic markers. Steiner (1998) notes that "language, any language . . . has in it these infinite resources of being" (p. 96). "In analogy with the organic, it undergoes incessant change. Languages live and die. They manifest epochs of enrichment, of acquisition, of political-cultural-literary dominance, and epochs of diminution and decay" (p. 96). On the individual level, languages represent forms of open expression, creations and interactions. Language, then, is a living organism that has no fixed or discrete markers, no imposed definitions of correct or incorrect, native or non-native or other artificial categories that are meant to control, limit and impose on people's external rules of interaction and use with regard to fixed notions of how they should act and express themselves. Rather, language is personal and unique and varies from one person to another, so that dictating to people how to use language in terms of accent, grammar and lexicon, etc., can be seen as a form of personal intrusion and manipulation. It is argued here that the imposition of specific linguistic behaviors, criteria and sets of orders, from outside bodies, represents a type of indoctrination of individual freedom by those who attempt to regulate people and their behaviors.

When viewed in general terms, language expands beyond its traditional boundaries towards the legitimacy of infinite mixes, combinations, hybrids and fusions. It embodies infinite devices, modes and codes of expression, which are useful for successful and effective communication and inter-action. Such devices include endless forms of creation and expression as well as a variety of modes of representation, such as music, dance, art, images, icons, visuals, clothes, architecture, gestures, silence and a variety of other "non-linguistic" or "non-verbal" markers. The way people use language varies, as language takes different shapes and forms for different people in different contexts and at different points in time. These uses represent broad and open means of expression, which can be free and creative. The term "languaging" is used in Chapter 1 to refer to language as an integral and natural component of interaction, communication and construction of meanings.

Chapter 2 shows how such views of language are in contrast to existing, widespread and commonly accepted views, often supported by linguists, where language is perceived as a closed and limited entity, governed by fixed boundaries and controlled by strict rules of correctness in terms of grammar, lexicon, spelling, syntax, discourse and accent. These views per-petuate the notions of language as "good vs. bad", "accurate vs. inaccur-ate", "acceptable vs. unacceptable", "native vs. non-native", "standard vs. non-standard", "official vs. unofficial", "grammatical vs. ungrammatical", "multilingual vs. semi-lingual", "oral vs. written". Similarly, terms such as "inter-language" and "fossilizations" represent categories that are socially constructed and create hierarchies of people and groups, i.e, "good" vs. "bad" language. Chapter 2 further argues that by using such notions, lan-guage is manipulated for political, social and economic purposes as it is used to dictate, regulate and create set orders of hierarchies in the name of clas-sifying and categorizing those who use the language in "the right way" in relation to those who do not. It will be claimed that such a view only serves as a device to differentiate people, to control their personal freedom and to perpetuate homogenous group memberships, loyalty, patriotism and the dif-ferentiation of the "haves" from the "have-nots". This way of using language has its origins in the notion of the nation-state, and other political bodies, where language is associated with a given political entity and becomes the major tool for defining and legitimizing people as members of "the nation" or "the group" or other forms of belonging. Such language manipulations continue in the current era where language continues to be used as a symbol of integration and belonging to the nation. While most nations nowadays, more than ever before, consist of diverse groups – immigrants, indigenous populations, transnationals and others, it is primarily through language that the battles between homogenous ideologies, hegemony and power vs. diversity, voice, representation and inclusion continue to take place.

Language policy, as argued in Chapter 3, is the major tool through which such battles and manipulations take place. It serves as a device to perpetuate and impose language behaviors in accordance with the national, political, social and economic agendas. It represents the wishes of groups in authority to promote the agendas of protecting collective identities, promoting globalization, stating "who is in charge", creating "imagined communities" and maintaining social and political orders. Yet, at times, mostly through the use of official and declared documents, language policies are also used to provide a means of expression, recognition and representation. However, it is argued in Chapter 3 and throughout the rest of the book that the "real" "de facto" language policy occurs through a variety of additional devices, or mechanisms, beyond the official policies that are included in language policy statement and language laws. Thus, the true and real language policy needs to be observed, understood and interpreted, *not* through these declared and official documents, but rather through a variety of these mechanisms, or policy devices, which are used to influence, create and perpetuate the actual policies. It is through these policy devices, discussed in detail in Part II of the book, that policy decisions are made and imposed, and through which ideologies turn into practices. Thus, the term "policy", referring mostly to declared and conscious statements, needs to include these policy devices in order to capture a fuller picture of language policy. Conscious decisions, surrounded by the different types of mechanisms, overt and covert, explicit and implicit, need to be included in a broader and more valid definition of language policy.

1 Expanding language

The universe as regular and ordered cosmo or as a chaotic proliferation. The universe perhaps finite but countless, unstable within its borders, which discloses other universes within itself. The universe, collection of celestial bodies, nebulas, fine dust, force fields, intersections of fields, collection of collections.

(Calvino, 1985, p. 33)

Language as individual, personal and interactive

Language is open, dynamic, energetic, constantly evolving and personal. It has no fixed boundaries, but is rather made of hybrids and endless varieties resulting from language being creative, expressive, interactive, contact- and dialogue-based, debated, mediated and negotiated.

Language is a unique phenomenon as it is personal and individual and varies drastically from one user to another. "Indeed, no two individuals speak exactly the same language" (Dawson, 2001, p. 1). Words are there, yet the choice of words and forms of expression differ among individuals, as they are used in different ways by different individuals at different points in time, in different contexts and domains, and on different topics. Individuals constantly make choices, consciously or not, with regard to how to use language, through the selection of words, grammatical structures and other linguistic features. This is similar to the way that individuals make choices with regard to other things in life, such as what to say and to whom, whom to associate with, what to do, what to wear and where to go.

When it comes to language, people have a large degree of freedom of expression as they can make choices with regard to intonation, speed, space, syntax, grammar, lexicon, length of sentences, repetition and tone, as well as a variety of content and topics. Individuals make decisions about the use of language according to what suits them best in given contexts as language is personal and individual. Some of these choices originate from the individuals themselves; others are influenced by the surrounding environment, especially by what people perceive as appropriate and convenient, as well as by a variety of contextual considerations. Languages portray the diverse personalities of different people.

The uses of language then, express and represent the unique individuality and personality of language users as they attempt to communicate and create meanings in ways that suit them best. Thus, when language is used for mediation as part of a social activity, each person has his or her own personal and unique ways and styles of using language with regard to content, topics and ideas. Even when similar or identical ideas and topics are expressed by two people at the same time, they are likely to express these differently as a result of individual differences and humans being unique individuals; they do it "in their own ways". The result of using languages in such ways is the infinite varieties and versions of "personal and individual languages". These languages are so individual that they make outsiders identify and recognize individuals by their "language personalities" which consist of these unique features as they are represented in terms of voice, style, accent, intonation, lexicon, intonation, syntax, discourse and a variety of additional characteristics.

This unique "personal language" of individuals is captured by Steiner in a number of places. In *After Babel* (1975), he writes: "The fact that tens of thousands of different, mutually incomprehensible languages have been or are being spoken on our small planet is a graphic expression of the deeper-lying enigma of human individuality, of the bio-genetic and bio-social evidence that no two human beings are totally identical" (p. 48). He claims that language is so individual and personal that an act of translation is needed in order to communicate from one person to another. "The affair at Babel confirmed and externalized the never-ending task of the translator – it did not initiate it" (p. 48). Speech was necessary once humans started to use verbal codes rather than other semiotic devices, such as smell, gesture and pure tone. "Speech would be . . . immensely profitable but also reductive, partially narrowing evolutionary selection from a wider spectrum of semiotic possibilities. Once it was 'chosen' translation became inevitable" (p. 48). Accordingly, the "human being performs an act of translation, in the full sense of the word, when receiving a speech-message from any other human being" (p. 47). In his later book *Errata* (1998), Steiner argues that "No two languages, no two dialects or local idioms within a language, identify, designate, map their words in the same way" (p. 97). "To speak a language is to inhabit, to construct, to record a specific world-setting – a *mundanity* in the strong, etymological sense of the word. It is to occupy and traverse a singular landscape in time" (p. 97). Finally, he states: "We speak worlds" (p. 99).

Language is thus very personal, unique and uncontrollable as it manifests the diversity of human beings. In the same way that we cannot control other things about people such as appearance, colour of skin, height, behavior and thoughts, we cannot control the language that people use. Lippi-Green (1997) notes that policies attempting to ensure that everyone speaks the same languages and the same varieties are no more realistic than policies attempting to ensure that everyone should be of the same height. There is no difference between the inability to control what and how people use language and attempting to control how they look. The claim, therefore, that there should be strict rules of how languages should be used cannot be substantiated; those who claim it overlook the unique and specific features of individuals and personal languages by trying to force people into narrow and closed boundaries.

It is the unique aspect of people that makes personal languages creative, fluid, dynamic, energetic, changing, fluctuating and varied in terms of functions, places, contexts, personality, age, gender, groups, cultures, history and individuality. If language is viewed as a reflection of the uniqueness of the individual and is a personal choice it also implies that there cannot and should not be "one correct" way of using it. One wonders therefore about the need to monopolize and impose rules on personal choices, personal characteristics and personal expressions and to make decisions about language use *for* and *about* people.

While language is personal, the free choice of an individual, it is also used for communication and creation as human beings are social creatures who use language in social contexts. Thus, they strive to maximize the efficiency of communication and are in constant search for common language elements that will facilitate such communication in the most efficient way. These are expressed in approximation, negotiations and accommodations of the languages of "the others" in terms of accents, lexical items, syntax, shared content, comprehension and other features that are instrumental to the process of facilitating communication. Ways of communication were examined by sociolinguists such as Labov with regard to accommodations of accent, pronunciation, lexicon and other features. These are especially noted in situations when language users share biological connections, geographical space, history, close social relations and a variety of other common features that cause their languages to become similar, so that communication is performed most efficiently. Thus, while language is personal, individual and unique, it is also social, dynamic and changing as common features are shared, negotiated and created by individuals as part of the need to maximize the quality of the communication and interaction.

Further, in relation to the socio-cultural theories of Vygotsky, language is also viewed as a tool of mediation, as part of mental functioning; it is language as well as other sign systems that are primary to human behavior, yet they cannot be understood in isolation from the social and physical environment in which they occur. Thus, "context" ranges from the immediate face-to-face setting of the individual person to the wider culture and society. A basic assumption is that an action is mediated and cannot be separated from the social context in which it is carried out. Human actions, on both the social and individual planes, are mediated by tools and signs. Thus, the child learns to speak because of the desire to communicate, and later language is used to represent thoughts. The primary function of language is social, for communication leads to a view of literacy as a communication, a form of using printed signs as the media for sharing meaning. Language also serves to mediate between environmental stimuli and individual response in school situations. Thus, language mediates thoughts and actions (Vygotsky, 1978; 1981).

Language as dynamic and evolving

All languages and cultures are continuously in the process of becoming, in recreating meanings. There are no "finite" and static languages as they constantly evolve as a result of language contact and interaction among people and groups, in relation to historical, political, and economic factors. As part of the effort to make meaningful connections and interactions, new language elements are created, used and exchanged.

Like any other element of our surroundings, languages tend to change over time: they develop, expand, shrink, borrow and mix as part of the dynamic processes of human interaction; they change and evolve and assume different colors, shapes and forms. Oral language is especially colorful as it has fewer restrictions than written documents with regard to how it should be used. Oral language therefore is manifested in terms of freedom of expression with regard to how it is used. Written languages change too, but at a slower rate as they often follow strict rules, restrictions and conventions in terms of how they *should* be used as there are more official documents that monitor it such as dictionaries, grammars and syllabuses. Thus, spoken languages and their varieties tend to emerge and evolve in more rapid ways with the infinite number of spoken dialects and varieties used by diverse communities. Such groups often share common social, political, biological, geographical and professional backgrounds influenced by factors related to age, gender, region and other features that affect how languages are used, resulting in endless forms of language varieties. In fact, all groups that come into contact with others, over time, develop their own unique "codes", "dialects" or "languages" that emerge through these interactions and shared knowledge, leading to the development of unique and collective identities. Thus, women of certain classes, of certain backgrounds, of certain ages, of certain regions, tend to develop "their own unique language". Likewise, youths, families and other collective groups that are engaged in close social and mutual interactions develop their own "languages". They constantly and regularly create and negotiate languages that share similar and unique features with others. Thus, the languages of individuals as well as of collective groups constantly evolve through a dynamic process.

Such changes also occur as a result of a variety of factors such as the media, the telephone and the more recent developments in electronic communication that make use of the Internet. Forms of literacy, then, are constantly changing as a result of technological changes affecting devices of communication, resulting in a move from writing letters on paper to writing electronic letters. These devices affect both the structure and the content of languages just as the telephone transformed the ways people communicated orally, removing the need for them to be geographically present. In these cases "different" types of languages evolve, both in terms of structure and content. Such language changes occur as part of a changing world, changing times and changing technologies.

Attitudes to specific languages and their uses also change and evolve over people's lifetimes, especially in multilingual societies. In these situations people tend to use different languages not only in different contexts, but also at different times of their lives, with different people, for different purposes, in different political and social realities, a phenomenon that is true of all human beings and is especially noticed among immigrants and indigenous groups who continually move from one place to another.

If languages are dynamic, energetic, creative and changing, questions need to be raised with regard to whether they need to be protected and if it is at all realistic and feasible to do so. Imposing on people certain uses of language may be viewed as a form of oppression and monopolization. In other words, if languages are personal, evolving and changing, it also means that issues such as "language correctness" and "language purity" and "language policy" may not be relevant. Forcing people to use languages in certain ways can also be viewed as a form of oppression as it is clear that "the correct way" is only a way used by certain individuals and groups. The view of language correctness and language standards are in complete opposition to the claims made about the nature of language.

It is therefore important to note the continuous battles taking place regarding language correctness between emerging new language varieties that are constantly being created vs. those who oppose them and seek to maintain languages as they are used at certain times by certain people and following certain prescribed rules. The latter resent changes in languages while seeking to maintain and preserve language, viewing such changes as "inappropriate", "bad", "wrong" and "corruptions". These varieties are positioned in comparisons with "official" languages, which are referred to as the "better" languages, often labeled "good", "correct", "standard" and "pure". The process that often occurs is that groups in power and authority take measures to ensure that "their" language varieties are maintained and preserved while these "new" varieties are erased, eradicated and stigmatized. The prestigious languages are recorded in dictionaries, text-books and other formal texts and are viewed as good models that are here to stay while "the other" varieties are rejected and forbidden from use, especially in educational systems. A case in point is the phenomenon of second- and even first-generation immigrants. With time, the language they develop is a mixture of their first language and the language of the place they have immigrated to as part of a natural evolution of contact. Yet, this language is not accepted by the dominant society and is perceived as "corrupted", "polluted", especially by native speakers. A similar situation occurs with those termed "indigenous", who continue to use languages other than the dominant majority languages.

In the same way, if we accept the notion that languages are dynamic, energetic, evolving and fluid, even their phasing out (often termed death) is a natural phenomenon of change which can also be viewed as an integral part of the evolutionary process of "change".

Crossing the fixed language boundaries

If language is viewed in such dynamic terms, languages cannot be viewed as fixed and closed systems capable of being placed in closed boxes. Such fixity is in opposition to the notion of languages as living and dynamic organisms resulting from interactions and the effects of a variety of factors. Regarding the language of bilinguals Brutt-Griffler (2004) notes that "Far from being monolinguals in two languages, as it were, they carve out their own space as *bilinguals* . . ." An increasing body of evidence shows that they do not use language the way monolinguals do. "Bilinguals simply do not obey the rules set out for them . . ." and "They refuse to hold their two (or more) languages as distinct, disconnected systems". (p. 93).

The need to cross traditional linguistic boundaries is noted by a number of scholars in the field of applied linguistics who are critical of traditional views of language. Pennycook (2004) states that ". . . the moment has arrived to argue that the language concept too has served its time" (p. 2) and that the ". . . over-determined sense of linguistic fixity, with its long ties to colonialism and linguistics needs to be profoundly questioned". The concept of language used by linguists was invented by European theorists to account for the diverse modes of articulation used by different human groups, but for all the supposed relativism of the notion of language, the concept's model of totality, basically organic in structure, is no different from the nineteenth-century concepts it replaced. "It is argued that the concept of language should at least no longer be tied to the notion of organic unity, traditional continuity and the enduring grounds of culture and locale." (p. 2).

Similarly, Makoni (1998) protests against the fixed categories of language and the fact that most language policies are organized according to discrete and defined boundaries such as *number* of languages and order of importance in strict and hermetically sealed units. He claims that viewing language in discrete ways is an invention of political entities such as nation-states and needs to be changed. It is particularly problematic in multilingual societies such as those of Africa, India and the Pacific islands, where there are no clear divisions among languages as they are embedded one within another. Makoni is especially critical of the language policy of South Africa which established eleven separate languages and argues that this way of looking at languages is "socially alienating and cognitively disadvantaging to the very people it is intended to serve" (2002, p. 1). These languages became separate and indigenous in colonial times as a result of "linguistic fixity" that colonialists and missionaries invented for bureaucratic convenience and are in contradiction to socio-historical facts. A more appropriate understanding, he proposes, would be in terms of a continuum acknowledging that there are considerable discrepancies between the official, standard version of the language and the one that is actually used. The use of languages as an organizing principle in societies, especially in the context of language policies and language education policies, is bound to exclude large sections of the population. In South Africa, in spite of the official status granted to the eleven languages, these represent only a proportion of the population while other languages and varieties are excluded.

Kubchandani (1997) confirms this view by claiming that "languages" when they are defined as closed entities represent a Western view that does not reflect reality in terms of contexts and entities where fluid multilingualism is an organic phenomenon. In India, languages blend with one another and users are generally not aware of when, and if, one language ends and another begins as they move from one language to another in natural and accepted ways. Kubchandani argues that questions such as "how many languages do you speak?" are irrelevant, in the same way that moving across genres and registers within "the same language" are natural and depend heavily on the sociolinguistic contexts such as home, work, school, family and intimacy.

It is therefore argued that fixed boundaries that are imposed on languages in terms of categorization with titles and names are artificial, given the endless number of varieties, hybrids, mixes and fusions. This is especially noticeable nowadays in the case of English with the endless number of varieties emerging from its use as a world language. English provides further evidence of crossing the fixed boundaries of language as it constantly creates new varieties, demonstrating the fluidity and flexibility of languages.

Something similar is happening in Europe, where languages are becoming closer and more similar to one another due to closer interaction. Gubbins and Holt (2002) point to the number of hybrids constantly emerging in Europe as a result of the breaking of political boundaries of the European market and the increase in communication among people speaking different languages. There is currently evidence of various types of hybrids as well as different varieties where people develop an ability to comprehend certain languages while speaking others. The endless number of spoken dialects in all languages but specifically of Arabic, German, Chinese and Italian point to this very phenomenon.

The fact that formal written languages are better preserved is rather a result of "purity movements" such as "standardization" as well as strict rules and regulations imposed by central bodies such as language academies, schools and other groups in authority imposing rules about what is "allowed" to be used in language and what is not. Yet, even written languages which are used for current communication via the electronic media manage to circumvent these strict regulations and create new and innovative written genres resulting in patterns of fluidity and changes and a variety of oral and written utilizing codes from different languages simultaneously. This is especially evident in text messages as well as other forms of electronic communication which manage to circumvent any prescribed rules and regulations.

There is ample evidence of a crossing of language boundaries at the personal level as shown in a number of biographies. We return to Steiner (1998), who describes the language interactions in a variety of contexts as a complementary activity with no contradictions whatsoever.

> My mother, so Viennese, habitually began a sentence in one language and ended it in another. She seemed unaware of the dazzling modulations and shifts of intent which this produced. Language flew about the house. English, French, and German in the dining- and drawing-rooms. I have no recollection of any first or bed-rock language. Later attempts to excavate one from within me, psychological tests, the hypothesis that the tongue in which I cried out to my wife when we were in a car mishap must be the linguistic base, have proved vain even in moments of panic or shock, the language used is contextual, it is that of the speech-partner or locale. Whether it be in daily usage or mental arithmetic, in reading comprehension or dictation, French, German and English have been to me equally "native".
>
> (Steiner, 1998, p. 87)

As noted, the use of a variety of languages is a frequently occurring phenomenon among people who move from one country to another, or are born to one language when another language is used in public life. They are often proficient in a number of languages and constantly cross linguistic boundaries. The phenomenon takes different shapes: from using a number of "fixed" languages, to mixing of codes within a language or using different codes within one language, depending on given contexts and a variety of factors such as topics (e.g., talking about intimate topics in one language, politics in another). Many immigrants use a number of languages or hybrids. Nobokov noted that not speaking English as his first language gave him the freedom to "bend" the language to his own liking (*Haaretz*, April 2, 2004), as opposed to the Israeli writer Meir Wieseltier, an immigrant from Russia who claimed that he had to "murder" the Russian language in order to write in Hebrew (*Misafa Le´safa* (From Language to Language), directed by Nurith Aviv, 2004).

The mixture of languages is especially common in urban areas with close and intensive interactions. Smooth language transfers in terms of codes, languages and varieties, with no defined boundaries, are also noticed in cross-generation talk and certainly with second-generation immigrants, and in colonial and post-colonial societies, where the codes used are products of political domination and where interactions in different languages take place.

Such cases are especially noticeable in family talk. Barron-Hauwaert (2004) reports on the language situations of families with mixed languages, where parents and others family members speak different languages, among themselves or with others. She studies the communication patterns of such families, finding that most parents were mixing languages as they found it hard to separate these languages. The parental language proficiency in two languages or more was high and they were often tri-cultural too. Yet, they all had concerns about the balance and input of each language and feared the community language would eventually dominate. They also found that the "One-Parent-One-Language" approach was frustrating and difficult to practice on a daily basis. In another study, Handoko (2003) reports on "the code-switching" that occurred during the interaction of three generations of an ethnic Chinese family in Indonesia. There were nine multilingual family members who were involved in the conversations she studied. She identified five separate languages: Nahasa Indonesia, Javanese, Mandarin Chinese, Hakka and English. These languages, in addition to a number of morpho-syntactically similar varieties, such as colloquial Indonesian, Malay/Peranakan, Jakarta dialect and Suroboyoan, were all employed in the family interactions. She refers to all these languages as codes; clearly "code-switching" occurs in almost any intergenerational conversation. She documented the phenomenon of code-switching from functional and socio-pragmatic dimensions, pointing to specific functions such as accommodations, regulating the distribution of turns among the speakers and satisfying socio-semantic constraints, "since some words or expressions are not readily translatable to other languages" (p. 33).

The use of such hybrids occurs frequently in written languages as well. In many situations, information from the Internet is obtained in one language while discussion about it is conducted in another language, pointing to the constant mix of languages and codes. In the public domain too, a variety of languages and codes are used simultaneously and organically as indicated in the languages of public signs, names of stores, streets, public announcements and advertisements. Mixes of languages are especially apparent in border areas such as those between the USA and Mexico, Finland and Sweden, as well as within many urban environments.

While some express fear that one language, namely English, will take over and dominate other languages creating a monolingual code, there is no convincing evidence for that phenomenon; rather a multi-code variety of national and local languages along with English is likely to become the dominant pattern. In fact the English used in different parts of the world is context-dependent and varies from one locale to another. Brutt-Griffler (2002) criticizes the view that world languages are dominant political languages that suppress all rivals over time within a limited territory. She shows how a crucial characteristic of a world language is that the majority of its speakers are bilingual or multilingual, noting that unlike a national language, a "world language" seems not to displace other languages.

While weaving and moving freely and smoothly among genres, registers, codes and languages is a natural phenomenon, beyond fixed boundaries, such patterns are often looked down upon and are degraded by linguists, who refer to them as pidgins, or even dialects, in comparison to "full blown" languages. Further, terms such as "fossilization", "semi-lingualism", "pigeon", "code-mixing" and "code-switching", as well as "interlanguage" and "intralanguage", are used to refer to them. Such terms are based on approaches whereby languages are regarded as homogenous and closed. Better terms to refer to such phenomena might include "hybrids", "fusions", "plurilingualism" as these represent more realistic views of languages that are not separated by closed, hermetic and discrete boundaries. Use of these terms can provide legitimacy for crossings among and between languages and other linguistic markers.

Specifically, hybrids apply to *un*doing languages in their closed forms of discrete categories and fixed boundaries arguing for the need to replace these categories with concepts that are anchored in reality and that legitimize crossing over among dialects, varieties and languages as these occur in natural and organic ways along a variety of dimensions and components. It is important to note that hybrids do not necessarily provide evidence that new languages are created but rather that there is legitimacy for the fluid, evolving and creative nature of languages.

As will be pointed out, the placing of languages in closed categories is reinforced by political entities perpetuating language as fixed and homogenous systems marking boundaries of national groups so that "the language" defines the collective identities and memberships of those using it as opposed to those who do not. This argument is transferred to language stereotypes and identities perceiving people as having fixed and constant identities and collective memberships based on their language. Such a categorization occurs in spite of the natural phenomenon, described here, of the use of different varieties and codes within given languages, codes, genres and registers in a variety of contexts at different points in time.

It is perhaps relevant to introduce here the statement attributed to Weinrach that "languages are dialects with an army and a navy" as it refers to the different language varieties that evolve naturally and yet how political factors determine whether they are termed as "dialects" or "languages". This phenomenon is clearly a result of the power and hegemony of groups to perpetuate and monopolize their own varieties, issues which are discussed in Chapter 2.

Languaging through multi-modalities

Viewing language in an expanded way also implies that it spreads beyond words and other traditional linguistic markers and incorporates multi-modal representations of different ways of "languaging": visuals, graphics, fashion, images, music, hip-hop, dance, food, silence, etc. Thus, the meaning of *hybrids* here is broader than mixing and combining of "marked" words; rather it refers to the use of additional features, especially non-verbal ones, referred here as forms of "languaging". There is a growing awareness today (Kress, 2003) that language is not limited to words and is broader than any accepted linguistic markers. This implies the acceptance of broader options of communication, spreading beyond conventional linguistic markers. This view originates from theories of semiotics that examine the different ways in which human beings choose to communicate, referred to often as multimodal means of representation, consisting of combinations of meaning and forms. According to Kress (2003), in social semiotic theory there is a motivated relationship between the signifier and the signified whereby meaning is made using an array of different possibilities, each signifying the interests of its maker. Thus, the making of meaning involves the use of several semiotic models as resources, all working together to create a communicative effect. Each mode has its own grammar and social languages, its own patterns that give it cohesion in given contexts (Kress and van Leeuwen, 1996).

Clearly, all communicative acts can be viewed in linguistic terms using metaphors. Stein (2004) notes that a foundational issue in the theory of multimodality is that communication is structured through modes and that "A mode is defined as a fully semiotically articulated means of representation and communication. The visual, gestural, speech, writing, and sound are all modes through or in which representation occurs" (p. 104). Accordingly, "A theory of multi-modality is concerned with the properties, uses, and effects of different modes in different contexts as well as with how these modes are connected to one another and work together to make meaning" (p. 104). According to semiotic theory several modes work together to create particular communicative effects.

If language is personal and creative and is not limited to "marked languages" with fixed borders, then a variety of devices can be used as part of an efficient act of communication. There are, in fact, an unlimited number of methods for languaging, for expression and communication, that go far beyond words and other linguistic markers.

Further, this also indicates that a language made of "words only" is limiting, as it places people in social modes that often incorporate a variety of filters and inhibitions, resulting in the suppression of thoughts, emotions and expressions. Thus words often represent a redundant, narrow and condensed manifestation of interactions and expression. Language is just not sufficient and statements about its insufficiency are commonly expressed as: "No words can express my thoughts"; "I cannot find the right words to say how . . ."; "It is beyond any words", "There are no words to tell you how sad I was . . .", or "I just can't do it over e-mail". An expression which is common nowadays in Israeli Hebrew is "*Xaval al hazman*", meaning literally, "It is a waste of time", referring to the notion that when words are not good enough to describe how wonderful something is (e.g., an experience, an item, an event), it is a waste of time using words to describe it, as they are inadequate tools for expression. Expressions about the insufficiency of words pointing to their limitations as a means of conveying feelings and thoughts are given even by those who are known to have high verbal skills and especially in situations that are loaded emotionally.

Major questions exist with regard to what and when words are needed; yet it clear that multiple devices are utilized in order to capture all social and psychological interactions; different devices complement one another, together creating meaningful forms of representation and interactions.

Languaging, therefore, refers to the multiple ways of representation that are not limited to words but rather include additional ways of expression consisting of a variety of creative devices of expression such as languaging through music, clothes, gesture, visuals, food, tears and laughter. Such messages can then be contextualized within the context of performativity (Butler, 1997, 1999) as a form of acting identities especially in the context of gender or of language identity (Pennycook, 2004). Thus, language in its broader definition includes a variety of codes such as prosodic features, movements, intonations, etc., all of which are integral ways of interacting using a variety of modes of representation. Languaging then adds new meanings and new and complementary dimensions to "language". Augé (1995) goes further in his discussion of non-places: "In the concrete reality of today's world, places and spaces, places and non-places intertwine and tangle together. The possibility of non-place is never absent from any place" (p. 107).

The following sections demonstrate how various devices such as food, clothes, architecture, visuals, images and numbers are used as acts of languaging. These represent a small sample of a much broader repertoire of devices used to "language" that include silence, art, music, dance, graffiti, hip-hop, paintings, public signs, billboards, photography, etc. These multimodal representations, each in its own way, contribute new and unique elements and together provide a more complete picture that facilitates endless forms of existence, creation and expansion, messages and mediations in private and public space. It is the repertoire of all these elements combined, that make up communication.

Languaging through food

Yisrael Aharoni, a well-known chef, describes a situation of languaging through food, when nobody around him knew any other language but Chinese. Despite this obstacle he managed to interact efficiently through food only, for eighteen months, referring to "fooding" as a most creative means of communication, not missing any "linguistic" codes.

Italo Calvino (1985) in *Mr. Palomar* describes the depth and multiple dimensions of the language of food in a cheese shop in the Cheese Museum:

This shop is a dictionary; the language is the system of cheeses as a whole: a language whose morphology records declensions and conjugations in countless variants, and whose lexicon presents an inexhaustible richness of synonyms, idiomatic usages, connotations, and nuances of meaning, as in all languages nourished by the contribution of a hundred dialects. It is a language made up of things; its nomenclature is only an external aspect, instrumental; but for Mr. Palomar, learning a bit of nomenclature still remains the first measure to be taken if he wants to stop for a moment the things that are flowing before his eyes.

(1985, p. 74)

Languaging through clothes and fashion

Appearance, especially clothes, is a powerful form of languaging used to communicate and transmit messages. For most people clothes represent an effective form of expression, particularly in the efforts of groups in authority and those seeking representation of their collective and individual identities. The word "uniforms" expresses this notion. Thus, military uniforms serve as devices for creating "uniformity"; school uniforms or dress codes are believed by some to be effective devices for transmitting educational messages of discipline, standards, decreasing violence, a serious approach to learning, control of permissiveness, the suppressing of radicalism and the increasing of respect towards teachers and society. Opponents argue that children find ways to undermine uniformity by constantly expressing individuality through other items not specified in the dress code and that it denies freedom of expression.

Clothes and fashion are often used as a form of resistance. Azar Nafisi, in 'Reading Lolita in Tehran' (*Haaretz*, March 8, 2004), states that the resistance of Iranian women to covering their head with scarves is shown in different ways, as they sometimes rebel even in the way they place their veils, with some hair showing, and some have varnished nails under their gloves.

A strong indication that clothes can be an arena of conflict is to be seen in the recent imposition of a law forbidding the wearing of the Islamic headscarf in French schools. Clothes, then, whatever interpretation a group places into it – religious freedom, separation of state and religion, or feminist statements of self-expression – can be seen as a form of languaging.

The image of Madonna is often used as a prototype of languaging through clothes to express her constantly changing identities. Speaking through clothes is a representation of ample identities such as age (young, old, middle-aged), gender (male and female clothing), professions (uniform and others). In many societies, grief is expressed through wearing black or white. A variety of colors in clothes represents moods of happiness, sadness, excitement, patriotism and loyalty, as well as group identities, the military, professions, etc. The fabric of clothes, as well, transmits identity and ideologies: leather, power; cotton, nature; silk, softness; polyester, durability, etc.

For a group of men marching through the streets of New York City, clothes imply equality, as was demonstrated in their parade in February 2004. Their main message was the right to wear skirts, in all lengths as well as dresses. They walked through the streets of Manhattan demanding an end to the domination and oppression of trousers, and claiming that they were fighting for the right of men to wear skirts.

Languaging through architecture

Architecture is a form of languaging used to express and transmit ideas and ideologies, mostly by political leaders, groups and individuals. In *Architecture and Democracy*, Sudjic and Jones (2001) provide examples of how architecture was used to language the concepts of democratic institutions. They report how the democratic concept of open discussions in Athens, equality before the law, opportunities to speak in the city's political assembly, the debates regarding important decisions that were carried out in a public forum and voted by citizenry as a whole, meant that political discussion was carried out in the open, in the fourth century BC. Languaging these concepts through architecture meant the creation of the semi-circular form of the Pnyx.

> In the fifth century the Pnyx was defined by semi-circular masonry which formed the base of a retaining wall that rose to a considerable height, supporting a theatre-like structure capable of seating several thousand people. The shape of the cube of rock at the center of the semi-circular area, approached on either side by a flight of steps leading to the top; its shape ensured that every participant could not see just the speaker, but all those present. The architectural legacy of the Greek and Roman civilizations, the temples of the Greek world and the religious, civil and military architecture of Rome, has provided the grammar of architectural language for most of the civilized world throughout the five centuries between the Renaissance and our own time.
>
> (2001, p. 17)

Languaging through visuals and images

Visuals, pictures, graphs and images are an integral part of languaging in literature. Yet, using these in adult literature and texts is rare although it could provide a complementary source of reading literature. Ronit Matalon, a well-known writer, argues for the inclusion of visuals as part of texts, since they provide deeper and more insightful meanings to writings. She claims that pictures were the main aid to constructing the text and she realized how useful they were for understanding the deeper meaning of the text and therefore decided to include them in her writings. Yet, she notes that she received major criticism from the literary community, especially from critics claiming that pictures did not belong in "serious" literary texts; pictures are so widely accepted in children's literature but not in adults' literature. Clearly, visuals and images are so very common nowadays in electronic messages, combining visuals, sounds and words; a new genre that is so widely accepted that it has obtained full legitimacy in a variety of texts.

Mitchell (1986) describes the broad repertoire of imagery that go by this name. "We speak of pictures, statues, optical illusions, maps, diagrams, dreams, halluncinations, spectacles, projections, poems, patterns, memories and even ideas as images, and the sheer diversity of this list would seem to make any systematic, unified understanding impossible" (p. 9). She argues that "It might be better to begin by thinking of images as a far-flung family which has migrated in time and space and undergone profound mutations in the process" (p. 9). She then classifies images into a number of categories to differentiate images from one another on the basis of boundaries between different institutional discourses.

Languaging through numbers

The use of numbers is another way of languaging that transmits important, meaningful messages. Orlee Shohamy (2000) describes a fashion in New York City of naming places, restaurants, bars and clubs after their street addresses. Examples are: "Bar 89, 23 Watts, Gallery 292, or 60 Thompson for a boutique (without the word hotel at the end)". She explains the meaning behind the number naming as follows: "With only the address as its name, the hotel upholds a fitting sense of anonymity" (p. 168). "How could New York, a city of extreme individualism, blanket its diverse establishments with such uniformity?" She notes that this is a new form of language, giving the following explanation: "This number madness might be a sign that figures have scored a final victory over words ... In American capitalism 'money talks' and the language of money is numbers." She further elaborates on the phenomenon: "In our cybertimes, names, thoughts, and even feelings are becoming more orderly, sortable, quantified. URLs might be word names, but we all know that they are really Internet addresses understood as binary code of zeros and ones" (p. 168).

Thus, the notion of language is expanded beyond the traditional and narrow scope of words alone. Yet, in spite of this reality these forms are rarely accepted as legitimate "languages". In the educational context, there is still an urge to limit languages to words and keep languages within their narrow boundaries with no crossovers. Mixtures of languages and hybrids are still not accepted as legitimate means of languaging and are often viewed as competing with verbal languages rather than complementing them or even substituting them. Yet, these forms of communication are rapidly penetrating the media and especially the Internet, consisting of a variety of forms of presentation, including text types, music, moving pictures and icons. It is a technology that is most likely to grant legitimacy to those means of languaging and multi-model representations in education and society.

Language as expression of freedom

Finally, an important dimension of an expanded view of language is its role as a free tool that enables personal and individual freedom of expression and its manifestation. An expanded view to language therefore implies that people are free to use language and express themselves in any way and form they wish. People are in charge of their own mouths just as they are in charge of their bodies and brains. They should therefore be allowed to use languages in their own ways, as long as this does not cause harm to others.

The right of people to express themselves can be considered a powerful act of "freedom of speech", implying that individuals, or "mouth users", can choose how to use language as part of their own unique identities, personal freedom and personal rights. Unfortunately, written languages are more restricted as they tend to abide by stricter rules; yet, the examples of graffiti and poetry indicate that people are seeking free forms of expression in writing as well. Accepting a free approach to language implies that there is a need to legitimize variations of expression so that people can decide what to say and how to say it, using different types of forms of expression. This is no different from the freedom associated with decisions such as what to read and what to listen to. Thus, users of languages need not feel that mixing and crossing languages is a forbidden act as a number of languages are able to live happily side by side and not necessarily be threats to one another. The right to express oneself in a variety of personal styles in terms of words and languages according to one's needs and desires should be viewed as a personal right. Statements such as: "It is my right to express myself any way I like" or "Don't put words into my mouth!" are frequently heard with reference to the desire of individuals to own their individual languages, to express themselves in open and free ways and in the languages of their choice in terms of words, intonations, accent, syntax, lexicon, mixing codes and languages, content and style and endless forms of "languaging". These should be viewed as personal forms of expression that make up the unique aspects of individuals; the forbidding of such uses should be interpreted as violations, invasion and intrusion into personal rights. Not allowing the free use of language in terms of what and how to use language amounts to totalitarian methods of controlling people's brains and minds. Issues of freedom of speech are discussed further in Part III and in the Epilogue, entitled "Language as a free commodity".

Summary

- Language is personal, creative, dynamic, open and free with no fixed or closed boundaries.

- A number of languages, dialects and codes are able to coexist harmoniously, creating varieties, hybrids, fusions, multi-codes and multi-modalities, beyond fixed and marked languages.
- This implies no need for strict and prescribed rules of correctness, choice of words and other means of expression as these can impose on personal freedom of expression.
- "Languaging" occurs not only through language itself but also through such means of communication as gestures, numbers, food, fashion, images, architecture and other means of expression.
- These things point to a view of language as a tool for free expression. To suppress language and speech is therefore to suppress, control and oppress a person's individual rights.

2   Manipulating languages

The construction of a model, therefore, was for him a miracle of equi-
librium between principles (left in shadow) and experience (elusive), but
the result should be more substantial than either. In a well-made model,
in fact, every detail must be conditioned by the others, so that everything holds together in absolute coherence, as in a mechanism where if
one gear jams, everything jams. A model is by definition that in which
nothing has to be changed, that which works perfectly; whereas reality,
as we see clearly, does not work and constantly falls to pieces; so we
must force it, more or less roughly, to assume the form of the model.

(Calvino, 1985, p. 109)

Overview

Chapter 1 saw language in an expansive way as personal, evolving,
dynamic, open and free with no fixed and closed boundaries. This implied
an absence of any strict or prescribed rules of correctness, of imposed words
or other means of expression, a language that is not limited to words or other
linguistic markers and which manifests itself through multi-modal forms of
expression and use. Yet, linguists, applied linguists, teachers and the public
at large view language in closed terms as a finite system with defined
boundaries, prescriptions and control. The results of such views are that
language is judged as correct vs. incorrect, grammatical vs. ungrammatical,
native vs. non-native, good vs. bad, high vs. low.

As will be argued in this chapter, one major reason for the above is that
language has become a tool for the manipulation of people and their
behaviors, as it is used for a variety of political agendas in the battle of
power, representation and voice. Such uses changed language from a free
and open device used for communication and interaction to a symbolic
political instrument. It is through language that group memberships
are determined, leading to categories of "us" and "them", inclusion and
exclusion, loyalty and "foreign-ness", "haves" and "have-nots". Language
is further used as a tool for legitimizing people, determining the right to use
language and speech vs. the need to be silent (Cameron, 1998) and the right

to use specific varieties and specific languages, so that language is expected to be correct, pure, native-like and grammatical. Thus, language turned from an open and free system to a tool for imposition, manipulation and colonialization, mostly used by ideologues and politicians with the support of linguists and educationalists. It is used in ways that require the following of strict rules of behavior, in terms of how, where and when. The chapter traces the historical processes through which this occurred and the motivations behind it. It describes the active role that linguists played by indirectly providing the tools for the imposition of such views. The second part of the chapter shows that in the new nation-state, which is more diverse than ever, it is again language that falls in the midst of the battles between those interested in continuing to perpetuate a homogenous and nationalist ideology and those seeking representation, participation and self-expression.

Manipulating language in the nation-state

In spite of the descriptions of language as open, personal and dynamic, the views and practices held by most linguists, applied linguists, teachers, students and the public at large is of language as a closed and finite system with fixed and well-defined boundaries. In other words, language emerges as a system that is finite, frozen, stagnated and rule bound.

It is only natural that people who are close to one another, physically and geographically, who live next to one another, who interact with one another and who share common interests (whether daily activities, thoughts or emotions) should develop similar codes of communication. These codes are used to transmit messages, as familiar codes are needed for efficient communication. This does not mean, as argued in Chapter 1, that people do not continue to use their own individualistic and personal languages and means of expression, or that they do not do so using the various different codes and devices of languaging. These familiar codes are used so that people are able to understand one another and transmit information efficiently and create meaningful connections in order to coexist socially, economically, cognitively and emotionally. Such types of interaction exist for any group, regardless of its size, the smallest being the individual who, according to Vygotsky, shares inner speech with himself or herself. This is relevant to couples, families or any other social units that share various levels of intimacy and interaction, and who utilize different forms of languaging for these purposes. These codes are not limited to people with similar biological traits, but also used by those who share other traits and features, such as profession, history, geography, intimacy and other experiences. It is a well-known phenomenon that groups belonging to the same group or trade – doctors, academics, prisoners, criminals, teenagers, teachers, students, etc. – develop similar and unique language codes in order to facilitate meaningful communication and to create intimacy (Fishman, 1998–99). With time, different groups develop their own unique and personalized ways of languaging, which are shared by their own members and often understood just by them. Since language follows the process of a dynamic organism, there are likely to be changes in the codes as different groups develop unique languages that may be more and more specialized and personalized in terms of lexicon, intonation, syntax, pronunciation and accent, as well as a variety of methods that employ multilingual and multi-modal devices in constantly evolving situations. The codes become more and more similar, especially if groups stay together and only interact within defined boundaries. Most individuals in the modern world are members of more than one community, which leads them to use different codes in these different contexts. Thus, a typical person would use different codes at home with his or her family than he or she would use at work or at leisure with friends as well as a variety of codes with other groups with whom he or she has different types of relations.

The situation of common codes among different groups continued for quite a while. May (2001) notes that "Empires were quite happy for the most part to leave unmolested the plethora of cultures and languages subsumed within them: as long as taxes were paid, all was well" (p. 130). Yet, this situation did not continue for long, as people started to interact in a number of more diverse and larger social circles within and beyond their own communities, especially when they needed to communicate for commercial and economic purposes. In most cases, these codes were understood just by these communities, so that for those not belonging to the community they seemed "foreign", which led to communication gaps which perpetuated their "foreignness".

It was the emergence of the nation-state, among other factors, that created a different reality. May (2001) argues that freedom of language use was the dominant pattern in most situations. Before the American Civil War, there was an attitude of laissez-faire with regard to language policy. In the USA, English was not an official language, as a result of a policy of freedom of choice, and multilingualism was evident in terms of communication *across* language groups. A large number of minorities were speaking different languages and there was great flexibility in terms of language use. In fact, May (2001) writes, there was "deliberate reluctance of the drafters of the Declaration of Independence and the Constitution to formalize English, or any other language, as the official language of the United States". "Underpinning this decision of the 'Founding Fathers' was the centrality of the principle of individual choice. This was exemplified in the notion of free speech and the related adoption of a laissez-faire language policy, deriving from the British model, which eschewed the legislative formality of granting 'official status' to English" (p. 210). This was connected, he notes, with the widespread multilingualism evident at the time, which was needed for communication across language groups.

Still, Crawford (2000) reports on a number of cases where schools that permitted the use of other languages were criticized and attacked in the second half of the nineteenth century, depending on the origin of the immigrants.

However, even in the USA there were a number of schools that used non-English languages as the medium of instruction. Spolsky (2004) reports that the Americanization campaign began around 1910 and was driven by fear of the revolutionary potential of immigrant workers and when Theodore Roosevelt believed that foreign-language-speaking immigrants remained divided in loyalty; the fear of non-English-speaking immigrants grew even further during the First World War.

What turned language from being dynamic and open to a set consisting of rules and regulations of how people *should* speak and write? What is it that changed languages into an imposed system that dictated, controlled and defined language behaviors in terms of "right and wrong", "correct and incorrect", "grammatical and ungrammatical" and "native and non-native" languages?

A variety of historical developments were instrumental in perpetuating the concepts of viewing language as a closed system. Two main developments took place at the end of the nineteenth century and they perpetuated each other. The first was the emergence and formation of the nation-state as the dominating political unit, especially in Europe as well as in the colonies, which were dominated by the European nations. The second was the emergence of descriptive linguistics, which was developed by anthropologist linguists, whose goals were to provide analytic descriptions of languages and the ways they are used. These very descriptions of how languages are used turned with time into a set of stagnated rules and laws governing how languages *should* be used within the political framework of the nation-states. Steiner (1998) writes that "Linguistic chauvinism, the exaltation of the official national tongue and its mythical roots, comes late. In the European instance, they hardly predate the sixteenth century" (p. 89).

With the emergence of the nation-state, a new situation was created whereby questions were raised about the boundaries of groups and especially about membership, i.e., who is/are eligible to belong and to be equal members residing in the same territory? In other words, once larger groups became formalized and institutionalized with the establishment of the nation-state, decisions had to be made with regard to membership, affiliation, loyalty, categories and affiliations. This is the time when communities started establishing criteria and rules, written and/or oral, regarding eligibility for membership of the dominant majority group who shared the same territory. Most of the criteria for belonging were based on biological features, such as "being born" into the group and sharing a certain type of personal appearance. Those questions became even more prevalent with the vast migration of people who did not belong to "the group" to these territories. It was then that language became one of the main identifiers of membership, and of inclusion and exclusion, and when the ruling groups started monopolizing language.

Language turned from being a free communicative means of interaction into a closed and stagnated system. From the early nation-state period, language and culture have served as major tools of the state apparatus.

it has been essential for the modern state to be perceived as having political boundaries that are isomorphic with language boundaries that are themselves isomorphic with cultural boundaries. Thus, political groups that aspire to independence within this broad ideology take as their first defining claim for a nationalist movement that they are a homogeneous language and culture group.

(Scollon, 2004, p. 272)

The establishment of the nation-state at the end of the nineteenth century started the association of nations with language (Safran, 1999). Thus, the use of language in the service of national ideology is relatively new, as the modern nation-state is a relatively recent phenomenon. Yet, such discussions and arguments as to the role of language in national identity had already been taking place in the eighteenth century. It was especially then that language began to be symbolized with power, ideology, nationalism, loyalty, patriotism and the drive for assimilation (May, 2001). In other words, national languages were inevitably an arbitrary and artificial process, driven by the politics of state-making. In some countries, such as Turkey, India, Israel and others more recently established, such as Latvia, Lithuania and Estonia, as well as some African nations, they were an integral part of "nation-building". Makoni (1998, 2002) writes that in some non-European nations the view of the nation-state was traced to the colonies. It was the colonialists who looked at tribes or ethnicities in terms of ethnolinguistic groups, mostly characterized by specific languages as one of the main features of the identity of the organism.

Thus, it was the nation-state in a number of areas in the world, not only in Europe, that was the ultimate example of the formalization of the collective group (Safran, 1999). The nation-state contained within it a large number of communities (families, tribes, villages, cities and towns) for the purpose of becoming a more efficient entity. In order for the nation-state to protect its existence it had to invent strict rules, regulations and a variety of symbolic markers to determine membership of who was "in" and who was "out". The first prerequisite was biological, being born to the "tribe" or "sharing the same blood", e.g., being German, Spanish or Chinese. But the nation-state constantly searched for additional symbolic markers that would provide clearer and more marked indications of memberships. Among the markers that were used in addition to biological and physical ones were those of a common history, a common culture, ancestry, religion and . . . *language*.

The method of classifying people into groups utilized a variety of identifiers, language being only one among them. In fact, as the case of Rwanda indicates, colonialists looked for *any* feature that would "mark" groups. The case of Rwanda is telling as the Hutu, Tutsi and Twa were tribes sharing the *same* language as well as a common history and cultural practices. They lived next to one another, attended the same schools and worked in similar places. A considerable number of Rwandans were mixed, the offspring of Hutu–Tutsi marriages, so it was difficult to know whether a person was Hutu, Tutsi or Twa. It was the Belgian colonialists who introduced the notion that Rwandans are made up of three *separate* "races". Thus, in an effort to create good order, they created closed categories of group affiliations – Tutsi, Hutu or Twa – so that it no longer was a flexible and amorphous situation. It is these categories that led the ruling elite to stress their separateness and their presumed superiority. This case illustrates how for colonialists in Africa and in other areas, categories were essential to an understanding of the colonies. Such categories were sometimes fixed via languages, but sometimes not. In fact, any group marker would have been legitimate for classification, categorization and the creation of hierarchies. While in some colonial situations language was able to serve as a major identifier and a marker of collective categories, in other situations it was not.

Thus, while language had been used as a means of communication for groups, it was the emergence of the political entities, especially of the nation-state but also of other political entities such as the colonies, that created the situation whereby language turned into a symbol of political and national identity and belonging, often in addition to other symbols of belonging. Language, then, was interpreted as a powerful symbol and indication of belonging and membership and an identifier of inclusion and exclusion. It is proficiency in the dominant, prestigious, majority language that has become the primary tool for obtaining citizenship and a prerequisite for membership of the collective group.

Gubbins and Holt (2002) note that language and identity were most noticed in Europe, where language became a key element in the emergent nation-states that replaced the old dynasties and empires and they came to share their names with the languages; a procedure needed for political legitimacy. The power of the monopolization of languages over whole nations can thus be seen in the close relationship of nations and languages and by the fact that a large number of countries in Europe and Asia share their names with the dominant and powerful languages.

Yet, the association of nation with language also meant that "the other" languages used in the nation had to be ignored and suppressed. May (2001) reports on the historical processes that made certain language varieties gain the status and prestige of national languages "while other languages have been 'minoritized' and, most often, 'stigmatized' " (p. 127). It became accepted to perceive all "other" languages as threats. Such was the case with the different languages used in Spain, with Spanish in the USA, Russian in Latvia and Yiddish in Israel, to mention just a few of the many cases that point to this widespread belief.

One such case is with Filipino, the national language of the Philippines, which is based on Tagalog, the lingua franca used in metropolitan Manila. Tagalog was named as the national language by President Manuel Quezon in 1939, and subsequently in 1959 the national language was renamed "Philippino" to give it a national rather than an ethical label. Although in the Philippines there are 168 languages and dialects and about 120 languages are spoken in the country.

The association of one language with the nation-state as the main identifier combined with the suppression of other languages can be illustrated in the following cases. In Quebec, Anglophones were forced to use French, to study it in schools and to use it in displaying public signs. "Jew, speak Hebrew" was a slogan echoed as part of the movement to revive Hebrew in the early part of the twentieth century. In the Baltic States, schools are required to use only the national languages, while not being proficient in these languages affects eligibility for citizenship and acceptance in the workplace. In English-speaking countries such as the USA or the United Kingdom, immigrants and their children are required to learn the "standard", "correct" and "unaccented" language of the nation as assimilation into the English language is associated with national identity, patriotism and belonging.

In each of these cases, the promotion of language is connected to nationalist ideologies so that these dominant languages have become integral parts of national agendas while at the same time other languages have become marginalized and denigrated. Language, then, has been manipulated to serve the agendas of the national and collective groups. The association of language and territory is not unique to the nation-states but extends to all other types of regional territories, as can be observed with the cases of Catalan, Basque and Galician in Spain and French in Quebec within Canada.

In the case of Quebec, the French language has been one of the major symbolic tools used by the Francophone movement to gain group recognition, status and power within Canada; its aim was the promotion of French along with the denouncement of English.

In the case of Hebrew in Palestine, it was the Hebrew language that has become the major symbolic tool for the early settlers in Palestine for promoting the Zionist nationalist ideology; it was specifically the promotion of Hebrew and the denouncement of other languages spoken by immigrants and indigenous groups, especially Jewish languages such as Yiddish, Ladino and Jewish Arabic, among others. The Yiddish language was the language used for communication among Jews living in Europe long before the Second World War. It had been used at the end of the nineteenth century as a cultural language in the service of the Jewish workers' non-Zionist movements (especially the Bunds) in Europe and more so in the United States. Hebrew and Yiddish, both languages of the Jews, were in a strong rivalry. Yiddish was a Jewish language of culture and secularity. The Chernovich committee of 1908 demanded that it be declared the Jewish national language, in contrast to Hebrew, the language of religion and Zionism. Although the decision was not accepted, the struggle between Hebrew and Yiddish as national languages was declared (Spolsky and Shohamy, 1999; Harshav, 1993; Fishman, 2001). Yiddish became the enemy of cultural Zionism. The language was declared as diasporic, which placed it outside the consensus in Palestine. Later, the Jews who continued to use Yiddish outside Israel, in

Russia and the USA, gave in to the Hebrew ideology, leading to the loss of the Yiddish language among secular Jews, a phenomenon that was accelerated by the destruction of the Jews in the Second World War. Yiddish has no major place today in the repertoire of languages in Israel; it is only used among Ultra-Orthodox Jews.

In the three Baltic States, language has become the main tool and symbol for re-creating national identity and for rejecting the remnants of the Soviet rule. It was the promotion of the three Baltic languages and the denouncement of Russian through strict language requirements in schools and language tests that high levels of language proficiency were imposed as a requirement for citizenship and entry into the workplace.

In the case of English, it is the "native-like", "unaccented" version that is promoted, believed by many to be the version that provides mobility, not only in nations where English is the dominant language but also in a number of post-colonial nations such as Singapore and Hong Kong.

In Brazil, many languages are used by its nationals, but only Portuguese has received legitimacy as the national language, while the value of "the others" is denounced. In Spain, as well, while a number of languages are used, it is only Castilian that has received recognition as "the" national language; however, this situation has changed drastically since the end of the Franco regime as other languages such as Catalan, Basque and Galician are gaining major recognition, particularly in Catalonia, where Castilian is giving way to Catalan.

These cases demonstrate that the use of the national languages, the removal of other languages and the need to use national languages according to specific and imposed rules became the main criterion of proper citizenship and acceptance. The formation of the nation-state is the key organizational principle underpinning the formation of linguistic and cultural homogeneity via the establishment of a common, usually single, hegemonic "national" language. It is the promotion of "good language" and the denouncement of plain, spontaneous, vernacular versions that became dominant ideologies, as language became the main tool for perpetuating homogeneous political ideologies. Thus, over the years, national languages have been legitimized as devices of power and control, and are symbols of inclusion and exclusion in most national societies. Language assumed the symbolic values associated with power and control, as those who knew "the standard variety" of the hegemonic language were associated with the power group, while others who used other languages or varieties were viewed as having low status and prestige, their languages not receiving any legitimacy, and often being referred to as "dialects". It was the domination of one or two languages over others that became an oppressive and discriminatory device in most nation-states for categorizing people and groups. Thus, language has become the major tool for political and oppressive actions, for manipulating and controlling the social order of nation-states and, naturally, the lives of groups and individuals.

It is by imposing a language requirement that the nation-state showed a definite preference towards some individuals on the basis of language. In most nation-states, speakers of the dominant language variety were immediately placed at an advantage in both accessing and benefiting from the civic culture and state services. One reason is that those speaking the prestigious and dominant language were also in control of major areas of administration, politics, education and the economy. Thus, knowing the language gave them preference and priority, while others were stigmatized and their languages restricted. It therefore became clear to those in authority in the nation-state that controlling language was an important symbol and indication of status and power and consequently of control over major resources and people in society. Once language was associated with the state and was used as such, knowledge of that language became an indication of loyalty, patriotism, belonging and legitimacy.

Role of linguistics in language manipulations

Linguists played a major role in providing the appropriate tools for carrying out these agendas and reinforcing the status of language in the nation-state. It was the combination of the nation-state with the emergence of the field of linguistics as a "scientific" discipline that resulted in the setting of defined and closed boundaries and the adoption of such terms as native/non-native, mother tongues and national languages (Hutton, 1999; May, 2001).

Linguists were instrumental in establishing language as a central component of the nation-state and in legitimizing it as a major identifier of collective groups. Specifically, this came about through the analysis of languages in terms of language families, organic differences between language types, language trees, etc. In *Language in the Third Reich*, Hutton (1999) claims that language was identified with race and that it was believed that the science of language could help show us the closeness of people: "Historical linguistics is the key to the history of the races. For philology has a method of analysis that is objective, one that is akin to methods of the natural sciences, and that has led to rediscovery of common bonds" (p. 265).

Hutton also argues that linguists adopted many of the terms associated with nationalism.

> Linguistics is a scholarly discipline, not a liberated nation, and many of its descriptive or methodological principles reflect the politics of European nationalism in the last two centuries. Notions such as "native speaker" and "native speaker intuition", and "natural language", "linguistic system", "speech community" have their roots in nationalist organism, and the fundamental "vernacularism" of linguistics needs to be seen as an ideology with a complex history and real political consequences.
>
> (1999, p. 1)

He also states that "Even the most superficial look at the problem makes it clear that ideas about an Indo-European (Indo-Germanic, Aryan) people (or race or tribe) derive from linguistics; race science took its lead from the study of language" (1999: p. 3). He condemns the field of linguistics by stating that:

> Linguistics is both the parent and the child of race theory. It is the parent, in the sense that nineteenth century physical anthropologists took their lead from linguistics and linguistic categories. It is the child, in the sense that linguistics has reclaimed the role as the premier science in the classification of human diversity, elaborating a "characterology" or "typology" of the world's languages, and therefore of the world's ethnic groups.
>
> (1999: p. 3)

Pennycook (2004), as well, argues that "linguists developed what Taylor (1990) calls an "an 'institutional' view of meaning whereby language comes to reside in a fixed, institutionalized system" (p. 4). Thus, "rather than words being a pale reflection of reality, a second cousin to the real world, they were in fact part of reality, that is, language was an objective fact and thus could be studied according to the same scientific principles as other objective domains of the real world" (p. 4). Language became a science.

Thus, a number of elements played significant roles in this process. First, it was the idea of a family of languages which was parallel to the family of people. Then, it was languages as complete and closed systems that included categories which were very fixed and final. The archetypes were languages which were referred to as closed systems and could be characterized as "correct" vs. "incorrect", "grammatical" vs. "non-grammatical", "accented" vs. "unaccented" and "standard" vs. "non-standard". But the most extreme categorization was the element of "native" vs. "non-native" as both languages and people, combined, were judged as being "correct" or "incorrect". In the same way that there were "correct" people who were associated with the "right" groups, there were also "correct" languages and those born into those languages, entitled "native speakers", who were born into the group and therefore belonged. Lastly, there was the issue of grammar and grammatical rules as these determine what belongs to the language and what does not, what aspects have the legitimacy to be included "in the language" and what do not; this was further enforced through the means of the standardization of language, i.e., legitimizing certain forms of language as "acceptable" as opposed to others that were not, i.e., pure and impure languages, pure and impure people.

The notion of language as a closed and finite system was in direct parallel to the idea of the nation-state as a closed and finite society to which only certain people had the legitimacy to belong. There was therefore a complete parallelism between languages and people. In the same way that there were complete and correct words and forms that belonged to the system, there were also correct and incorrect people who belonged to the nation. There were "ins" and there were "outs"; there were those "who had the right blood" and those "who did not"; there were "native speakers" and there were the "non-natives".

Hutton also points to the term "mother tongue" as creating close connection between language and biology. Equating "mother tongue" with "native tongue" means that the child is joined to the community through an organic bonding. "Reverence for the mother-tongue reached at points a mystical level. It was expressed in the language of the cult, and had complex links with the Germanic-pagan ideal of a pre-patriarchal matriarchal order" (pp. 6–7). "It related to the mother as 'life giving', intense veneration ('unshakeable love') from which radiates life-giving and life-sustaining forces." This was differentiated from "father tongue", which was the language of the scriptures and was granted to Hebrew or Latin. "The mother tongue gave life and energy, it was grounded in the earth" (p. 7). The approach was "to conceptualize the language-system as an organically-structured 'mother-tongue', and to see in the bond between mother and child the primal site of socialization. In this bond, the link between race and language was determined indirectly, but at a fundamental level by the primary socialization of the child" (pp. 8–9). This view, according to Hutton, contributed to the notions of purity and was part of racial theory: "Under these circumstances the linguistic system can be conceptualized by the totalitarian lawyer: as an autonomous force that determines the boundaries of the acceptable. The linguist is the gate-keeper of the language, just as the lawyer is the guardian of the rules of law" (p. 8).

Linguists, then, provided the nationalists with tools for domination by accepting languages as strict, defined, closed and objective systems. This was based on families of languages which were all based on a combination of language and nationalism with very defined boundaries. According to Hutton (1999), linguists were used by nationalists to support nationalistic ideologies. Linguists took the stand that language is a finite system with one solution, one formula and one way to be used, i.e., language purity. The purification of the language was also perpetuated by the invention of terms that refer to language as impure, such as "code mixing", "error", "borrowing", "pidgin", "creole", "contrastive analysis", "error analysis", "focalization" and "inter language", to name just a few. Such terms lend a firm legitimacy to the notion of purification of people. If languages can be pure, so can people. The consequences were that every language item as well as every person that did not fit the mould or that did not follow the purism ideology was considered a pollutant, an interference, an error, a problem and an alien.

Pennycook and Makoni (2001, 2004) also claim that the nation-state was seen as an entity requiring clearly defined borders, that perceived language narrowly by "purifying" it of anything that did not belong. Further, language was viewed as a science to which only linguists had access, along with its knowledge: "by concentrating on internal linguistics and rejecting external linguistics, there was no longer any mode of reflection for looking at what linguistics was and what it had invented. Thus, language could be viewed as a 'scientific entity', an objective fact, constructed by experts. Real knowledge about language is only available to the real linguist" (p. 5). Linguistics managed to preserve this idea of the narrow nature of language for a long time due to the association of knowledge and power, as linguists were the ones who knew about language and thus had a major advantage over others. Thus, while language was a domain of use, linguists were the only ones who knew *how* it should be used.

The field of linguistics, then, played a major role in the process of language becoming a tool of domination and oppression in the nation-state, specifically in controlling the quality of language that was legitimate and that lent itself to notions of memberships and categories. Thus, ideas such as correct and standard languages became other forms of domination. Rather than just describing languages, linguists started dictating strict rules regarding how languages *should* be used. Specifically, this meant that not only should all people in the political entity speak the same recognized and standardized language, it also meant that languages should be used in certain homogenous and fixed ways. These concerned not only the choice of language but also the choice of the ways in which languages should be used in terms of words, grammar, pronunciation, syntax, spelling, etc.

This trend has taken different shapes and forms but it had special ramifications in schools as national languages, framed as "mother tongues" were enforced as the mediums of instruction across whole nations. In this way, the association of languages and national membership, patriotism and loyalty was reinforced in the educational context. Teaching the "mother tongue" in schools reinforced the creation of myths about the need for "national languages" to be taught to children that opposes early multilingualism and thus excludes immigrants and other groups from "the nation". This was relevant to how languages were taught as noted by Reagan (2004) that once language was objectified and became a subject on its own to be learned in schools and mastered, it lost its function as a means of communication, as it became "an object to be studied". It was then boiled down to a set of rules to be acquired as part of the study of "mother tongue", which was in fact another way to perpetuate homogenous national ideologies.

Hutton (1999) criticizes these limited views of language as manifested in "the science of language" and claims that these approaches still persist. "The widespread belief held by linguists today that some great conceptual distance separates them both from nineteenth century German linguistics and from linguistics in the Nazi era, this is unfounded" (p. 2). "Modern linguistics sees itself as a forward-looking discipline, and regards the activity of linguistic analysis as either ideologically neutral ('scientific') or ideologically positive, in that most linguists rhetorically claim the equality of all language systems" (p. 1).

This was also relevant to speakers of the majority languages with regard to equating spoken and written languages. Native speakers, too, were expected to speak the written languages, while oral languages had a substantially lower status; "street" languages, jargons and vernaculars were not considered "real" languages and were viewed as "low" languages. This was clearly an unrealistic demand given the nature of language as a dynamic process, as described in Chapter 1. In fact it is not possible to find any language where the oral is identical to the written, given the endless number of oral varieties, some more distinct than others, although there is always a drive to use written languages, especially in schools.

Accent was another identifier supported by linguists. Accent is the most overt and visible language feature used to determine and mark membership. It was already used as a categorizing marker in the Old Testament, with the tribe of Ephrayim pronouncing the word *shibboleth* in different ways. It is considered a powerful feature given the fact that it is overt and enables one to differentiate among people according to their association with specific speech communities. But, like other language features, it is socially constructed as certain accents considered prestigious by one community may not be accepted by others as is the situation even in nations where the national language is English.

Thus, language and its derivatives – national languages, language standards, oral varieties, language correctness, nativity, accent and educated language, became markers and tools for domination and for making categorical decisions about people. Knowing the right language became a criterion for acceptance and rejection, inclusion and exclusion and was seen as an indicator of patriotism, loyalty, class, education and mobility in society and in the workplace.

The association of people and language spread beyond the territories of the nation-state through the process of colonialization. In this way, the views of language and nation were incorporated into an ideology of diffusion, which implied the imposition of certain languages also in territories outside the nation-state. Errington (2001) demonstrates how languages were used as collaterals and resources for perpetuating the inequalities in colonial territories along with gender, race and class. Pennycook (2001, 2004) notes that in colonial policies, languages were used as markers to measure, describe and classify people, like places, territories and cultures as part of the definitions of spaces. Standardizing languages and scripts was one such means used within the domain of language. Both Pennycook and Errington claim that the notion of language and ethnicity emerged in the colonial era and that it then developed into modern linguistics with its hierarchies, fixed languages, language trees, and so forth. It carried with it many of the assumptions of the colonial collateral that brought about its emergence: "This led to the construction of language families, organic differences between language types, language trees, and so on, and became closely tied to the scientific racism of the 19th and 20th centuries" (p. 4). Thus, it was the diffusion of languages and their imposition on other groups, especially in Africa, Asia and the Middle East, that spread the "language equals ethnicity" notion beyond the nation-state as well.

The current nation-state

Yet, as Holt and Gubbins (2002) note: "Yesterday's dialect may become tomorrow's language claiming political independence for its speakers" (p. 1). It is the politics of state-making that to a large extent determined the politics of language. It is clear that the same language can sometimes be of high status and the national language of a certain nation-state, while in other circumstances it can be considered a minority language with no status at all, as is the case of Spanish in Spain and South America as opposed to in the USA, or French in France as opposed to in Canada.

The nation-state is currently going through major change in terms of fluid national identities, recognizing the existence of diverse groups with different collective identities – indigenous, immigrants, transnationals, locals, global and everything in between. These realities challenge the ideology of the homogenous nationalistic state and affect the roles and places of languages and their manipulations. Yet, many of the same strategies of imposing national languages continue with greater force as national ideologies are beginning to feel threatened by these diverse communities who use a variety of other languages. Thus, fierce battles are taking place between those who strive to maintain the homogenous nation-state and others who challenge it, and it is through the medium of language that these battles are taking place.

Recognition of indigenous groups

An important feature of the current nation-state is the *recognition* of different groups, especially those who are *born* there but nevertheless use different home and community languages than the "national" ones. Those groups are currently seeking personal and language rights, voice, recognition and representation. The term "indigenous" is being challenged nowadays, as it is perceived as derogatory, since it was used by prestigious and powerful groups (often colonizers) for those who they viewed as less powerful, i.e., "the natives". It is often the case that those termed indigenous were residing in the territory before those who claimed the territory through colonialization and occupation.

In terms of *language*, along with the willingness to obtain recognition of the group comes their demand to recognize their "different" languages, which they want to maintain as part of their other differences and unique collective identities. A new generation emerges, refusing to accept the derogatory classification as well as to "buy" the nation-state ideology of associating culture and language of the homogenous nation. They therefore seek to maintain their own languages and/or along with the acquisition of the "power" language and to develop bilingual patterns. As will be shown in Part II, although nations will demonstrate recognition of these rights in official policies, these rights are not manifested through other devices, such as textbooks, allocation of learning time and tests, or languages of instruction.

Immigration

Most nation-states are currently characterized by vast migration from within the nation as well as from outside nations. These groups, as well, often seek recognition and rights and refuse to assimilate. At times, they are willing to assimilate, but on their own terms, such as when they assume multiple affiliations of the new place and the place they came from. Thus, while in the past these immigrants accepted the ideology and behavior of the nation and the majority groups and adopted assimilative patterns in one generation or two, current immigrants demand recognition and the right to disagree with the hegemonic ideology as they strive for legitimacy for maintaining their differences. Yet, in most situations, the nation-state refuses to recognize their rights to remain different. The term "immigrants" is also being challenged nowadays as it has connotations of a lower status, of people who will always be referred to as "the others". Further, it is often the case that many immigrants aspire to return to their country of origin.

In terms of *language*, it implies that many groups of immigrants refuse to accept an assimilative ideology of the need to acquire the hegemonic and homogeneous national language and would rather maintain their home languages. More common is the situation when immigrants seek to acquire the hegemonic language in an additive way, so they can maintain their own home languages and at the same time obtain the recognition and rights for their languages. Opposition to this demand on the part of those in authority in the nation-state is manifested especially in schools, where immigrants are ordained into the national languages with no opportunities to learn their own languages, let alone as mediums of instruction; this policy is further manifested through the different LP mechanisms, as will be demonstrated in Part II.

Transnationalism

Transnationalism is a relatively new recognized phenomenon (Shain, 1999), that refers to those who change their place of residence from the place they were born but at the same time continue to maintain close connections with their kin society. Thus, they create an entity of "diaspora" that plays a unique role of rejecting older patterns of total assimilations in favour of open and fluid affiliations following different patterns and taking active roles in a number of societies and countries. They no longer see themselves as obliged to have *full* loyalty to the "new" place, especially in terms of ideology; alternatively, they view themselves as loyal to both places in different ways and assume different, and often multiple, identities and demand recognition as such. Thus, they continue to maintain contacts with their kin countries, often reside in both places, and assume multiple or partial affiliations in terms of political interests, voting, social benefits as well as citizenship. Shain (1999) and Shain and Barth (2003) described the special roles and unique functions of diasporas in nation-states; for example, "they are regarded as a force of identity formation. Because they reside outside their kin-state but claim a legitimate stake in it, diasporas defy the conventional meaning of the state. The are therefore defined as the 'paradigmatic Other' of the nation-state, as challengers of its traditional boundaries, as transnational transporters of cultures, and as manifestations of 'de-territorialized communities' " (p. 450).

In terms of *language*, transnationalists and diasporas often adopt a variety of different language patterns from the acquisition of bilingual patterns resulting in additive forms, multilingual patterns as well as the use of new languages consisting of fusions and hybrids or even other, neutral global languages. Complex loyalties and affiliations are part of the current nation-state and so are the languages.

Globalization

This refers to the trend of most nation-states to view themselves as part of the global world, international affairs and world markets. Nations have different patterns of such affiliations, such as belonging to the European Union and NAFTA, the United Nations, etc. Thus, national boundaries are becoming more fluid and less rigid as nations become closer to one another within the world, while their fixed borders are becoming less defined.

In terms of *language*, this means that the world's lingua franca, English, and/or other prestigious regional languages are needed for use in international communication, as is the case with German, Swedish, Chinese, Arabic, Swahili, etc. It also implies a radically increased role of English in most of the world. Local languages are no longer useful beyond the specific territory of the nation-states, while other languages are needed. Nations realize this situation and demand that their residents acquire a variety of additional languages that will be useful for such international and global functions and for economic and academic purposes.

Language practice patterns and categories

Various patterns of language practices are created as a result of these changes. The closeness among speakers of different languages results in the emergence of various complex types of hybrids as languages of the different nations do not remain distinct and homogenous. Trim (2002) suggests that new versions of languages in the form of hybrids are produced as a result of the closeness of groups of speakers. Gubbins and Holt (2002) write that "language identity in Europe is diverse, complex and ever changing as boundaries of language, citizenship and borders are breaking up, resulting in emerging languages which are not distinct and homogenous". Brutt-Griffler and Varghese (2004) note that it is ofteñ the case that bilinguals do not hold their two (or more) languages as distinct, disconnected systems but transform the languages they speak in unexpected ways, with still less anticipated results: "They refuse to submit to attempts to regulate their behaviour according to the accepted norms of monolingualism, no matter how strident the attempts to do so" (p. 93).

The current nation-state being in a form of transition means that it is no longer homogeneous but rather consists of a variety of different types of groups, ideologies and languages that produce complex types and patterns of language practices. There are those who are born in the territories but speak other languages, and those who have moved, permanently or temporarily, to the nation-state and use varieties of language forms of the national languages, if at all; there are others who refuse to accept the ideology and hegemony of the state in which they reside, and yet others who want to assume all identities simultaneously. At the same time, the global markets require new means of communication, resulting in different languages and identities, and implying that nations are becoming closer to one another as borders lose their original meanings, open up and are less marked, as is currently the case especially in Europe. This is especially relevant with the joining in May 2004 of new countries to the EU, where nation-states are currently in a fluid and transitional form as the older forms of fixed boundaries in terms of languages, culture and ideology are losing their original meanings. One can easily argue that such diversity existed in the early days of the nation-state as well, since it always consisted of "different" groups. Yet, it is nowadays that the ideology of the nation-state in terms of language and culture is being openly challenged.

These changes are not viewed in the same way by all groups, as those in authority in most nation-states still strive to keep and maintain the original form of the nation-state in terms of ideology, culture and language (Taylor, 1998). The battles continue as the nation-state still perceives itself as the "bedrock" of political world order and continues to exercise internal political and legal jurisdiction over its citizens and claim external rights of sovereignty and self-government. This is indicated for example by the growing number of nations that stipulate strict language requirements for citizenship in order to become "full" members of the nation-state.

With all the above changes, questions arise as to the status of the nation-state, pointing to the constant battles that are taking place about the status of the different languages within its borders. This refers to local, national, regional, global trends and various patterns of combination among all of them. At the same time, it is being asked whether there are signs that the nation-state is losing its unique features or whether the nation-state is maintaining its power but in a different form. Thus, Ralston Saul (2004) argues that while it seems that globalization was successful for a while, current political events provide evidence that the nation-state is recapturing its power, as there are signs of a return to the traditional nation-state after what he claims is the "fall of globalization". He argues that while there were expectations that globalization would provide a new kind of international leadership, free of local political prejudices, this did not happen and did not lead to the stability of societies as "globalization required no one to take responsibility for anything" (p. 35). "The next logical step was to think of those trans-nationals as new nations unto themselves – virtual nations, freed of the limitations of geography and citizens, freed of local obligations, empowered with the mobility of money and goods." Globalization was organizing itself not around consumers, but corporate structures that sought profits by limiting personal choice. He claims that "The idea of trans-nationals as new virtual nation-states missed the obvious. Natural resources are fixed in place, inside nation-states and consumers live in countries, we are all residents and consumers of nation-states" (p. 35).

The boundaries among the local, national and global are very fluid and creative, moving from one to another and creating various forms of hybrids of the local, national and global, connected to the heterogonous populations as described above. Yet, evidence of this transitional phase can also be observed from the fierce battles that are taking place between those groups. On the one hand, there is the abolishment of passports in the European Union as well as state borders, but on the other hand, strict nationalistic policies are imposed, especially against immigrants, such as new citizenship tests requiring immigrants to become proficient in national hegemonic languages in a most homogeneous form as a condition for becoming a citizen. Thus, language continues to serve as a symbol of loyalty, as was the case in the early days of nationalism.

Negotiating and battling languages in the current nation-state

The debates and tensions are manifested in the representation and use of languages as these fall in the midst of the battles of those seeking to maintain the "order" of the nation-state and national languages versus those attempting to change it toward local, global, hybrids and regional languages. Language, in its different forms, continues to play a major role at the center of the debates and at the center of the arena of the battles for power, control, manipulation and domination by central government. In many entities, fierce conflicts take place between and within groups (as well as with central authorities) due to demands for recognition and the acknowledgment of difference and special linguistic rights.

Another layer is the widely recognized need for knowing the global and world language, represented by English, as the implications of these debates concerning languages focus on English. Can English serve as a neutral and free tool in this new world? If there is a return to nationalism, does it imply a stronger emphasis on national and local languages or even a return to "linguistic chauvinism" and monolingualism, as can be deduced from the growing number of citizenship tests in many states? Although it is more likely that bilingualism, in its different variations, as mentioned, will continue to be the dominant pattern, such battles between the national and the world languages and between the local and national languages, especially with regard to the legitimacy of different varieties, may still continue.

It is still the case, where many of these battles are fought over languages, that nations try to preserve and maintain national identities through national languages and suppress others, viewing them as threats, as in the case of the "English Only" group in the USA. This is so since the control of languages and linguistic rights facilitates or hinders access to resources in various societal domains, such as the workplace, education, or government, and enhances or denies status in society; languages confer power.

> With the rise of the modern nation state, language policy has become a common method of determining membership of and access to the state's institutions. In the market-place, it is the buyer who determines policy, for a seller depends on being able to communicate the qualities of the items he or she is selling. In a governmental setting, it is the bureaucrat who is able to decide what languages he or she is prepared to understand. If you can't speak the national language, you might be blocked from access to banks or police or even hospitals. Language policies then apply to members of speech communities who are in some way in the power of policy makers.
>
> (Spolsky and Shohamy, 1999, p. 50)

In response to this struggle, state authorities adopt a variety of approaches, ranging from repressing differences to providing solutions that reflect democratic pluralism. Within this spectrum of possibilities, it is expected that dominant groups are rarely inclined to give up their advantage and accept pluralist policies, especially because changes are likely to lead to a redistribution of wealth and a realignment in political power.

In the current nation-state, these types of battles that take place are on behalf of all groups and especially minority groups who seek representation, visibility and power. At the same time, among the different groups of the territorial entities, languages continue to be used as major tools by those in authority, as well as by those seeking representation.

In order to emphasize the dynamic nature of these battles, distinctions are made between public and major corporations and those of autonomous status, referred to as top-down vs. bottom-up. The first relate to public and economic authorities and the latter to local businesses and private citizens who enjoy freedom of action within the framework of general relevant state regulations. It is the interaction between these two flows that is of interest in discussing the use of language in the battle for control and representation.

As will be shown in Part II, in most situations, those in authority, government agencies and big corporations have greater accessibility to a large repertoire of mechanisms that they can use for imposing and perpetuating policy agendas. They use these mechanisms to perpetuate de facto language behaviors and practices in the midst of the struggles for power and representation.

Language in the current nation-state has a number of crucial roles to play as groups realize its value for manipulation and for obtaining power; they therefore use it as a tool in the battle for control, visibility and representation. It expresses "national" (or other entities) identities, often embedded in shared history and cultures; it is "ideological" because it is associated with aspirations of unity, loyalty and solidarity, patriotism; it is "social" because it is perceived as symbols of status, power, group identity and belonging, and it is 'economic' because knowledge of a language can be linked to different types of economic consequences, positive as well as negative.

Thus, on the one hand those in authority use language to create ideologies of uniformity, cohesion and control. At the same time, various groups in the society (immigrants, indigenous groups, teenagers, women, gays, etc.), use language to seek and create their own individual personal or collective identities in the form of recognition, visibility, consideration, manipulations, imposition and power, through languages.

The role of language in these battles can especially be observed in the USA, where language continues to be viewed in symbolic political terms. English is associated with patriotism, speaking good English is equated with being a "good American" (Auerbach, 2000, p. 181), and language is very much associated with loyalty. So, while minorities refuse to submit to the attempts to regulate their behaviour according to monolingualism, Brutt-Griffler and Varghese (2004) claim that the languages of bilinguals is perhaps the most politicized issue in linguistics, as different agencies, policy makers and educators intrude deeply into the personal domains of the bilinguals in terms of the languages in which they choose to express themselves. Bilinguals are viewed as violating and betraying essentialists' views of language in the nation-state along with such notions as mother tongue, first and second language, native and non-native, monolingualism, language deviations, standard language and positivist thinking about languages.

Language, then, continues to be an instrument for creating group identity within the global world or within regions such as the European Union. Now that it is used by groups other than those residing in the nation-state where the language is its symbol, language acquires a new symbolism. Thus, the English language seems to have a number of symbols and different meanings for different people. For those living in English-speaking countries, the English language may have a nationalist symbolism, yet for those elsewhere who speak English, generally as an additional language or as a hybrid,

English may have very different meanings, perhaps as a natural language, as claimed by Brutt-Griffler (2000), of English as a world language, as a symbol of an imperialist language or as a phenomenon described by de Swaan, regarding the "big" language swallowing the "small" ones (de Swaan, 2004).

Yet, national languages are used not only as tools for manipulations in the nation-state itself but often to create special status for the nation-state within the global community, as in the example of the use of English in a number of academic institutions around the world. Further, since English is recognized as the language of status and globalization, the nation-state promotes the use of English in order to gain status in the world community. In Singapore, for example, the English language, as spoken throughout the world, is being promoted above local languages such as Singlish. Similarly, in Hong Kong the English language is being promoted, especially at some higher education institutions, to mark Hong Kong as different and of higher status (more Western) than China, especially since the 1997 handover. Mongolia has just established English as a required language for schools, for world trade and status but also as a backlash against the history of imposed Russian. The current nation-state, then, uses languages, national or global, to create status and international recognition and as an international marker of identity. But also within the realm of national languages, clearly control of the "right" language that should obtain legitimacy still exists. As Lippi-Green (2000) notes, English not only varies from one nation to another but also within nations, so this is another proof of the vagueness of the boundaries among languages.

These battles are clearly not restricted to languages in the narrow definition of words, but are rather viewed in expanded perspectives, as can be seen in the recent battle over "languaging" through clothes in France. Clothes have become a major medium in this battle, with Muslim women being forbidden to wear coverings on their heads in a number of European countries. Thus, the language of clothes, through the wearing of a veil and/ or other religious symbols, becomes a manipulative "languaging" tool. Azar Nafisi (2004) notes that the veil has become an ideological political issue rather than a religious one, claiming that today in Iran, even religious women like her own grandmother oppose the veil because they feel that the regime has eliminated its spiritual significance, and has taken away from them the opportunity to choose it for religious reasons (p. 9). However, in France it is becoming a symbol for many women, given the French law of suppressing religious freedom, of their desire to dress as they wish, framing it as a personal right, or rather a "language" right.

An additional battle over language is currently taking place in the USA, referring to languages being considered as part of "national security". In the USA since 9/11, there has been a drive by the government to teach the "languages of the enemy", in order to increase the security of the nation. Accordingly, languages are framed in terms of secret codes that need to be acquired in order to increase the security. The lack of proficiency in Arabic may have been one of the main causes of 9/11, which could possibly have been prevented had there been more control over those languages. This is similar to the argument that was behind the study of Russian in the USA during the Sputnik era. It is a similar argument to the teaching of Arabic in Israel. In the USA, the establishment of the new CASL (Center for Advanced Second Language), funded generously by the US government, was driven by the association of language and security. Yet, this drive to teach languages of the Middle East and especially Arabic for the purpose of security, representing governments' nationalist views, receives heavy criticism. Edwards (2004) draws our attention to the conflict and contradictions associated with this type of policy, relating to the tension between different types of competing policies, the promotion of languages for academic and humanistic purposes vs. language for security.

> The present tension, then, between bilingual education and national security is indicative of a much larger problem: tension between national security and education in general. We are now aware that languages are important and that we have a national language crisis, but we are not addressing long-term solutions, so to prepare citizens to deal with the rest of the world.
>
> (Edwards, 2004, p. 271)

Summary

- Language has become an essential tool for manipulation, especially within the nation-state but also within other political and social entities, playing an integral role in the creation and perpetuation of unified, homogenous ideologies.
- The preferred use of a particular language over others often serves to establish and maintain the social superiority of members of a dominant central group in relation to those outside the group. Here indicators of social acceptability include such features as "native"-style speech, grammatical correctness, accents, "mother" tongue and favored dialect.
- Linguists have played a major role in this process by defining language as a closed, limited system with fixed boundaries.
- In the same way that nation-states define their members as belonging to a homogenous group of people in "the nation", there are languages that consist of closed systems and categories that dictate the language elements that belong to "the language" and those that do not. Languages, like nations, consist of similar systems of differentiation.
- In the current form of the nation-state consisting of diverse populations, language again is used as a symbol and as an ideological tool whose purpose is to create and consolidate group membership and indicate the degree of inclusion, patriotism, loyalty to the state, economic status and classification of its residents.

• Language use has become associated with legitimacy in the midst of this conflict. The widespread acceptance within political entities of a particular favored language along with its supposedly correct and pure grammatical form and appropriate accent, has resulted in language policy (LP) becoming a prime means of ensuring that certain types of ideology are put into practice as opposed to others.

3 Expanding language policy

In Mr. Palomar's life there was a period when his rule was this: first, to construct in his mind a model, the most perfect, logical, geometrical model possible; second, to see if the model was suited to the practical situations observed in experience; third, to make the corrections necessary for model and reality to coincide. This procedure, developed by physicists and astronomers, who investigate the structure of matter and of the universe, seemed to Mr. Palomar the only way to tackle the most entangled human problems, such as those involving society and the art of government. He had to bear in mind the shapeless and senseless reality of human society, with all its monstrosities and disasters, and, at the same time, a model of the perfect social organism, designed with neatly drawn lines, straight or circular or elliptical, parallelograms of forms, diagrams with abscissas and ordinates.

(Calvino, 1985, p. 108)

Overview

In most political entities, language policy (LP) is the primary mechanism for organizing, managing and manipulating language behaviors as it consists of decisions made about languages and their uses in society. It is through LP that decisions are made with regard to the preferred languages that should be legitimized, used, learned and taught in terms of where, when and in which contexts. Thus, LP acts as a manipulative tool in the continuous battle between different ideologies. These manipulations occur on a number of levels and in a number of directions but especially in relation to the legitimacy of using and learning certain language(s) (e.g., the right to speak and to learn) in given contexts and societies (status) and their forms (corpus), i.e, how they should be used (pronunciation, lexicon, grammar, genre, etc.). LPs refer to specific documents, laws, regulations or policy documents that specify these language behaviors.

   The main claim made here is that the real LP of a political and social entity should be observed not merely through declared policy statements but rather through a variety of devices that are used to perpetuate language practices, often in covert and implicit ways. Moreover, it is claimed that these devices, which on the surface may not be viewed as policy devices, are strongly affecting de facto policies, given their direct effects and consequences on language practice. Thus, it is only through the observations of the effects of these very devices that the real language policy of an entity can be understood and interpreted.

LP falls in the midst of the battles currently taking place in nation-states between the demands of the different groups for recognition, self-expression and mobility and those in authority eager to maintain national and homogenous ideologies in relation to local, national, regional and global languages. It is these very agendas that are perpetuated through LPs by a variety of mechanisms that directly and indirectly affect language behavior. As was discussed in the previous chapter, it is in the current political environment, where nation-states are becoming more diverse, multilingual, transnational, multinational and global, that language is used as a major tool for political, social and economic manipulations in the midst of these battles. A specific context in which this phenomenon can be observed is in the introduction in democratic societies of LPs and LEP that on the surface may follow the rules of pluralistic, democratic societies, including the promotion of language learning, yet the actual LP, as observed via these different mechanisms, is often in contradiction to these policies.

The chapter begins with a brief overview of LP; it then argues for the need to apply an expanded view of LP that incorporates the different policy mechanisms, in order to gain deeper insights and understanding of the true policies. The effect of these mechanisms is often implicit and covert, hence, the term "hidden agendas".

LP in the current nation-state

As was noted in Chapter 2, the current nation-state, because of its being composed of different ideologies and rules of representation (e.g., common history) and its connections to the global world, stands in stark contrast to the traditional nation-state and can even be viewed as threatening it, because of the many "others" it introduces as social actors. As a result, authorities often use propaganda and ideologies about language loyalty, patriotism, collective identity and the need for "correct and pure language" or "native language" as strategies for continuing their control and holding back the demands of these "others". A particularly instructive site for observing this tension-filled dynamic is the development of LP in democratic societies in which minorities have begun to demand and gain power. These minorities make these demands at the same time as established groups fight to retain their privileged status, while appearing, on the surface, to follow the rules of pluralist democratic societies, including advocating that all citizens should have the opportunity to learn a variety of languages.

As a result, a number of countries have introduced new language policies that are multilingual and include national languages plus English, as well as local and community languages, following a formula of one or more official or national language that gains high priority and represents some national or dominant group identity, ideology, loyalty, or common history. Then, given the role of English as the world's lingua franca in commerce, academia and technology, it is included as well as a local language that represents a regional, heritage, indigenous or community language used by a section of the population. Such policies were adopted by states such as the Netherlands, South Africa, France and Spain. Thus, a large number of democratic countries that were the prototypes of the "one nation, one language" policy are adopting more plurilingual and inclusive policies that involve a number of languages.

Types of language policies

The past few years have witnessed a renewed interest in issues of language policy that are emerging from a changing world, where nation-states are becoming more varied and diverse and at the same time more global and international. Yet, given the changes in the structure of the nation-state, as described in Chapter 2, where nation-states are becoming more varied and diverse and at the time same time more global and international, there is a renewed interest in issues of language policy, but this time from a critical perspective. Definitions of national and official languages, and consequently the language(s) that should be taught in educational systems, are being questioned and challenged. These developments have also led to other related questions about the political and ideological forces behind language policies as described in the previous chapter. Specifically such questions address the legitimacy of making sweeping language policy decisions for whole populations, the focus on languages as unidimensional units, the involvement, or lack thereof, of a more diverse constituency of citizens and especially of the educational establishment (teachers and schools), the relation between language policy and actual language learning and the mechanisms by which language policies are made and managed as well as the effect of language policy on democratic systems and individual rights (Schmidt, 2000).

LP attempts to make order in society in terms of language use and it is believed to be instrumental in settling some of the conflicts discussed in Chapter 2. For example, LP can address such issues as the languages that should get status and priority in societies – global, national, local, regional, or others – and which languages will be considered as "official", "correct", "standard" and "national"; it can also assist in legitimizing the revival of marginalized and disappearing languages such as aboriginal languages as well as languages that society considers important for its economic and social status, such as business languages like English.

In a large number of nation-states, LP implicitly or explicitly is the main mechanism for manipulating and imposing language behaviors, as it relates to decisions about languages and their uses in education and society. It is through LP that decisions are made with regard to the preferred languages that should be used, where, when and by whom. Thus, when certain entities, as small as neighbourhoods and communities and as large as cities, nations or global regions, for a variety of reasons, grant certain language(s) special priority and status, raising and/or maintaining the status of specific languages and lowering the status of others, this is included in the LP documents.

The scope

While LP is often perceived on a national political level, it is not always the case, as LP can exist at all levels of decision making about languages and with regard to a variety of entities, as small as individuals and families, making decisions about the languages to be used by individuals, at home, in public places, as well as in larger entities, such as schools, cities, regions, nations, territories or in the global context. Immigrant families often make decisions about the languages they want to use at home, in interaction with children, among themselves and in a variety of other contexts and domains. Likewise in a given environment, children make decisions, conscious or not, as to the language(s) they want to use at home, with their peers and in the public domain, depending on a variety of considerations. Similarly, decisions regarding language policies are made in the educational systems and the workplace by larger political entities such as the European Union (EU), which has now made language policy decisions regarding the use of 25 languages, as well as the United Nations (UN). As noted, LP decisions are not limited to the languages to be used but also include decisions about grammar, vocabulary, genre and the styles appropriate to given contexts.

Corpus vs. status

Of the multiple ways used to classify, examine and analyze LP, *corpus* vs. *status* policy has been a distinction that has been traditionally used as a way of differentiating between decisions concerning the structure of language itself (corpus) vs. decisions relating to language use and choice (status). Status of language may be determined through laws and regulations that determine the required languages in certain situations such as proclaiming a certain language as official. Corpus sets out the approved forms of a language, such as official lists of approved spellings, terms or grammatical rules or a new lexicon. Thus, corpus planning sets out to change or modify a named language.

Yet, Fishman (2000) questioned this distinction by examining the linkage between the two. He disagrees with the belief that corpus is less ideological than status and claims that this differentiation is more complex, as corpus planning can be hidden and issues that can "be advanced on purely linguistic grounds, can often imply a hidden status planning agenda" (p. 44). "In either case, corpus planning is likely to reveal more signs of status aspirations than has been admitted in the literature" (p. 44). He presents a number of such cases and introduces a new set of factors in which all policy cases can be placed: purification vs. regionalization, status vs. corpus, classization vs. vernacularization and uniqueness vs. internationalization. In fact, he claims: "If all language planning boils down to one heavily status-flavored super factor of independence/interdependence, then it makes no difference which solution we select, for both embody degrees of explicit status emphasis at different states of a total process" (p. 45). Thus, there is no language planning that is detached from some aspect of ideology.

Language planning and language policy

Another common distinction in LP is between *language planning* and *language policy*. Language planning was the term used in the 1950s and 1960s to refer to sweeping intervention and control of language behavior. In terms of language, it means determining exactly the language(s) that people will know in a given nation; policy, on the other hand, refers to a set of principles regarding language behavior, although this tends to vary from one context to another. Yet, in many situations, there are policy attempts to influence and manipulate language behaviors via different mechanisms, as will be shown in Part II.

Thus, while language planning refers to control, it does not leave anything to the individual to decide, as the governing body determines not just what the person will know but also how he or she will arrive there. This is where language planning is combined with practice. Language policy attempts to be less interventionist and to refer mostly to principles with regard to language use. Thus, it may include a statement that a number of languages should be learned in a given country or that indigenous groups should have the right to maintain their language, but it often does not go into which groups or which languages or how this should be implemented. With the increase of less interventionist approaches, the role of planning is subsiding and policy is becoming the bona fide. Yet, it should be noted that the boundaries between planning and policy are far from clear. There may therefore be LPs, especially language education policies, that specify in very accurate terms the exact languages, even the exact hours and methods, students will be required to learn as well as the specific situations in which these languages should be learned and the language tests needed to demonstrate knowledge of the languages; at other times these statements are more vague and subtle.

LPs around the world differ in their scope and type. Some are very vague and not specific and mostly state a general principle while others are as detailed as the language policy of Quebec, which is expressed in terms of language laws. In the Quebec policy, the language laws refer not only to principles, but more specifically to the implementation of these laws and to the most minute elements of the implementation, such as the languages on signs, the number of hours children will learn a language in school and so on. For further elaboration on types of language policies, see Spolsky, 2004; Spolsky and Shohamy, 1999 (Chapter 2); Ricento, 2006 and others.

Language policy and language practice

Explicit–implicit/overt–covert

In some contexts, language policy is stated *explicitly* through official documents, such as national laws, declaration of certain languages as "official" or "national", language standards, curricula, tests, and other types of documents. In other contexts, language policy is not stated explicitly, but can be derived *implicitly* from examining a variety of de facto practices. In these situations language policy is more difficult to detect as it is subtle and more hidden from the public eye. Implicit language policies can occur also at national level as many nations do not have explicit policies that are formulated in official documents. In the case of the USA, for example, there are no explicit and stated language policies that specify the status and uses of the English language. Yet, it is clear that English is the dominant majority language and this observation can be derived via a number of indicators. It is important to note in this context how the US English movement still perpetuates English by passing state laws that state explicitly that English is the official language.

In a somewhat similar distinction between explicit and implicit, Schiffman (1996) differentiates between *overt* and *covert* LPs. Overt LPs refers to those language policies that are explicit, formalized, de jure, codified and manifest. Covert LPs, on the other hand, refer to language policies that are implicit, informal, unstated, de facto, grass-roots and latent. Schiffman states that what are usually ignored are the covert aspects of language policy. Specifically, he claims that "many researchers (and policy-makers) believe or have taken at face value the overt and explicit formulations of and statements about the status of linguistic varieties, and ignore what actually happens down on the ground, in the field, at the grass-roots level, etc." (p. 13). The explicit and overt policy is according to differentiation between narrow and broad meanings of the term language policy. The implicit language policy is an integral part of the culture of the specific entity and is supported and transmitted by the culture, irrespective of the overt policy with regard to the various codes in questions" (p. 13). Schiffman therefore argues that it is not enough to study the overt and declared policies but rather that there is a need to study the covert and de facto policies.

Evidence of this distinction is demonstrated by Schiffman with examples of entities such as the USA, where there is no overt policy but certain policies are practiced. Alternatively, there are a number of cases where overt policy exists, yet different policies are practiced, de facto. Yet, Schiffman discusses also the "cleavages" which take place between the overt and the covert policies as observed especially through the study of the overt policies, such as official documents, statistics and ignoring the grass-roots developments of various sorts that in fact lay the groundwork for phenomena such as language shift. He brings up a large number of language policy cases where such distinctions are being ignored and calls for an examination of the linguistic cultures of a society and for language policy not to be viewed as the explicit embodiment of rules. Specifically, he calls for the study of language policy in terms of how policies are formed within a broader framework and how they are influenced by the covert and implicit grass roots of different linguistic cultures.

Policy and practice

Language policies are mostly manifestations of intentions while less attention is given to the implementation of policy in practice. It is often the case that even when policies are stated explicitly it still does not guarantee that the language policy will in fact turn into practice and there are situations when the use of languages are in opposition to declared policies. Thus, those who introduce language policy are often skeptical about the extent to which policy will actually be implemented and adopted by the population. Baldouf (1994) therefore warns that language planners should not have the illusion that they will be able to control the language scenes of a country, as there will always be those who want to create their own language agenda and resist from bottom-up the policy that is imposed from top-down. They will want to do it at their own pace and through their own processes. He demonstrates how, in a large number of cases, language policies and planning are often totally ignored as there are bottom-up forces in society that will try to introduce their own language ideologies and agendas within their own priorities, pace and processes. They develop a variety of strategies to ensure the implementation, practice and use of its policies. Description of such battles between top-down and bottom-up in terms of implementation or "de facto" practices of policies will be the focus of each of the chapters in Part II in the context of specific strategies, policy devices and mechanisms, which are used to introduce language policies by different interest groups, as well as methods of resisting those policies.

The typical LP that existed in most nation-states consisted of national languages in congruence with national state ideologies of loyalties, belonging and group solidarity, often termed "mother tongue", assuming that it was acquired in infancy, as discussed in Chapter 2. This language also became the medium of instruction in schools and its grammar was studied as a separate subject. This language was imposed as a requirement even when it was in contradiction to home languages of people who lived in the nation for whom it was not a home language, or a mother tongue, such as immigrants and indigenous groups. Recently, there has been more recognition of other languages of those born in the state who do not use the national language at home. Yet, it is still assumed that they will "adopt" and acquire the national hegemonic language as soon as possible. Thus, even in situations when the languages of immigrants are recognized as official languages in various policy documents, this is mostly lip service as there are no rights associated with this recognition, as will be discussed later. The main result is that, with time, these languages cease to be used and eventually stop existing in the given political territory, while the national languages take over as they are perpetuated through overt and covert language policies and a variety of mechanisms, as will be described in Part II. At the same time, it is important to note the observations made by Crowley (1996) and others that in spite of such ideologies and strong propaganda where this ideology seemed to be successful in the public domain, in private, people continue to use their own languages in their homes.

A recent proposed framework for language policy that differentiates between policy and practices has been introduced by Spolsky (2004) in a book entitled *Language Policy*. Spolsky identifies three components of LP: *beliefs, practice* and *management*.

Language beliefs refer to ideologies about language that lie behind each policy. Examples are when a group believes that nation equals language so that language can provide a unifying factor of the nation; another ideology may be when the nation perceives other languages as irrelevant or as intrusions to the monolingual ideology or unity.

The second component is *language practice*, referring to the ecology of language and focusing on the kind of language practices that actually take place (are practised) in the entity, such as when, regardless of policy and beliefs and for a variety of reasons, certain languages are used in certain places and contexts. When English is widely used in a growing number of countries nowadays, this is part of language practice and ecology.

The third component, according to Spolsky, is *language management*, referring to specific acts that take place to manage and manipulate language behavior in a given entity.

The framework proposed by Spolsky, is especially relevant here as it serves as the foundation for the introduction of the concept of mechanisms, or policy devices, as means through which policies are introduced and incorporate the hidden agendas of language policy. The graphic description of the framework introduced by Spolsky is displayed in Figure 1.

An expanded view of LP

It is argued here that there is a need for an expanded view of LP, whereby even the most multilingual declared policies do not always reflect the de facto and real LPs, as these provide only lip service, declarations and intentions.

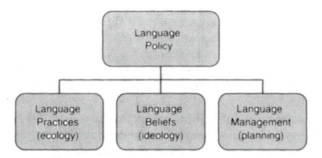

Figure 1 A model of language policy.
Source: Based on model in Spolsky (2004).

Yet, the de facto policies are determined somewhere else, by a variety of mechanisms that indirectly perpetuate LPs and that serve as a tool to turn ideologies, mostly in the traditional nation-states, into homogenous and hegemonic policies. Thus, in order to understand real LPs, there is a need to examine these other indicators beyond language policy documents. These are the different mechanisms that dictate and impose, often covertly and implicitly, the de facto language practices. It is through the multiple types of mechanisms that these "real" policies are manifested and they will be described and discussed in Chapters 4–7. The totality of all these provides the true picture and of de facto policies, and creates alternative language realities. It is often the case that formal language documents become no more than declarations of intent that can easily be manipulated and contradicted. Yet, it is essential that these mechanisms, or policy devices, given their direct effect and consequences on de facto language policies and practice, must be included in the general picture for understanding and interpreting LP.

Spolsky (2004) also claims that it makes sense to look generally at the policy revealed in the language practices of the society as

> the real language policy of a community is more likely to be found in its practices than in management. Unless the management is consistent with the language practices and beliefs, and with the other contextual forces that are in play, the explicit policy written in the constitution and laws is likely to have no more effect on how people speak than the activities of generations of school teachers vainly urging the choice of correct language.
>
> (Spolsky, 2004, p. 222)

The mechanisms described in Part II are often used covertly, not only in specific nations but also in transnational and global domains as they are accompanied by propaganda and ideologies. Such is the case when, through the use of English as the language of instruction and as a requirement for acceptance to institutions of higher education, the power of the English language and its speakers is perpetuated. The policy of schools and programmes that present English as "the language of world democracy" and the "language of freedom and openness" perpetuates the domination and influence of the West and its ideologies and creates de facto LP with regard to the English language. It is through these mechanisms that ideology turns into practice.

The expanded view of LP, then, argues that LP should not be limited to the examination of declared and official statements. Rather, the real policy is executed through a variety of mechanisms that determine de facto practices. There is a need, therefore, to examine the use of the mechanisms and study their consequences and effects on de facto LP, as it is through the mechanisms that the de facto language policy is created and manifested.

Mechanisms, as they are defined here and discussed in detail in Part II, represent overt and covert devices that are used as the means for affecting, creating and perpetuating de facto language policies. They expand LPs beyond official documents and towards an understanding of LPs in terms of the means used to influence policies. Within the LP framework proposed by Spolsky (2004), mechanisms lie at the heart of the battle between ideology and practice. Figure 2 describes the place of the mechanism within the ideology and practice.

Some of the mechanisms are considered hidden and covert since the public is not aware of their power and manipulative capabilities of affecting de facto policies. These will be demonstrated throughout Part II of the book. It should be noted that mechanisms, or policy devices, are used by all groups in society, top-down and bottom-up, whenever they use language as a means of turning ideology into practice and of creating de facto policies. Yet, it is those in authority who can use the mechanisms more powerfully, as they have better access to sanctions, penalties and rewards, including financial sources.

For example, with regards to the first set of mechanisms (Chapter 4), which focus on declared policies, those in authority have easier access to the laws, while other groups may be far more powerless, even financially in using the law to support their cases. Their access means that they can

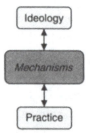

Figure 2 Ideology–mechanism–practice.

influence whether certain languages will be official and others will not; it is clearly within their power to influence educational systems or legislation to introduce language tests for citizenship. It is also in the hands of government agencies to stipulate that public signs will use certain languages and not others in a given territory, be it a city or a state or the educational system. While mechanisms are widely used as legitimate devices in most democratic entities, the new perspective introduced here is the need to become aware and knowledgeable about the use of these mechanisms to influence and create de facto language policy. It is often the case that people are not aware of these devices as powerful tools capable of influencing language behavior and practice. This lack of awareness implies that there is no protest and resistance to these manipulations. It also means that people comply unquestioningly with the demands set by the mechanisms as they are unaware of their often negative influences in terms of language rights and democratic processes, issues which are discussed in Part III.

One example, described in Chapter 6, is the use of tests as a mechanism for affecting de facto language practices. When tests are given in certain languages, those tested are not aware that even the very fact of using one language and not another as the language in which the test is administered sends a direct message as to the de facto priority of one language over another. This is being accepted as a given with no resistance and no negotiations. Rarely are there any questions or protests about the administration of the test in that language and the possibility of administering it in another language, although this can result in discrimination against students for whom it is not their home language. Those tested are not aware of how influential this mechanism is in affecting their view of which languages count and which do not, not least the effect of the language on the scores they obtain on the tests and the consequences it has on their lives. Neither students nor parents are even aware of the possibility of resisting this imposition.

Since language is not neutral but is embedded in political, ideological, social and economic agendas, these mechanisms are not neutral either and serve as vehicles for promoting and perpetuating agendas. Thus, the different mechanisms reflect the fact that languages express national (or other) identities that are embedded in shared history and cultures; they are also ideological because they are associated with aspirations of unity, loyalty and patriotism; they are social because they are perceived as symbols of status, power, group identity and belonging; and they are economic because knowledge of languages can be linked in different types of economic consequences, positive as well as negative.

Thus, it is through these mechanisms that the battles for power and control, visibility and voice, described in Chapter 2, take place. As such the mechanisms serve as major tools affecting language perceptions, people's behavior and eventually the de facto LPs. Mechanisms then are tools for managing language policy, but they are also considered forms of policymaking in terms of perceptions, choice and actual use.

Some of these mechanisms are official and declared such as LP documents or language education policies; others are more subtle and influence language behaviors indirectly. While much of the research in this area focuses on top-down agents, it will be shown in the different chapters that a dialogue is taking place between those in authority, big corporation, global and national agencies and smaller grass-roots groups, that tend to resist and protest these manipulations. Each group uses the mechanisms to serve its own purposes and battles, although as noted, it is those in authority that have more power of imposition due to their greater ease of access to powerful places in society; they can therefore make better use of those mechanisms for manipulations and for moving agendas and can maximize the probability that the manipulations will actually be carried out. Bottom-up groups, on the other hand, different ethno-linguistic groups, parents, students and the public at large, can also manage to use mechanisms to turn their ideologies into practice, but rarely do so. This issue is brought up again in Chapter 9 in the discussion on LP and violations of the democratic principles and to some extent in each of the chapters.

Summary

- Language policy has become a major tool used by those in authority seeking to manipulate language behavior and practice.
- The term encompasses a range of forms including overt and covert, implicit and explicit methods and policies (see Schiffman, 1996; Spolsky, 2004).
- A strong case can be made for the formulation of a new, expanded kind of language policy which would take into account the many and varied mechanisms involved in the creation of language practices. These mechanisms include rules and regulations, language educational policies, language tests, language in the public space as well as ideologies, myths, propaganda and coercion.

Part II

Mechanisms affecting de facto language policies

Mechanisms, or policy devices, are part of the expanded view of language policy where LP is interpreted not through declared and official documents but is derived through different mechanisms used implicitly and covertly to create de facto language policies. Specifically, mechanisms are overt and covert (i.e., hidden) devices used as means of affecting, creating and perpetuating language practices, hence, de facto LPs. As was noted earlier, it is via these different mechanisms that ideology is meant to affect practice. As will be shown in each of the chapters, it is also through these very mechanisms that violations of democratic principles and personal rights occur. Yet, it is also through these mechanisms that practice can affect ideology and that different language policies can be resisted, as practice can also influence ideology. Unfortunately, in most situations, those in authority have better access to power and can use the mechanisms more powerfully. It is through the consequences of the different mechanisms in practices that real/de facto LP can be observed and studied. In fact, all mechanisms are forms of marketing language ideologies.

The specific mechanisms discussed in Part II fall into four categories: Chapter 4 discusses laws, rules and regulations, standardization and officiality; Chapter 5 addresses *language education policies*; Chapter 6 focuses on *language tests*, as a policy device, as a branch of language education, but also as having its own power as a policy device that has a most powerful effect on language practices; and Chapter 7 discusses *language in the public space*, as well as ideology, propaganda, myths and coercion which are often not addressed in the language policy literature, but nevertheless have a powerful influence on language practices. Each of these chapters will define and describe the specific mechanism, show how it affects de facto LP and will address the relationship between the device and de facto policies as well as democratic principles and personal rights. Figure 3 provides a graphic representation of the mechanisms within the framework of ideology and practice, demonstrating also the bi-directional flow.

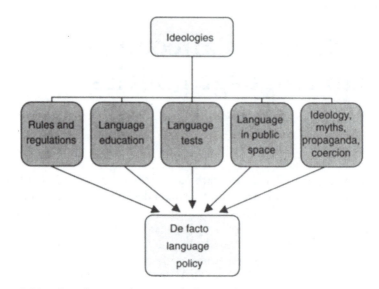

Figure 3 List of mechanisms between ideology and practice.

4 Rules and regulations

Overview

Of the different types of mechanisms discussed in Part II, rules and regulations are the most commonly used devices that directly affect and create de facto language practices and thereby turn ideology into practice, in private as well as in public domains. It is often the case that central governments develop a series of official mechanisms and devices to maximize their control over language behaviors. Being in authority, governments have the tools that enable them to do so, as they can produce policy documents and create laws and regulations that declare the official languages to be used in society. Yet, such policies are often introduced by other groups, such as religious communities or other collective groups as the languages to be used in different contexts. The mechanisms discussed in this chapter includes policy documents, language laws, officiality, nationalization, language academies and citizenship laws. The extent to which they can really affect language practices will be discussed as well, pointing to the "bottom-up" and grass-roots initiatives taking place to resist, protest about and negotiate on these declared policies and to propose alternatives. The main purpose of this chapter is to examine the mechanisms and devices that are used by different agencies to perpetuate these declared policies so as to put the language ideologies into practice.

The policy devices

Language laws

These refer to legal and official devices used by central authorities to perpetuate and impose language behaviors, in political and social entities, such as nation-states and other social and political groups; these may include global and international groups, municipalities accompanied by some type of abiding legislation. Laws are especially powerful mechanisms for affecting language practices, as they are supported by penalties and sanctions and can therefore ensure that policies are carried out and turn from ideologies into practice. Thus, it is in the power of language laws to affect the personal freedom of individuals and groups with regard to language behaviors. Language laws are considered, therefore, to be among the most powerful devices used in democratic states. Once there are language laws that grant certain languages a preferred status and rights in public and private domains, most people have no choice but to comply. Thus, language behaviors can be imposed, since those in authority have the power of enforcing on people the use, or forbidding the use, of certain language(s) in private as well as public space. Violating and not obeying laws can lead to harsh penalties, fines and sanctions, and even imprisonment. Language laws are manifested in various ways, such as through the use of the language(s) of public signs and businesses, studying certain languages in schools and as mediums of instruction, and the use of those languages in public domains, especially in government offices. A common situation in a number of countries is for language laws to be mandated through parliament. It is also important to note that even laws that state that people should not be discriminated against because of language are considered to be language laws.

One known example of language laws is in Quebec, which granted preferred status to the French language over English. This was accompanied by a series of laws as to the use of language in public spaces, especially with regard to the stipulation to post signs in French forcing businesses to display the languages on shops, road signs and other public places of representation. Similar laws were introduced in the Baltic States after they obtained their independence in 1990.

While the introduction of language laws "have the power of law" and can at times perpetuate the domination of languages as is the case in Quebec, which led to the actual changes of all signs and the introduction of French in public places, there are numerous cases where such laws are not obeyed, as people continue to use languages according to their own ideologies, especially in the private domain.

It is important therefore to discuss language laws in the context of an expanded view of languages, as described in Chapter 1 with regard to laws as they relate to other forms of "languaging" as in the case of using clothes as a languaging device.

Take, for example, the situation in Scotland, where the parliament decided unanimously to give support to a bill that would give Gaelic an official language status. Currently, the number of people able to speak, read or write Gaelic has dropped by 20 percent in 20 years. The legislation would require every public body in Scotland to draw up a Gaelic plan and the recruitment of Gaelic teachers would be stepped up. This involved also the creation of a special board to oversee the development of the language in order to secure its status as an official language. The bill also proposes turning Gaelic into a medium of education; the language would gain equal status with English, framing Gaelic as the gateway to an entire culture, setting beliefs and values, leading some speakers of Gaelic to become language teachers, and producing a plan that would consider intensive language courses to help potential Gaelic teachers reach the language requirements. The raising of Gaelic's status by law to that of English is being viewed as a central step in declaring this new policy. Clearly, a certain amount of money is devoted to the cause as well, but Jon Farquhar Munro, a Gaelic speaker, said: "For effective revival of the language, its status needs to be secured in legislation" (*BBC News*, February 7, 2005).

Officiality

Officiality is another device used to grant preference to certain languages in given territories and to take the power away from other languages. Although officiality is often determined by law, it is often the case that various entities, even families, town, schools, hospitals, prisons, can make decisions regarding the languages that should be used in all domains of interaction in the public arena. In most cases, "official" decisions of institutions reflect national policies, such as in the case of South Africa, which has declared eleven languages as official. Officiality can refer to local and municipal levels when certain municipalities or even neighborhoods declare certain languages to be official, given the composition of the population. Yet there are situations when private and public institutes, such as hospitals, prisons, schools and especially ethno-linguistic communities, make decisions regarding "the official" languages that should be used in certain places and situations. Thus, the United Nations declared that official languages should be used in its meetings and public documents. Similarly, the European Union declared twenty-five languages to be official. Clearly, decisions about officiality can change over time, especially with new regimes or with a variety of agendas and motivations for declaring certain languages as more important than others for a variety of reasons.

The manifestation of officiality is not always clear and often varies from one situation to another. In most cases, officiality means different things in different situations. In some situations, officiality may relate to the use of language in the public space, at others to the use of languages on official documents, yet at others to government offices, especially in terms of the languages of forms and publications, names of building and the languages that should be used at the workplace (i.e., in meetings), in public institutions and especially in the educational systems, as will be discussed in Chapter 5.

As is often the case, the mere act of declaring certain languages as official does not carry with it much meaning in terms of actual practice in all domains and it does not guarantee that officiality will be practiced. It often remains at the level of "declaration", even if the officiality is anchored in law. Such is the case when certain languages are declared official as part of historical events, especially as a result of colonialization, but the official status does not carry with it any aspects of practice, in both the oral and the written domains. This is the case in Hong Kong with English that is considered official but has no meaningful implications in actual use, especially in the oral domain. The case of Arabic in Israel is another example that points to the confused interpretation of officiality. While Arabic is an official language in Israel, there is very limited meaning to this in terms of de facto language practice, as there are hardly any public and official signs displayed in Arabic and no use of the language in either written or oral forms. While some ministries may have specific regulations for the use of Arabic, such as the Ministry of Health with regard to instructions for medicines stipulating the use of Arabic, there is very little visibility for Arabic in either public or private domains. However, a Supreme Court decision of 1999, in response to a request by the activist group, ADALA, stipulated that the officiality of Arabic needs to be exercised in public signs on freeways as well as in the signs of six mixed towns where both Arabs and Jews reside; it remains to be seen whether this court decision will have any meaning in practice, given the complex political situation with regard to the Arabic language in Israel.

At the same time, *not* declaring certain languages "official" does not imply that they will not be used in public spaces and on all official documents. Such is the case nowadays with English in many places in the world, where there is no need to declare it official for the public and government offices to realize its importance in one way or another. While in most of these places English is not an official language, it has high visibility and it is displayed and used widely within society, academies, government, commerce, schools and public spaces.

Still, the main advantage of declaring specific languages as official is its standing in court, as this can lead to decisions and sanctions regarding the obligations to minimize language discrimination by "forcing" groups and institutions to use the language in specific contexts. While a decision to declare certain languages as official may at times be arbitrary, at others it carries with it a variety of political, social and economic agendas, especially in situations where people view a minority language as threatening but also when majority groups try to gatekeep unwanted groups by declaring their own language as official. Such is the case with the powerful movement in the USA demanding to declare English an official language, while English is already the powerful and dominant language without any declarations. The motivations behind such a drive may be to exclude and reject immigrants and perpetuate the power of the dominant majority groups. A similar situation happened in the three Baltic States, after the fall of Communism, that declared their national languages as official in order to regain national identity and reject Russian speakers. Officiality is exercized as a powerful tool in the battle for manipulating political situations and as an indication of loyalty in the effort to maintain or re-create homogenous states. Officiality also acts as a propaganda tool, since most people will support such a notion as it symbolizes a need to maintain identity without understanding what it really implies. Officiality is generally viewed by the public in subtractive terms rather than in additive ones. It is rare to find people who will reject the notion of English as an official language, as they are not aware of the fact that by declaring a specific language as official, the meaning is actually rejection of "other languages", especially with regard to weak languages in society. In most cases, officiality should be used for weaker languages as one step for protecting language rights, so it should not imply any legitimacy to exclude others; although the sole declaration of officiality does not guarantee implementation but only intentions.

Another criticism of "officiality", even when it is most inclusive and multilingual, is that it rarely represents the whole population, as there will always be those whose languages are left out. Such is the case in South Africa where eleven languages were declared official but other languages were omitted; as much as the officiality policy is inclusive it almost always represents only a portion of the population and this device is often questionable.

Clearly, while officiality is a widespread mechanism for manipulating languages in most nations, it is often criticized on the grounds that it is undemocratic, since it is a means for imposing language policies top-down, and thus turning various ideologies into practice, using the device of languages. At times, it indoctrinates and perpetuates the power of the majority group, as is the case in "US English", a language that is widely used in the USA, implying that the main reason for declaring a certain language as official may be to perpetuate the powerful and reject the others. On the other hand, as was noted, officiality can lead to decisions that may empower language groups whose languages are in a weak position and the intention, along with penalities and sanctions, can work in their favour, in relation to situations when no such official status exists.

Standardization

Another device used by central governments to impose and manipulate language behavior is standardization, referring to decisions made by recognized bodies about "the correct" ways of using a language, mostly in terms of "corpus" policy. Standardization is often implemented through language academies, such as in the Basque Country, Friesland, and France, and is often used in situations when there is the motivation to reverse the language shift of certain languages and to upgrade the status of certain languages.

Yet, the very notion of "standardizing" language implies the imposition of specific uniform and homogenous norms. Standardization therefore enters the midst of the battle between language creativity and language preservation, mostly in terms of lexicon and grammar, but also in terms of status planning as to which languages should be legitimized. Crystal (2004) notes that "Standards exist to avoid the dangers of variability" (p. 222). He then describes the different ways in which standards arise.

They can evolve over a long period of time associated with a particular body of religious or literary writing. Or an official body can be created (an Academy) which "institutionalizes" a language by organizing the compilation of dictionaries, grammars, and manuals of style. In a further scenario, a standard can arrive, quite literally, overnight: a government selects a dialect of a language, prepares its people, and on a certain legally defined day it becomes the medium of national communication.

(p. 222)

It is possible, as in the case of Norway, to have two standards, i.e., Bokmal and Nynorsk (see Crystal, 2004, chapter 10, for a detailed description of the emergence of Standard English in Britain).

Standardization means that languages need to be used in certain ways, often in sharp contrast to how they are actually used by people, especially with regard to oral varieties, which are known to vary greatly from one person to another and from one speech community to another. It is therefore considered a form of linguistic engineering and imposition on personal freedom, as it strives to force people to use languages in uniform ways. Most standardization acts impose written forms on the oral language and thus overlook the wealth of creativity and varieties of spoken languages. It is a clear case of top-down imposition by those in authority, with the support of linguists, on the speech behavior of people and thus places major limitations on the freedom of expression and speech.

It is especially important to discuss the notion of the standardization of languages with regard to languages such as English, which is used as a second language among large communities in the world today and as a lingua franca with a large number of varieties. These varieties of English demonstrate how problematic standardization can be, as it is difficult to think of a homogenous "Standard English". Can Standard English ever be a realistic goal, let alone the difference between the US, British, Australian and South African varieties of English? Since English does not owe its existence to any nation, group, or individual, English today can be viewed as the language of many different individuals and communities in different parts of the world, and not the possession of its native speakers. Clearly, any attempt to standardize it is not realistic and not needed. In fact, when it comes to English, one can use local forms for local purposes, but if communication is done internationally, then there has to be a more serious engagement with intelligibility and linguistic norms shared across cultures. It is interesting to refer to Pennycook (1994), in this context, who refers to "A 'World Standard Spoken English', noticing that that any such a standard is bound to be based on Anglo-American mother tongue norms" (p. 166). Thus, the phenomenon of the widespread nature of English and its use as a world language, as well as a home language for a number of people, challenges the notion of standardization. Although the case of English is a clear one, similar questions need to be asked regarding other languages, such as Arabic, when spoken languages are constantly being criticized as "non-languages", because they do not follow standard rules. The gap between spoken and written languages and the inability of most people to speak the written language provide the best proof that standardization is a political notion with no foundation in real language use.

Nationalization

This term is associated with the notion of the nation that certain languages are viewed as representing the ideology of the nation-states, although there may be other languages that can be considered official. It is especially noted in situations in which there are a number of official languages in a given political entity, often competing with or complementing one another. Declaring a given language as the national language implies granting higher status to the speakers of the languages over others as they become the public representation of the nation-state. Gubbins and Holt (2002) note that for most European countries the name of the country is the same as the name of the language. Thus, in Spain it is Castilian that is considered "Spanish" and thus representing Spain. France is associated with French. Recently, Zuckermann (2003) has suggested that the name *Israeli* refers to Modern Hebrew, thus perpetuating Hebrew as "the national" language of Israel. Highlighting Hebrew and suppressing Arabic and the other languages that are used in Israel can be interpreted also as an agenda for nationalizing Modern Hebrew, leading to the displacement of other languages that are widely spoken and used in Israel, quite apart from the fact that Arabic is an official language. It is clear that the nationalization of a certain language communicates the message about the power of certain groups over other language speakers; thus, nationalization perpetuates power and hegemony, and the marginalization of others.

Language academies

These are bodies intended to make abiding decisions with regard to language use, mostly in terms of corpus policy, i.e., the correct forms to be used, grammar, lexicon and other decisions about how languages should be used. In most countries, language academies are integrated with purist approaches and they serve as branches of standardization ideologies. Thus, academies also have the roles of making major decisions in the midst of the battles between language creativity and language preservations and purism. Most of the decisions are in the domain of lexicon (corpus planning), but relating to the point made above with regards to standardization, decisions made by the academies also affect the status of the language, given the strong interaction between the two (Fishman, 2000).

Language academies are often considered to be institutions of prestige, authority and power in terms of their views. Thus, they provide the stamp of approval as well as impositions, often implying inferiority of those not following the rules set and stamped by the academy and consider them as outsiders, or as violators. At times, academies are responsible for policing and enforcing language correctness.

Language academies have a variety of goals but most often they are responsible for introducing new words, imposing and promoting official policies, guarding against foreign intrusion and serving as the final and most authoritative word on how languages should be used, both in terms of corpus and status.

While language academies are more flexible nowadays in accepting oral language varieties as legitimate, they still tend to follow native language standards; and "native" usually implies those who are considered of higher status. The fact that immigrant varieties, even in countries that consist of large number of immigrants, are still not considered legitimate is the prime indication of how language is viewed by academies as a tool and marker of inclusion and exclusion.

Yet, in spite of the authority of academies, especially in renewing "foreign" words that did not exist in the language and giving the flavor of the national language, it is not really clear how much influence they really have on de facto language use and in affecting the actual speech of people. They are considered authoritative in terms of the written language; yet, even that is in doubt, as the media, especially newspapers and the Internet, do not see the need to follow such prescriptive rules and tend to use languages in their own ways, with hybrids and fusions, phenomena that most language academies will not accept.

Citizenship laws

Language as a condition for obtaining citizenship is another form of official mechanism for imposing language practice that is widely employed nowadays in a large number of countries, especially in Europe (e.g., Germany, Slovenia, Latvia, the Netherlands, the UK and others). The ideology behind it is that residents of a political entity need to be proficient in the national language in order to be fully accepted as part of the nation. It is a requirement and a prerequisite for granting citizenship (i.e., legitimacy) for residing in a given state that a growing number of countries impose. Further, it is accompanied nowadays by a growing number of countries that administer language tests that are supposed to determine the level of proficiency in the national language; the results of the tests are used to determine the eligibility of people to obtain citizenship and be considered as members of "the nation". Language as a requirement for citizenship often has the power of law and it is therefore considered a very strong device for affecting language practices as it perpetuates the ideology that knowledge of the language is associated with loyalty and belonging and thus language can be used as a device to legitimize people.

Citizenship has always been a device used to legitimize people in the nation, ever since the times of the Greeks. But it is lately that proof of language proficiency in the dominant national language has become a major prerequisite for accepting people as members of the society. It is clearly connected to the growing number of immigrants moving from certain countries to others where different languages are spoken and looking for ways to select among these immigrants. But it is also for the nation to examine the intention of the immigrants to identify with the ideology of the nation and their willingness to assimilate; language is again used as the symbol of power. It should be mentioned that arbitrary criteria are often used to determine the level and quality of proficiency that is considered "accepted" to fulfill the citizenship language needs. In Germany, for example, the law in some states declares that second-generation immigrants will be allowed to become citizens; at the same time, they are required to pass a language test in German with arbitrary criteria. In Latvia and Estonia, and a number of other countries in Europe, there is a demand to pass language proficiency tests in the national languages for obtaining citizenship; it is often the case that passing citizenship tests is a condition for being qualified for employment as well. The UK has just introduced a language citizenship test. The USA, it was reported on July 13, 2004, plans rigorous English tests for immigrants from 2006. These tests will include those in the English language, US history and civics. The announcement said that the new English standards would include having applicants participate in a conversation, give simple directions, express needs and preferences, respond to warnings, read and comprehend simple material, describe in writing a person, object, place or situation and fill out forms such as a job application or a driver's license form. The article states also that "Some would like the new test to include specifically patriotic material to help inculcate love of the United States in the new citizens."

Here are some excerpts from the website of the US government regarding the language needed for citizenship now: "Applicants for naturalization must be able to read, write, speak and understand words in ordinary usages in the English language" (US Government website). Yet, the problems of defining proficiency for immigrants can also be learned from the different phrases about what it means to know English in one of the pages, entitled "Sample sentences for written English testing". It is also stated there that "To be eligible for naturalization, you must be able to read, write, and speak basic English. The questions will be read aloud or written during your interview. The INS officer who interviews you may ask you to read or write other sentences." The connection between these language tests and ideology can be learned from the type of questions the candidate is presented with: "All people want to be free. America is the land of freedom. America is the home for the brave. America is the land of the free. Many people have died for freedom, etc."

With the growing number of countries requiring language proficiency as a basis for citizenship, it is still difficult to see the relationship between good citizenship and language proficiency. Yet, language for citizenship is clearly becoming a major mechanism that manipulates and imposes language practices and national languages as symbols of loyalty and identity. It is an indirect way to create de facto language policy and to show how language is used as a symbol of loyalty, patriotism and perhaps an indication of intentions to assimilate in the nation-state. It is again an example of how the public has no choice but to obey this decision, not being aware of how this test serves as an imposing mechanism influencing de facto language policy and practice. In the same way that language academies are the bureaucratic solutions for corpus policy, language for citizenship is the major device used by governments to perpetuate status priorities.

Effect on de facto language practices

While rules and regulations are considered powerful ways of creating policy as they are driven by powerful institutions, supported by legislation and are capable of imposing sanctions of different types, including financial ones, there is still no guarantee that they will actually be applied and implemented. In fact, it may very well be that declared policies, as stated in various official documents and those described in this chapter, only reflect intentions and "nice words" and are not practiced. It is important therefore to examine the extent to which the content of these policy documents becomes a reality.

Most rules and regulations are not fully implemented, but it is also the case that the effect of most declared policies is not properly assessed. There are only very few studied that examined the effects of such declared policies on actual de facto practices and the reasons for their implementation or lack of. Thus, it is not known whether de facto language practices result from declared policies or from other factors. Immigrants, for example, are constantly being told that keeping their home languages will damage and harm their success in acquiring new languages and their eventual success in the new societies. They may have internalized such ideologies and these may have affected their behaviors and not the official policies. Immigrants realize very fast, given such propaganda and myths, that the languages they used in their home countries have no relevance in the new place, are of no value in the new societies and may communicate disloyalty, resulting in negative language stigmas and stereotypes about belonging and exclusion that can also cause discrimination in terms of language rights.

As noted, very few studies examined the connection and effect of declared policies and their derivatives with actual de facto language practices. Clearly, had such studies been conducted they would need to be administered over time and in relation to a large number of contextual variables.

Pavlenko (2003) provides an example of an analysis where she examined the success and failure of language policies in a number of contexts. She claims that in the case of banning the teaching of German in the USA during the First World War, the policy had long-term effects and was able to influence the entire foreign language teaching system in the USA until today. Specifically, she attributes the fact that foreign languages are still only taught in secondary schools in the USA and rarely before that level to that declared language policy.

With regard to the teaching of Russian in the former Soviet Union, Pavlenko shows that the language policy of introducing Russian was successful during the Communist era but it was not successful over time as once Communism fell there was a radical shift in language policy when new languages became national symbols especially in the newly freed Baltic States.

Resistance to official policies does take place in many forms: through using the languages at home, offering private language classes, holding meetings to read literature, municipalities creating local policies to protest against national ones, continuing to use languages in private and in clubs, and inventing new secret languages and codes.

The lack of systematic and solid research on the ramifications and consequences of various language policies is noted by Spolsky (2004) who nevertheless poses the question: "why do language policies fail?" Such questions need to be addressed with regard to the definition of "failed policies". Does failed policy refer to resistance on the part of the people and a continuation of what makes more sense to them? Do they continue to use language in mixed or bilingual forms? Do they totally suppress their home languages? Do they code-switch and use a variety of languages as fusions and hybrids? How much do they really comply? And what are the results of this compliance? An important question with regard to effect is: what is considered "success" and what is considered "failure" in terms of language policy? Success, as perceived by one group, may be "failure" for another. Thus, there is not much evidence to show whether policies declared through various mechanisms had any actual effects on people's behavior; and if they did or did not, whether these are considered successes or failures, by whom, where and when.

Clearly, such declared language laws and regulations are considered aggressive and powerful forms of policy mechanisms, since they have the potential for imposition and sanctions. Yet, as was noted, it is not clear how effective they are in changing and imposing language behaviors. There are ample examples where officiality and standardization and even laws are not put into practice. Yet, these laws and regulations also enable those who are interested to demand that these language laws should be enacted. Such is the case when laws and regulations are used to protect languages and the rights of individuals and groups who are incapable of communicating, benefiting and participating in democratic societies because of language. Thus, when new laws are created so that public signs, for example, will be comprehended by more people, this should be considered as success. Yet, there will be others, especially those believing in one language/one nation ideology that having a uniform sign system for the whole political entity will be considered a success in spite of the fact that they result in situations when less people, especially in multilingual contexts, can understand, a phenomenon that is viewed by many as discriminatory.

Similarly, when only a small number of languages become official while others are left out, these can be considered failed policies as well, while for others, such as in South Africa, this is often being viewed as a success, especially in comparison to what had been the situation before. Yet, when the Māori language is official in New Zealand, and all other indigenous languages are not, this is viewed by some as success. But for those of other language groups this means that they do not receive the appropriate language services and the right to learn in their own language and their language rights are violated. Similarly with regard to French in Quebec. While French speakers do have official rights which are anchored in laws and regulations and all other language groups do not, Anglophones are disadvantaged.

Laws and regulations vs. de facto policy: The case of Israel

The case of Israel can provide a good example to demonstrate the relationship between declared mechanisms and de facto language practices.

Background on the LP in Israel

The society of Israel consists of a large number of ethnic, linguistic and cultural groups who use a variety of languages and have varied backgrounds and identities. Out of a population of 6.3 million, the majority use Hebrew for everyday communication. 1.1 million are Arabs (of which 81 per cent are Muslims, 10 per cent are Christians and 9 per cent are Druze), whose home languages are a variety of different Arabic spoken dialects (depending on geographical regions) and the written form is Modern Standard Arabic (MSA). In addition, about 1 million are immigrants from the former USSR (mostly arriving since the beginning of the 1990s), for most of whom the home language is Russian but which is augmented by a variety of other home languages used in the former Soviet Union. About 80,000 are immigrants from Ethiopia whose languages are Amharic and Tigrinia. Further, the approximately 250,000 foreign workers currently residing in Israel use a variety of languages such as Tagalog, Romanian, Turkish, Bulgarian, Spanish, Turkish and a large number of African languages. A large number of ultra-Orthodox Jews use Yiddish as their language for everyday communication. For many other Jews, Yiddish, Ladino, a variety of Arabic dialects (e.g., Jewish Arabic) and other territorial languages (e.g., Polish, Russian, Bulgarian, Hungarian, English, Spanish) are considered heritage languages as they arrived in Israel with immigrants. English is a dominant language of a high status used in commerce, business, academia and public interactions, although it has no official status. (See Spolsky and Shohamy, 1999 for a detailed description of the languages of Israel.)

In Israel, ideology drove the language policy. Hebrew was and still is the mobilizing symbol of Zionist ideology for the new Jewish society created in Palestine, later Israel (Shohamy, 1994). All other home languages of the immigrants were to be rejected for public use, especially Jewish languages such as Yiddish and Ladino as they were not part of the ideology. Thus, the ideology applied only to the Jewish immigrants and not to the Arabs, non-Jew as well as ultra-Orthodox non-Zionist groups. Another ideology aspect was the legitimacy of English as an international language and a bridging language with Jews outside Israel.

The situation in Israel is very similar to that in other nation-states where groups in authority and power are eager to maintain their language and identities and thus their power. In Israel, as in other countries, there is a still continuous policy and practice of using language in service of ideology and creating situations of "us" and "them". Language is therefore still used as a means of creating "Jewish Israeli identity" and the Hebrew language continues to be used as an ideological tool that perpetuates different identities including negative attitudes to "other" languages as they are being viewed as threatening to the existence of the nation-state. This attitude is not just typical to the foreign languages which are spoken in Israel by immigrants but also towards Jewish languages such as Yiddish and Ladino. In this respect the current situation is not at all different than the policies and practices argued in Shohamy (1994), May (2001), Scollon (2004) and Valdes (2004), where "the other languages" are perceived as threats to the dominant and powerful languages, in this case, the authority of the Hebrew language as a symbol of ideology. This approach continues as the dominant language is perpetuated at the expense of the other languages spoken in the state.

Rules and regulations

Israel does not have official documents that declare language policy. In terms of officiality, both Hebrew and Arabic are considered official languages. In terms of standardization, in Israel it is only Hebrew that went through a process of standardization, as determined by the Israeli language academy that takes responsibility for the corpus planning of Hebrew only. In terms of laws, there are no language laws as such, but the Supreme Court decision stipulating the need for public signs in Arabic implies that the officiality may be viewed as manifestation of the law. In terms of language for citizenship, there is no such requirement at present (in Israel, being Jewish is the only requirement for obtaining citizenship, although the issue of the need to demonstrate proficiency in Hebrew is currently being debated publicly). In terms of nationalization, Hebrew is considered to be the national language of Israel, as a manifestation of the Zionist ideology. Hebrew is also the language used in all government offices.

The de facto practices that can be derived from these ideologies are as follows.

De facto practices

In terms of Hebrew in Israel, it is the major language that has the status of a national languages used in all domains of life. Thus, the ideology of Zionism to promote Hebrew and to identify it with the new nation of the Jews, in place of other languages of immigrants as well as to introduce it in place of other Jewish languages, has been successful as it is in fact the main language.

In terms of English, there is no connection between the declared policies and statements and de facto practices. While English is not declared anywhere as an official language, the reality is that it has a very high and unique status in Israel. It is the main language of the academy, commerce, business and the public space.

In terms of Arabic, while it is considered an official language, the de facto situation is that Arabic has very limited presence, visibility and a very low status. It is not used in public places where Jews reside, and there is limited use in mixed towns of Jews and Arabs, no use even in government agencies, not even in Parliament. There are hardly any government documents that appear in Arabic and it is not a required language for obtaining any government or public positions. The places where Arabic has any visibility in terms of use is in homogenous areas where Arab speakers reside; even in these places there is a fast-growing presence of Hebrew. While Arabic continues to be used as the medium of instruction in Arab schools, there are signs of the loss of Arabic, especially in these mixed towns.

With regard to the other languages, especially languages of immigrants, these are not stated as desired languages to be maintained or learned in any of the declared channels, except in the new Language Education Policy, discussed in Chapter 5. These languages continue to be used by immigrants for one generation and often disappear in the usual pattern, described by Fishman, of three generations. By then all immigrants have acquired Hebrew and lost their home languages. Yiddish, a Jewish language widely used by Jews living in Eastern Europe, has no use except among ultra-Orthodox communities who use Yiddish to avoid using Hebrew, considered to be a holy language and only to be used for holy texts. Thus, immigrant languages have no official status at all. Yet, the continual flow of immigrants from a number of countries guarantees the use of a variety of languages, at least for a while, in addition to Hebrew.

Resistance

The effects of the declared, top-down, policies need to be examined also in terms of de facto policies that oppose or "violate" the declared and official policies. These can be viewed according to the following evidence.

In Israel, while English is not stated in any of the official documents as official, all evidence demonstrates that it is used widely in most domains of life, in the academy, almost all texts are in English, it is also the language used in commerce and science and almost all public signs are displayed in English as will be shown in Chapter 7. It is certainly the language of wider communication and status in school and society in Israel.

Another indication of resistance to declared policies is the appeal to the Supreme Court by an activist group to display Arabic as the language of public signs and thus to implement its official status. Yet, other evidence of resistance to the top-down impositions is the large number of immigrant languages that continue to be used in society in a variety of contexts such as social clubs and schools and on private occasions, especially those of foreign workers. The use of Yiddish by the ultra-Orthodox communities is yet another indication of bottom-up resistance of a community that made its own policy decision with regard to language use according to its own ideology.

Thus, the effect of the declared policies on de facto language in the case of Israel is very mixed. In the case of Hebrew, the official status means that it is also practiced; in the case of Arabic the declared policy has no meaning other than a legal stipulation. In terms of immigrant and other languages, there are no official statements about it and they are not used de facto. Yiddish continues to be used by the ultra-Orthodox group regardless of official national policies. Further, while all immigrants strive to acquire Hebrew and eventually lose their home languages, the Supreme Court decision regarding the use of Arabic in public places and mixed towns indicates that these policies are negotiated. Further evidence can be obtained from the large number of languages that continue to be used in the home such as Russian, Yiddish, French, Jewish Arabic – at least for one generation.

Democratic principles, personal rights, consequences

The extent to which these declared policies in Israel actually follow democratic processes of decision making needs to be posed in the following terms. How were the decisions made and who was involved? Did they follow democratic processes of decision making? How involved were citizens in these types of policy decisions? In none of the declared policies was the public involved in making the decisions.

In terms of consequences, even if these declared policies followed demo-cratic principles of inclusion and open debates, there is a need to ask a ques-tion with regard to whether these rules and regulations violate personal rights in terms of the ability of residents living in the country to comprehend and participate in the society. The consequences of the declared policies in Israel is that speakers of all other languages, besides Hebrew, have no language rights and are not included. They therefore have great difficulty in participating in the society in terms of public discussion, debates and representation. At the same time, there are not enough opportunities to study Hebrew and no policy for maintaining home languages. There is therefore a clear message that other languages are not appreciated and the message given is that it can be erased once the person lives in Israel. For the Arabs too, their language has no value, no public representation outside their own communities; the languages of foreign workers are marginalized as well and such people have no linguistic rights as far as health care or the workplace are concerned.

Questions need to be raised with regard to how these official policies were made and the extent to which democratic processes were followed, by whom, for how long, and the extent to which these declared policies reflect all groups in society. The criteria for success and failure, as noted, are also not clear. Do these policies violate or protect the rights of people to under-stand and participate in democratic societies? Some would claim that it was a big success, as it proved instrumental in reviving Hebrew; others would say that the cost was too high and that there was no need to "kill" and "des-troy" one language in order to revive another; others would say that the language repertoire of Israel lost a major cultural resource and yet others would examine the psychological effects and its various ramifications on people who were not allowed to use their home languages while still having major problems in using the new languages. Yet, others would say that there was a need for such a subtractive view as it was the only way to "revive" a new language, Hebrew. They would claim that without such aggressive and indoctrinating acts it would not have happened. Yet, others would say that there was a need for Jews in Israel to have a common language in order to facilitate the Zionist ideology and to create a new Jewish nation-state. In light of the recent efforts to give more attention to Yiddish and of a number of groups protesting the loss of a language that was a central cultural resource, it is possible also to see that what was considered a success at a certain point in time in the history of the nation may not be seen as such at a later time.

Summary

- Declared language policies and rules and regulations as policy mechan-isms become established through a variety of devices including policy documents which are designed to fix policy, making it public and visible through written documents.

- Policy documents aim to perpetuate the ideology behind language policies and transform it into language practice. Examples include documents relating to such issues as language laws, standardization, citizenship rules and the setting up of language academies.
- Declared policies will thus be seen to have only a limited effect on de facto language practice, as it is through language practice that declared polices can be openly challenged, changed, negotiated and resisted.

5 Language education policies

Overview

Language education policy (LEP) refers to a mechanism used to create de facto language practices in educational institutions, especially in centralized educational systems. LEP is considered a form of imposition and manipulation of language policy as it used by those in authority to turn ideology into practice through formal education. Yet, at times, LEP is also used as a bottom-up, grassroots mechanism to negotiate, demand and introduce alternative language policies. Thus, LEP is another mechanism through which ideology is meant to turn into practice or practice into ideology.

Specifically, LEP refers to carrying out LP decisions in the specific contexts of schools and universities in relation to home languages (previously referred to as "mother tongues") and to foreign and second languages. These decisions often include issues such as: which language(s) to teach and learn in schools? When (at what age) to begin teaching these languages? For how long (number of years and hours of study) should they be taught? By whom, for whom (who is qualified to teach and who is entitled or obligated to learn) and how (which methods, materials, tests, etc.)?

LEP and its power as a mechanism

In most countries with centralized educational systems decisions regarding LEP are made by central authorities such as government agencies, parliaments, Ministries of Education, regional and local educational boards and schools. In all these situations LEP serves as a mechanism for carrying out national language policy agendas. LEP are imposed by political entities in top-down manner, usually with very limited resistance as most generally schools and teachers comply. These policies are then reinforced by teachers, materials, curricula and tests. For bureaucrats, LEP offers a very useful opportunity for exercising influence as they can enforce various political and social ideologies through language.

Thus, when entities grant language or languages special priority status in society, this language policy is especially manifested through the educational systems of the entity. This may imply using specific language(s) as medium(s) of instruction; it will often be the prestigious language(s) of the entity that most often have been declared as "official", an issue that may have special problems when the official or national language(s) are different than the home language(s) of some of the learners. In the current political environment where states are becoming more multilingual, multinational and at the same time more global, students are asked to learn language(s) that reflect and affect the interests of different groups in quite different ways. Such preferred languages may include languages that are considered important in the global world, as is the case with English in most countries. It may also include decisions to teach certain language(s) as a foreign/second language in the educational system. In the current environment of recognition of different groups for their differences, indigenous and immigrants, the LEP may also include a decision to include to teach foreign/second languages that are used as heritage, community, immigrant, indigenous languages.

LEP, then, cannot stand alone but is rather connected to political, social and economic dimensions. While LP is concerned with decisions people make about languages and their uses in society, LEP refers to affecting these very decisions in the specific contexts of education, schools and universities, most often in relation to languages which are considered home, foreign and global.

It is often the case that LEPs are stated explicitly through official documents such as curricula or mission statements. Yet, at other times LEP are not stated explicitly but are rather derived *implicitly* by examining a variety of de facto practices. In these situations the LEP is more difficult to detect as it is "hidden" from the public eye. It is in these situations that LEP needs to be derived from actual language practices through the study of textbooks, teaching practices and especially testing systems. The issue of tests as a policy mechanism is addressed in the next chapter.

LEP is considered a powerful tool as it can create and impose language behavior in a system which it is compulsory for all children to participate in. It can further determine criteria for language correctness, oblige people to adopt certain ways of speaking and writing, create definitions about language and especially determine the priority of certain languages in society and how these languages should be used, taught and learned.

As was argued in Chapter 2, the composition of the new nation-state with its different ideologies and rules of representation and its connections to the global world, stands in strong contrast to the traditional nation-state, and can even be viewed as threatening it because of the many "others" it introduces as social actors. As a result authorities will often use propaganda and ideologies about language loyalty, patriotism, collective identity and the need for "correct and pure language" or "native language variety" as strategies for continuing their control and holding back the demands of these "others". These ideologies will be carried out through LEPs. Thus, in countries with centralized educational systems (and occasionally also with decentralized ones), decisions regarding LEP are made by central authorities in order to exercise influence.

Another way of describing the function of central authorities with regards to LEP is to note that they introduce, establish, and often impose LEP as ways of creating order, managing and controlling the linguistic repertoire of the nation (or other entities). In turn, educational institutions, schools and universities, serve as the vehicles through which this order comes about. In other words, since language policy is not neutral but is rather embedded in a whole set of political, ideological, social and economical agendas, likewise LEP serves as the vehicles for promoting and perpetuating such agendas.

It is important to note the indirect and covert agendas behind LEP, not only in specific nations but also in transnational, colonial and global entities as they are often accompanied by propaganda and ideologies. For example, such is the case when, through the use of English tests as requirements for acceptance to institutions of higher education, the power of the English language and its speakers is perpetuated. Another case is when a newly opened university in Central Asia (previously in the USSR), funded by the USA and other Western countries, declared English as the language of instruction it simultaneously overlooked and devalued the local languages of the area. The school's policy that presents English as "the language of world democracy" and the "language of freedom and openness" perpetuates the domination and influence of the West and its ideologies and created a de facto language policy with regard to the English language.

The agents of LEP

LEP represents a very strong form of language manipulation, also from the manner in which LEPs are introduced in most countries and contexts. Some of these procedures will be described below.

In most cases, educational staff and personnel which includes teachers, principals and inspectors are responsible for carrying out the language education policies in the educational systems, classes, schools and districts as they see it as part of their job to carry out these LEPs. These are often implemented with no questions asked with regard to their quality, appropriateness and relevance especially their validity in terms of successful learning for students in schools. Thus, they serve as "soldiers" of the system who carry out orders by internalizing the policy ideology and its agendas as expressed in the curriculum, in textbooks and other materials and the very perceptions of language. They are the ones who make decisions not only in terms of which languages will be taught but what will be considered "appropriate" and "correct" language in terms of its quality. It is the role of supervisors, teachers and inspectors to ensure that these policies are implemented by mediating between the LEP and their implementation; they all are, therefore, servants of the system. Teachers, therefore are viewed as bureaucrats that follow orders unquestioningly. Further, it is in their power to perpetuate the educational policy in terms of additional mechanisms which ensure that the policy is implemented and in which form by applying specific teaching methods, controlling the number of teaching hours, allocation of resources, in-service training and especially through language tests as will be discussed in detail in Chapter 6.

Thus, teachers and other educational personnel become the main agents through whom the ideology is spread and turns from political statements about LEP to de facto practices of language learning. Thus, most decisions regarding LEP are made at the political level with no teachers involved. In the rare cases when there is some representation of teachers they are rarely listened to.

Auerbach (2000) draws attention to the role of classroom within the implementation of LEP. She claims that there are no instructional approaches where knowledge, language use, and literacy practices are neutral. Access to literacy and languages are limited to unequal power relations. Within this framework, classrooms can be seen as sites of struggle about whose knowledge, experiences, literacy and discourse practices, and ways of using language count. She further elaborates on the role of English as a second language in the USA claiming that teachers play a major role in the various types of LEP, especially relating to the English Only movement. She notes the push for fast English for Speakers of Other Languages (ESOL) instruction, in order to move newcomers as quickly as possible into minimum wage jobs, which reduce their dependence on government subsidies. She then argues that "Most ESOL educators vehemently oppose these policies as politically reactionary and educationally unsound; they are often at the forefront of the struggle to uphold language rights and oppose linguistic repression" (p. 177). Yet, at the same time many of those who oppose the English Only movement embrace the commonsense perspective that English is the only acceptable medium of instruction once students enter the door of the classroom. "They insist on English on *pedagogical* grounds, arguing that excluding the first language is in the students' best interest" (p. 178). Teachers then devise elaborate techniques to enforce the use of English Only with no function whatsoever given to first languages. "The common rationale is that total immersion in English is the quickest route to English acquisition; there is no function for the first language in the United States so there is no role for it in education; and students will rely on their first language (L1) if they are permitted to use it" (p. 178).

Policies often take the form of specific curricula that ensure that the policy is implemented; it is then translated into textbooks and other types of materials. Clearly, language tests play a major role in this process; they are so powerful in terms of mechanisms that the next section of this chapter will focus specifically on them. The content serves as an additional tool whereby teaching is accompanied with the material that is embedded by a variety of ideological and political agendas. There are abundant examples of the use of language ideological stereotypes in language teaching material. Thus, many of the textbooks for teaching English portray the English speaker in ideological terms as wealthy, well established and having ample opportunities and choices.

One reason that teachers internalize the ideology is that they are not part of the process of making LEP and do not obtain training in issues of LP and LEP and its relevance in the social and political contexts. In other words, one reason for such a role of teachers is that teacher education programs in many countries do not include language education policies as part of teacher knowledge, preparation and training. By framing LEP decisions as political acts, their creators remove teachers from providing professional input and action. This is especially problematic since, as noted, teachers are those who are expected to carry out the LEPs through their teaching practice in their classrooms. The outcome of such an approach reduces teachers to bureaucrats who are agents of big government policies without having any say in their shaping and delivery.

Further, most schools as well as teacher-training institutions define teachers as agents of specific languages (e.g., French, English and Spanish teachers) and not as "language" teachers so they obtain their theories still from the language and not from theories of applied linguistics and language acquisition, learning and teaching. Such a situation perpetuates issues of language correctness, of using the language with native-like proficiency as the goal rather than accepting the variety of a second/foreign language learner, an issue that has a powerful effect on the criteria for success and how students view their own success in the language. It also creates artificial boundaries among the different languages, does not encourage cooperation of the language teachers representing the different languages who, rather than support one another in the commonalities, focus on the differences.

Surprisingly, language teachers themselves all too often buy into this official view, unaware that decisions about the languages they teach are embedded in a variety of ideological and political agendas. The study of how to influence LEPs has not yet become an integral part of the basic intellectual preparation of language teaching professionals. This point will be taken up later in Chapter 9 where ways for increasing teachers involvement in language policies will be discussed.

LEP and de facto language practices

A number of countries have introduced LEPs that range from policies stating the need to learn one national language plus English (such as in Japan) to those that advocate two or more national languages with a large variety of local and community languages such as South Africa. The general formula seems to be this: first, one or more official or national language considered of high priority and representing some national or dominant group identity, ideology, loyalty, and/or common history; second, given the status of English as the world's lingua franca in commerce, academia and technology, in most non-English speaking nations the choice is to learn English as the main foreign/additional language in schools (at times even as the language of instruction), normally to begin at some level of elementary school; third, regional, heritage, indigenous and/or community languages that represent some portion of the population, considered for some reason to be significant.

Yet, strict categorizations of languages is especially harmful for students in schools where there is no consideration of the many languages students possess. Most educational systems perpetuate the discreteness and thus ensure that languages continue to be considered as separate entities. Yet, given this fluid view of languages, as described in Chapter 1, it is difficult to think of numbering languages as "first" "second", as if there were a certain order of languages of priorities and fixed boundaries. As was noted earlier such an approach has serious implications for the perception for bilingual and trilingual students and especially in schools. As was the view at the beginning of this century, children who spoke a number of languages were perceived as having serious mental problems. Such approaches are still in evidence today as students who are not using languages in the "pure" way but rather in fluid and hybrid ways are considered as not really mastering the power languages and are viewed as having lower intelligence and lacking in academic skills. After all most intelligence tests are given in one language, and most high stake tests employ one language, in all cases, the power language. Yet, as studies by Bialystok (2001) and others on children who use a number of languages show, many of these children demonstrate high cognitive advantage in schools. Educational systems, on the other hand, view languages in fixed units measuring people according to discrete units of languages rather than in terms of what they can do with the languages, and thus de-legitimizing the mixing of languages in schools and especially on tests. A similar situation applies to numerous cases worldwide, when LEPs assume a uniform standard language even though a large number of dialects are spoken by different groups, especially immigrant students with no clear and defined language boundaries. Schools as well still demand that the standard language be used in school although this requirement is far from realistic. Makoni (2002) argues that the discrete approach to languages and the great divide between the official, standard version of the language and the version that is actually used can be harmful in the educational context. Specifically, students enter schools speaking a non-standard version of the official language which by itself draws on a number of other languages (e.g., English, Afrikaans and some African dialects and languages). In such contexts assigning a "mother tongue" to a student may have little to do with sociolinguistic realities so that students are constantly misplaced and are expected to function in non-realistic situations.

In the USA, Valdes (2004) demonstrates how the one language ideology continues to be perpetuated with regard to immigrants through the teaching of English as the only alternative:

> In the United States, all public discussions relating to academic language, no matter how neutral, are currently taking place in a context that is influenced by ideologies about the standard language. For example, discussions of academic English are informed by ideologies about Standard English as well as by ideologies about the place of English in multilingual America. To those concerned about the erosion of Standard English, any mention of the teaching of academic language necessarily refers to the teaching of the "correct" language to all students but especially to students who are speakers of non-standard varieties of English. To those concerned about maintaining and protecting the status of English as the language of education in this country, on the other hand, discussions of the teaching of academic language necessarily focus on the use of English as the only language in which instruction is offered, especially to newly arrived immigrant students.
>
> (Valdes, 2004, p. 105)

The example in Figure 4 displays a written sample of a student who is in the process of learning English as a foreign language. The test task asked the students to write a recipe and procedure for preparing a chocolate cake. The student used both languages, Hebrew and English, each complementing one another. The words in Hebrew refer to the very words that the student knows in English, assuming that the reader of the test knows Hebrew. The student allowed himself to include words in the two languages in the task of communicating the recipe to the reader. It is possible that had he not been sure that the reader knew Hebrew he would have replaced the words he did not know by either paraphrasing or by choosing other words in English. The interesting thing is how the words in the two languages complement each other in a continuous flow of syntax. He is clearly making use of available resources of both languages to construct the text and to convey meaning. Hybrids existed in the grammar area, as the syntax and grammar are presented in English while the lexicon was almost exclusively in Hebrew and the mixture of languages makes the text very comprehensible. Yet, one wonders how such a text would be evaluated by the tester and what score he or she would obtain, on the basis of such a text that contains a mixed code.

Mixes of languages occur in a variety of educational systems, especially in higher education as most academic texts nowadays are written in English. It is often the case that the texts are read in one language, often English, while the discussions take place in the local language.

The mixing of words and codes within and among languages is natural in a world where immigration is such a central component of society, as was described in Chapter 2. In this transnational and global world people constantly move back and forth from one entity to another and from one area

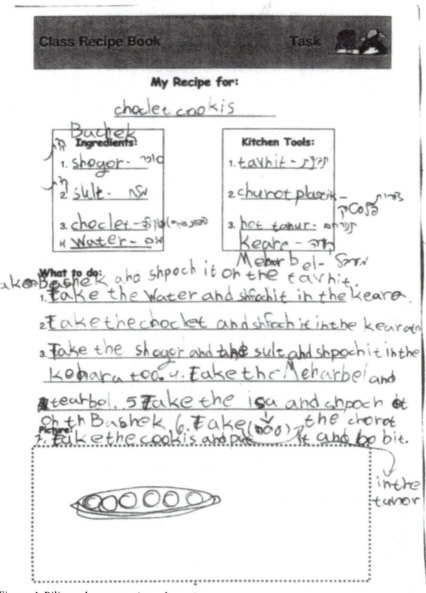

Figure 4 Bilingual construction of a recipe.

to another and use different codes and languages within these contexts. Yet, in spite of this obvious reality, the mixing of languages and codes have not received recognition and legitimacy and immigrants are still expected to comply with the dominant language. Educational systems in most societies still strive for purity of languages, both within and across languages as exemplified both in textbooks and language tests with their fixed monolingual and purist criteria. While the languages of teachers often consist of a variety of codes and languages, they still insist that students use a single code while the use of a number of codes is considered a violation. It is clear that mixture of languages and the various types of hybrids are not considered acceptable ways of language communication in the educational context. Most probably, the student who wrote the above note will be penalized for using Hebrew as there are no existing rubrics and descriptions in the rating scales that are supposed to evaluate the sample that legitimize the use of "another language" in the same text.

The illegitimacy of hybrids as part of educational ideologies of language purism has negative ramifications for immigrant populations. In a study on the academic achievement of immigrants (Levin *et al.*, 2003) it was demonstrated that it takes immigrant students in school between 7 and 11 years to acquire academic achievements in Hebrew and mathematics, compared to those who were born and raised in the dominant language. It is clear, therefore, that those who were not born and raised in the dominant language (i.e., immigrants) will be using home languages and the new languages in mixed forms. In this study (which will also be discussed in detail later), it was shown that success in mathematics for immigrant students coming from the former Soviet Union was significantly higher once the students were given the mathematics test in two languages, their L-1 (Russian) and the newly acquired language, Hebrew, in comparison to immigrant students who were given the test in a monolingual form of Hebrew. This positive advantage of performing significantly better on a test that uses two languages lasted for a period of more than 8 years after immigration. There is growing evidence, then, that for immigrants operating in two languages actually offers an advantage, in production, comprehension and in a variety of academic and cognitive tasks, throughout school and possibly later as well. Yet, no such realization has been accepted in the educational context.

LEP: The case of Israel

The introduction of a new LEP in Israel can provide a good case to demonstrate a number of issues in terms of the ideologies behind the new LEP, the connection between the LEP and de facto language practice, the cost of the LEP in terms of language rights and the extent to which the introduction of the policy followed democratic practices.

A new LEP

Until 1996 there was no official document stating the LEP for Israeli schools, yet various languages were taught in the educational system. Hebrew and Arabic were the languages of instruction for both the Jewish and Arab communities respectively, students of both communities studied English as a foreign language throughout school, and Arabs studied Hebrew as a second language. French or Arabic (primarily MSA) was taught to about 40 percent of the Jewish population. Some ultra-Orthodox schools taught in Yiddish, but very few additional languages were taught in the education system.

Yet, in 1996 the first consolidated document of LEP was introduced by the Israeli Ministry of Education for the educational system with the principle of "3+". It followed, in fact, a multilingual principle, reflecting the language diversity of the society in which a number of languages are used, each fulfilling different purposes. The principle of "3+" meant that each community was required to learn three languages and there was strong encouragement to learn other languages as well. Thus, the LEP document stipulated Hebrew as the language of instruction in all Jewish schools, English is to be studied from fourth grade onward and Arabic (MSA) or French as additional languages from grade 7 for a period of three years. For the Arab community, Arabic continued to serve as the language of instruction in schools, Hebrew to be taught from grade 3 and English from grade 4 onward. As stated, additional languages were encouraged for both communities such as community languages (e.g., Russian or Amharic), world languages (e.g., German, Spanish, Japanese, Chinese), and heritage languages (e.g., Yiddish and Ladino). Immigrants were encouraged to maintain home languages (not as languages of instruction) through special classes. The LEP also specified the starting age and duration but did not specify the methods of teaching, as these were to be decided through national curricula for each language.

The LEP of Israel may seem progressive and pluralistic. Yet, it is argued here that such declared and official policies are no more than lipservice and possibly statements of intention, while the de facto policy needs to be derived from a variety of hidden mechanisms that create and affect actual language educational practices.

Further questions need to be raised with regards to the extent to which the introduction and practice of the LEP followed principles and practices of democracy, ethicality, inclusion, rights, representations and educational principles as well as recognition and acknowledgement of linguistic realities.

The LEP and de facto policy

While LEPs are specified directly in various types official LEP documents, a number of hidden agendas can be identified through the use of these mechanisms which can affect a variety of language practices.

First, while the LEP encourages multilingualism, it is mostly Hebrew and English that are taught in Jewish schools. While the stated LEP promotes the importance of the Arabic language for Hebrew speakers, Arabic is taught with limited scope and limited success. The only Arabic that is taught in schools is the literate Modern Standard Arabic and not the type of Arabic that can be used for actual everyday communication with Arabs. The teaching of this variety cannot promote personal connections and cannot create a situation whereby the language will create a bridge of communication between the two groups, given the conflict that exists between Arabs and Jews in Israel.

The testing of all immigrants only in their national language, Hebrew, communicates a clear message of priorities which is in contradiction to the official policy that encourages the maintenance of home languages of immigrants, thus resulting in a situation whereby home languages are very soon lost.

Thus, the message that the LEP delivers is of significance of Hebrew only. Students of other languages have no language rights, are forced to learn Hebrew with very limited support. There is no recognition of previous knowledge of L-1, although it is considered instrumental to learning. Clearly, such an approach negatively affects these students' academic performance in schools, as can be seen in Figure 5, 6 and 7, which are taken from the study by Levin *et al.* (2002).

It is clear from the graph that it takes students a long period of time to arrive at high levels of achievement in schools, in subjects such as mathematics. It is important to note that the students from the former Soviet Union come from an environment that is a very rich and supportive academic environment, especially in mathematics and literacy. Learning in the first language, with limited support in acquiring the language occurs in spite of the fact that it takes students 7 to 11 years to gain an achievement similar to those of native users, especially for the speakers of Russian who arrive with high levels of mathematics. This is in spite of the research findings that show that knowledge of L-1 helps in academic achievement, as is demonstrated in the next chapter in Figure 8 with regard to the bilingual test accommodation

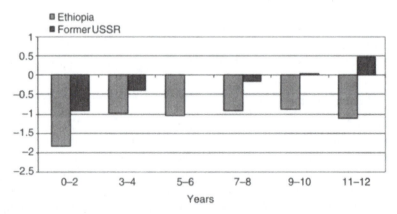

Figure 5 Research on academic achievements of immigrants in schools.
Graph 1: 5th grade mathematics standard grades according to years of residence.

Source: Levin *et al.* (2003).

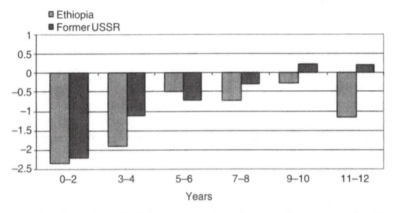

Figure 6 Graph 5: 9th grade Hebrew standard grades according to years of residence.
Source: Levin *et al.* (2003).

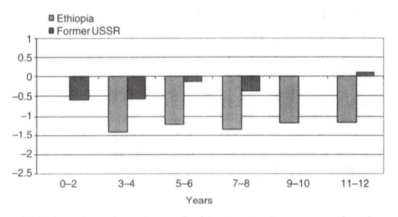

Figure 7 11th grade mathematics standard scores according to years of residence.
Source: Levin *et al.* (2003).

that significantly enhanced achievements for 11th grade students in
mathematics.

The LEP and democratic principles

Questions need to be raised also with regard to the methods through which
LEPs are introduced. In most centralized educational systems LEP is introduced in undemocratic ways. Specifically, this means that the educational
policies are introduced in a top-down manner, whether on national, state,
municipal or local levels, often without any input from the constituents. It
therefore represents authoritarian ways of making policies. As will be
pointed out in the next chapter, these methods of enforcing policies are

another arm of enforcing and perpetuating the LEP. Further, there is often very limited representation of broad sectors of the populations in decisions and implementation, even though they are the ones who are strongly affected by it.

In the case of Israel, the LEP was introduced by government administrators through consultation with academic experts. But given the loaded agendas representing of LEP and the variety of ideologies, as discussed in Chapter 2, such a way of introducing policy can be viewed as violating democratic principles. The lack of representation of constituents is especially noticed with regard to teachers. By framing the LEP as political acts, their creators remove them from professional input and action, even though teachers are expected to carry out the policies through their teaching practice in their classrooms. Such an approach reduces teachers to bureaucrats who are the agents of big government policies without having any say in their shaping and delivery. There is also generally no involvement of citizens and the public at large, students, language learners and residents of the different geographical entities. In addition, as is the case with most LEPs that perpetuates the knowledge of the power language, in the case of Israel, the Hebrew language. Thus, the LEP contributes to the creation of hegemonic groups whereby speakers of the other languages, Arabic and Russian are marginalized and excluded.

Another aspect that violates democratic practices which happened with the LEP in Israel was the fact that it addressed only language learning in *schools*; it is only schools which are viewed in most societies as the places that are in the control of central government and as essential arms for shaping populations. By contrast, the LEP did not address higher education while these are just as much instruments of states or special interests as are all other cultural institutions. As a result, broad gaps and extensive contradictions exist between the two educational levels. The LEP of Israel refers only to schools while universities could create their own policies and these are in contradiction to those stated in the national LEP. It is interesting to note here that while the LEP for schools declares Arabic and Hebrew as languages of instruction, Hebrew is the only language of instruction in higher education, thus discriminating against those students in Arabic-speaking communities who went through school using Arabic as the language of instruction.

The LEP did not come out of extensive negotiations, research, need analysis or discussions, as are required of decisions in democratic societies. There were also no plans to examine its implementation. Thus, it is not known whether the LEP even represented realistic goals of language learning; it may reflect more ideological wishes and statements of intention than reality.

The LEP and language rights

In terms of violation of language rights, students of the other languages besides Hebrew have no language rights at all as they are obliged to study and learn Hebrew. This applies specifically to students who are Jewish and are forced to study in Hebrew, not only as the national language but also as part of the ideology of the Jewish state that still follows the ideology of Hebrew being the national language of the Jewish state. This is in contrast to the Arab students who can study in Arabic.

Violations of language rights in the mechanisms of LEP are manifested in situations when students of languages which are not the power and official languages have no language rights when they are forced to learn in the national and prestigious language with limited or no support. At the same time, there is no recognition of previous knowledge and of their home languages. This results in a loss of academic knowledge. Further, often the declarations of LEP are totally unrealistic and unattainable, resulting in situations where students are viewed as failures. Thus, the graph demonstrates as well the violation of rights by showing how LEPs often pose unrealistic demands and goals on students. These represent mostly wishful thinking and not the reality; thus students are bound to fail. For example, the goal that students need to study all academic subjects in the new language is in violation of language rights given the research findings reported earlier showing the length of time it takes to attain achievement in academic subjects. Similarly, not providing students with bilingual accommodations may be viewed as a violation of their rights as research shows that such accommodations can enhance achievement when the tests are presented in a bilingual form. A number of additional accommodations seem to help, such as providing texts which are familiar to the immigrants, that focus on issues of immigration as well as texts that are simplified. These findings provide crucial evidence that using tests and learning materials in the majority language only and the study of all academic subjects in the new language is unrealistic and can be considered a violation of language and personal rights. Additional cases of violations of language rights are when immigrants have no meaningful opportunities to learn the new language, or when there is no recognition of the previous knowledge of students.

Not all rights can be viewed as positive. Often, there are cases when rights are granted at a certain point in time but taken away at another point. For example, certain languages are used as mediums of instruction only in schools and not at higher education level. In these situations, the language education at tertiary level is not taught in the home language but rather in the dominant language.

Conclusions

Language education policy is considered a powerful mechanism for creating de facto policies in society as all children must attend school. Educational institutions in general, and literacy education in particular, are among the primary mechanisms for promoting ideological power in societies. Auerbach (2000) notes the role of education in socializing learners for particular life roles, not just at the level of policy and planning but also through differential content and processes of educational interaction. "To the extent that the knowledge, life experience, language and discourse of the dominant class are valued in educational institutions, it is their power that is perpetuated." (p. 179).

While mechanisms of ideological control exercised through language policy have been examined extensively at a global level, they have been less fully explored at the level of day-to-day interaction. By referring to Fairclough (1989) she (2000) shows how the insistence on using only English in the classroom represents precisely "these everyday taken for granted practices that Fairclough (1989) calls 'ideological power', one of the central mechanisms of ensuring control by consent. He argues that discourse plays a particularly important role in exercising this control: authority and power are manifested in and perpetuated by institutional practices around the ways language is used and the purposes for which it is used" (p. 179). Thus English Only instruction has come to be justified in pedagogical terms, it rests on unexamined assumptions that originate in the political agenda of dominant classes, and serves to reinforce existing relations: precisely because its mechanisms are hidden and it is therefore a prime example of covert ideological control. It is important therefore to unveil and examine the ways in which language teaching movements such as "English Only" are grounded in invisible but powerful ideological assumptions that the dominant classes exert through institutional practices (Auerbach, 2000).

It is often the case that the fluctuations of LEP have been determined by political rather than pedagogical factors. Thus, Auerbach (2000) notes: "In the nineteenth century, for example the decentralized and locally controlled nature of public schooling allowed for bilingual education in accordance with the political power of particular ethnic groups. It was the resurgence of nativism and anti-foreign political sentiment in the late nineteenth century that triggered the decline of bilingual education. The advent of the First World War, the increase in immigration from southern and eastern Europe, and the growing role of immigrants in the labour movement contributed to an increasing xenophobic atmosphere in the early twentieth century; 'foreign influence' was blamed for the nation's political and economic problems, and the Americanization movement was promoted as a means of countering this influence" (p. 181). This led to the spread of the teaching of English as a second language as a direct outcome of the Americanization movement and especially from the teaching of oral English rather than the students' home languages. Thus, "English only" became the norm in the teaching of English and "English was associated with patriotism – speaking 'good' English was equated with being a 'good' American." Thus, Auerbach (2000) states, "practices which have come to be viewed as natural and that we take for granted as pedagogically grounded have antecedents in overtly ideological tendencies" (p. 181).

In spite of the powerful role of LEP in determining de facto policies and the role it plays in manipulating language and ideologies, there is very little research on the actual effect and consequences of LEPs. Very little is known as to how effective LEP is in determining language practices and questions are often raised as to their real effect.

In the case of the LEP in Israel, no study was planned to examine its consequences and impact and a proposal to examine the effects and the consequences of the policy did not get funded; it seems that the Ministry of Education that introduced the policy is not really eager to know its consequences. LEP may reflect more statements of intention by those in authority than real practice. There is therefore a need to conduct research that will examine the interpretations of these policies by teachers, parents, students as well as the intentions of those who introduced these educational policies, i.e., the connection between ideology and practice.

It is therefore important to examine both the intentions and the effects of the LEPs that are taking place in given entities, in given schools, programs, which are not part of the top-down LEP. For example, bottom-up initiatives to introduce the study of certain languages, especially English, in earlier grades than specified in the policy documents, or the drive by parents in Israel for the teaching of spoken Arabic in spite of the LEP specifying only MSA, or the schools in the Arab community who start teaching Hebrew and English at an earlier age, or the initiative of immigrant populations to teach immigrant languages in private institutions, especially Russian, or the initiative to open bilingual schools of Arabic and Hebrew. These initiatives provide a clear indication that LEP need not necessarily be used only as a tool in the hands of centralized educational systems but that there is a need to legitimize it as a mechanism that can serve other groups according to their needs and priorities. One of the main problems of LEP is the attempt to create policies for whole nations, for large groups of learners, not realizing that different people and different groups may have different needs, in different times, in different locations, not always in congruence with hegemonic national ideologies.

Yet, in spite of the top-down pressure of most LEPs, initiatives may also be allowed, even in contradiction to the declared and "official" policies. Bottom-up and grassroots initiatives can at times put pressure on centralized bodies to change and alter the LEP. Such has been the case with numerous examples concerning the teaching of English at an earlier age, a move often urged by parents. The pressure exerted by parents affected the ideologies of the ministries and resulted in the adoption of different educational policies, which were more in the spirit of the "clients". In the case of Israel, this occurs through the study of English earlier than stated in the LEP, the early study of Hebrew and English among Arabs, through the study of Russian in private schools and through the study of spoken Arabic in a number of cities in opposition to the policy of the Ministry of Education. It is clear then that the LEP provides an arena for resistance but also an arena for negotiation, as will be discussed in Part III.

Summary

- Language education policy (LEP) can be seen as a powerful mechanism for creating de facto language policies given the fact that children in most countries are obliged to attend school.
- Educational institutions in general and those concerned with literary education in particular are among the chief mechanisms for promoting language ideologies within a society in accordance with the interests of certain powerful groups.
- Fluctuations in language education policy have often been determined by political and ideological considerations rather than pedagogical factors as the history of social attitudes to bilingualism demonstrates.
- These policies are in contradiction to research findings about language learning and language use, about the length of time it takes immigrants to acquire academic proficiency of the dominant language, and about reliance on L-1 as a valuable source.
- Bottom-up and grassroots initiatives have been successful in persuading central bodies to alter certain aspects of language education policy.
- Language education policy has thus been shown to be an arena for negotiation as well as resistance.

6 Language tests

Overview

Language tests refer to a set of mechanisms which are used in subtle ways to manipulate language and create de facto language policies. Language tests are widely used mechanisms that are considered covert since the public is not aware of their effects and impact in creating, affecting and imposing de facto language policies, often in contradiction to declared policies and for perpetuating ideological agendas. Language tests are considered a powerful device that is imposed by groups in power to affect language priorities, language practices and criteria of correctness often leading to inclusion and exclusions and to perpetuate ideologies. Tests are powerful also because they are imposed on all students in all schools, with no way of resisting them.

The power of tests

While testing can be viewed as part of LEP, it is discussed here in a separate section, since it acts as a most powerful mechanism for affecting and manipulating language behaviors and the use of students, teachers, parents and society as a whole (Shohamy, 2001; Broadfoot, 1996). In recent years, tests have been viewed not only as pedagogical tools, but especially as social and political instruments that have a strong impact on education and can determine social order. The term "use-oriented testing" refers to a view of testing whereby tests are not viewed in isolation but rather as connected to psychological, social and political variables that have effects on curriculum, ethicality, social classes, bureaucracy, politics and knowledge (Messick, 1981, 1994, 1996, 1998). Thus, in recent years, there has been a major emphasis on the roles that language tests play in society. Specifically, these questions relate to what happens to test takers taking tests, the knowledge created by tests, the teachers preparing their students for tests, the materials and methods used in preparation for tests, the decisions based on tests' results, to the motivation of policy makers in introducing tests, the intentions and motivations for introducing tests, the effects of tests on language knowledge and language teaching, and the consequences of tests on education and society.

In Shohamy (2001), there is a detailed discussion of the power of tests in manipulating language behaviors, especially in terms of deciding the priority of specific languages in society and education. Given the power of tests, even the act of testing itself already provides a message as to the importance of certain languages over others. It shows that the tests of specific languages and of a specific content can determine which languages will be studied and the content and methods of teaching that should be used.

Thus, in the case of a new national reading comprehension test, it was shown how the introduction of the test forced teachers to engage in teaching "test-like" materials, such as texts and questions in the classroom, rather than teaching reading in a more integrated way. Similarly, the introduction of an English oral test in the 12th grade resulted in teaching test-like content in the classroom and only the particular tasks that are included in the test and not others. Also, in the case of learning Arabic as a second language, a new test created a pedagogy that was identical to the test.

Tests as tools for manipulating language

In all these cases, tests were used as the main mechanism for manipulating languages, and decision makers were totally aware of the effects of tests in imposing language policies. They specifically and intentionally introduced the tests as policy tools in order to control and manipulate language policy: "It is the realization by those in authority that test takers will change their behaviors in order to succeed on tests that leads them to introduce tests to cause a change in the behavior of those affected by the tests in accordance with their own priorities" (Shohamy, 2001, p. 17). In the case of reading comprehension, the tests for this subject were used to create a situation whereby reading comprehension was given special teaching time in schools. In the case of the English test, the national supervisor was convinced that oral language would only be taught if it was imposed through testing. Finally, in the case of Arabic, the national supervisor tried to ensure that Arabic script would be taught efficiently by setting a national test designed to compel teachers to use specific teaching methods and thus also raise the status of the language. Tests also demand a certain level of proficiency as they demonstrate not only an individual's ability in a particular language but also the criteria used to assess the quality of the language he or she produces. The yard stick for correctness is almost always the language of the native speaker.

Davies (1997) warned against such uses of tests, by noting that "While the growing professionalization of language testing is perceived as a strength and a major contribution towards a growing sense of ethicality, the increase in commercial and market forces, as well as the widespread use of language assessment as an instrument in government policy, may pressure language testers into dangerous and (and unethical) conduct" (p. 236).

Language tests are therefore powerful tools that are instrumental in manipulating languages in three major directions:

1   determining the prestige and the status of languages;
2   standardizing and perpetuating language correctness; and
3   suppressing language diversity.

Each of these purposes will now be discussed:

Determining the prestige and the status of languages

Tests serve as a major tool for determining the status and power of specific languages in society, and especially perpetuating national languages. Thus, most entrance criteria to universities and other educational institutions are applied through national languages. One way to abolish de facto bilingual education in the USA has been to make it compulsory for students to be tested in the national language, English. Graduation tests in the USA, even in states that are populated by immigrants, are *all* in English. In Israel, as well, all graduating tests of high schools are in Hebrew, even for Arabic students who go through their schooling with Arabic as the language of instruction, as will be described later. A recent debate has taken place in the USA with regard to the No Child Left Behind policy as they are conducted only in English. Schools that are populated by immigrants feel they are being penalized as immigrants cannot demonstrate their full proficiency as the tests are conducted in English.

Tests are also capable of determining the status and hierarchy of other languages, as is the case with the testing of English in a large number of countries in the world today. The role of tests in determining the prestige and status of languages is especially noticed in the case of the English language and the role of international tests such as the TOEFL (Test of English as a Foreign Language) in perpetuating the English language. There is no doubt as to the power of the English language in the global world today. But it is the introduction of tests in the English language that perpetuates their power. Thus, educational systems use English tests to perpetuate policies. The entrance to schools and universities is determined exclusively nowadays by passing an English test. By introducing tests in the power language, given the power of tests, the power of the language is reinforced. Scenarios that describe such situations will be presented later in the chapter.

Thus, in the case of English, language tests drive forward, perpetuate and reaffirm the status of English. Further, English tests act as mediators between politics and education. The process is unending as the testing of English and the teaching and learning of English affect and perpetuate one another and together affect its power; at that point, it is not clear what is the chicken and what is the egg.

Standardizing languages and perpetuating correctness

One of the most powerful uses of tests is in determining and perpetuating language correctness and standards. The fact that tests have one criterion for correctness means that they are capable of perpetuating uniformity and standardization according to the predetermined and defined criteria.

Most tests have specific norms and criteria for correctness and, as Milroy and Milroy (1999) note, these tend "to characterize speech in terms of writing" (pp. 139–40), while spoken norms are ignored in most tests and thus "normal spoken features tend, as a result, to be stigmatized" (p. 140). Thus, tests are capable of influencing the definition of languages and in creating new genres. Milroy and Milroy (1999) also note that language tests have a weakness in that they allow only for standardized answers in terms of grammar and lexicon. "They do not usually attempt to measure these more subtle but important aspects of language ability" (p. 142). As such, tests oversimplify language, which, they claim, is characteristic of most doctrines of correctness, "and it is clearly these popular correctness doctrines, rather than careful linguistic analysis, which underlie the design of many language tests". In fact, they claim that "results of tests are often used to support arguments that non-standard English-speaking testees lack language ability in some unspecified way. Scores are thus used to lend apparent objectivity to judgments based on prescriptive ideologies" and that "unjustifiable notions of correctness are inherent in the design of tests" (p. 145). Moreover, "This widespread use of standardized testing as a mode of assessment is predicated on the assumption that standardized tests are objective; this assumption in turn does not appear to take into account differences in communicative competence between different groups of speakers" (p. 145). This point will be brought up in a different way in the next section about tests that suppress diversity. Most tests determine the criteria of correctness according to the native variety of language, and all other groups, including immigrants and the indigenous population, are expected to comply and use language according to this standard.

Suppressing language diversity

Multiculturalism is characteristic of most nations of the world today, as most nations consist of different ethnic groups, whether these groups have been residing in the country for some time or have recently arrived. As noted in Chapter 2, these groups define themselves as different with respect to dimensions such as culture, language, religion, ideology and politics, and have begun to demand recognition of their differences. They are resisting pressures to conform to the dominant group and would rather preserve, maintain and even enhance their uniqueness. In the past, however, these "different" groups were expected to conform to and assimilate with the dominant or majority group and assume its values and ideologies.

One important outcome of multiculturalism, with regard to education, concerns conceptions and definitions of "knowledge". In earlier *assimilative* models, there was no appreciation of the knowledge that minority groups had; rather, they were expected to relinquish it and acquire the knowledge that is associated with the dominant group. A later model is referred to as *recognition*, implying that there is appreciation and acknowledgement of different forms of knowledge as valuable and important. In this model, different groups are granted credit for their knowledge and are often encouraged to maintain and cultivate it, at least for a temporary period. Current models are referred to as *interactive* in that the knowledge of the minority groups is seen to affect that of the dominant group and enrich it in a two-way interaction. Thus, the minority groups no longer simply *accommodate* and *adjust to* the majority. In this model, it is also not enough to *recognize* the knowledge; rather, the knowledge must be viewed as part of a new enriched knowledge, perceived as important "funds of knowledge" for the society as a whole.

Clearly, the two-way interaction model is not simple to apply as there is often resentment by the dominant groups who are eager to maintain and preserve their place in society and who view the "other" forms of knowledge as challenges to their values and existence. Thus, elite groups tend to deny interactive models in overt and covert ways and continue to perpetuate assimilative models by viewing the knowledge of the different groups as deficient. In most societies, it is still the assimilative model that is being practised, in which minority groups acquire the language of the dominant group, often with no encouragement to maintain their home languages. Tankersley (2001) notes that "the majority of people are of the opinion that minority language speakers in a country need to speak the language of the majority speakers in order to be seen as productive citizens" (p. 109). In some situations, the different groups are encouraged to maintain their languages, but it is rarely the case that the dominant group acquires the other languages spoken in the society.

This pattern is most apparent in schools where various types of mechanisms allow for the perpetuation of policies in formal ways. In schools, the knowledge of minority students is not being acknowledged because immigrants and other groups are generally not granted any credit for it. Their different knowledge is viewed as deficient, and the knowledge of the dominant group is considered the only knowledge of value. Even in situations where multiculturalism is recognized, tokenism prevails, and educational systems use a variety of overt and covert mechanisms to strive for homogeneous knowledge, which they believe should be owned by all. Thus, Tankersley (2001), for example, quotes a teacher who comments on the status of the Albanian language in Macedonia: "the majority in a country usually don't want to learn the language of the minority because they fear that the majority could be easily dominated that way. They would lose their superiority that way" (p. 120).

Tests provide effective tools for carrying out such assimilative agendas. Tests of language as well as types of school content play major roles in the process of maintaining and perpetuating the dominant knowledge. They serve as tools to suppress and eliminate the unique knowledge of minority groups, eventually leading to its elimination. At times, curricula may contain statements that *recognize* diverse knowledge, yet the tests, which are based on homogeneous knowledge, represent the de facto educational policy. Minority groups rarely take part in the deliberations over the content of the tests and are not considered as partners in the decision-making process (Taylor, 1998). Further, in many cases, minority groups internalize and accept the domination and relevance of the dominant knowledge.

Language tests play a special role in multicultural/multilingual societies in accepting certain languages and rejecting others and in promoting assimilative notions instead of recognition and interactive models. Below is a list of testing scenarios that demonstrate how language tests perpetuate de facto assimilative models. More information about these scenarios is presented by Shohamy (2004) in an article devoted specifically to the uses of tests in language policy, entitled "Assessment in multicultural societies: Applying democratic principles and practices to language testing", where it was shown how tests are used to impose monolingual language policies and suppress multilingual diversity. Specifically, these scenarios describe how the knowledge of minority groups is not valued and appreciated, and how the mechanism of language tests serves mostly as a tool to maintain and perpetuate the dominant knowledge of majority groups and to suppress other languages. In a series of articles (Byrnes, 2005), a number of policy makers, teachers and other scholars report on specific changes that have occurred at schools in the USA as a result of the No Child Left Behind Act. Specifically, they relate to the fact that foreign languages are not included in the testing. They claim that this had a major effect on the number of students enrolled in languages classes and that switching foreign language teachers into English as a Second Language (ESL) classes reduces the number of foreign language classes as well as the number of foreign language teachers. This impact, they claim, will be very difficult to reverse. The message given through the testing policy is that foreign languages are not relevant in the USA today.

Language testing scenarios*

Scenario 1: No recognition of previous language and content

Russian immigrant children arriving in Israel are proficient in the Russian language. In Israel, Hebrew is the dominant language and the avenue to success in society. Since it takes immigrant students approximately 7–11 years to acquire a level of proficiency in the new language that is equivalent to that of native speakers, many of the Russian students fail the mathematics tests. It is clear that the Russian students have to, and in fact do, acquire Hebrew, but they are not granted any credit for their knowledge of Russian. All the learning is taking place in Hebrew and the tests that determine their achievements and their entrance into higher education are conducted in Hebrew.

In the above case, the educational system does not recognize the knowledge that the immigrants possess. This is expressed both in terms of the language of instruction as well as in terms of the language of all the tests. Since the tests are conducted in Hebrew, a language that Russian immigrants are in the process of acquiring but are still not proficient in, the students cannot demonstrate the full range of their competence. In this scenario, the language and the knowledge that Russian students acquired in their home countries is not valued. It is clear that such a policy keeps the immigrants in a powerless position compared to the dominant group, and their unique knowledge is erased from the educational repertoire.

Scenario 2: Language and content are recognized but the testing policy is in contradiction

In Israel, both Hebrew and Arabic are official languages. Israeli Arabs study in their first language, so Arabic is the language of instruction. Israeli Arabs also learn Hebrew beginning in third grade, but as a second language. Yet the main criterion for entering Israeli universities is passing an end-of-high-school test that requires a high level proficiency in Hebrew. Clearly, the Arab students get no credit for their knowledge of Arabic, their language of instruction throughout their years of schooling.

In the above case, the dominant group recognizes the language of the minority group and in fact encourages it. In the Arab communities in Israel, Arabic is

* Taken from Shohamy, 2004.

used as the language of instruction. Yet, without getting into the specific reasons for recognizing Arabic as the language of instruction (and not granting such rights to other groups such as the Russians), it is the performance in the Hebrew language tests (the dominant language) that serves as the main criterion for entrance into higher education. Language tests perpetuate the dominance of Hebrew and grant no value to Arabic. Clearly, such a situation is likely to result in low motivation on the part of the Arab students to maintain their home language because Arabic has no recognized status and no legitimacy as a rite of passage. In fact, there are already signs of this happening as more content areas in Arab secondary schools are being taught in Hebrew. Thus, the policy of maintaining the home language by using it as the language of instruction is in contradiction to testing policies; since tests are such powerful instruments, they create and dictate the de facto educational policies.

Scenario 3: The cultural interests of minority groups are not validated through testing practices

Israeli Arabs are required to study Jewish content such as the Talmud, the Bible, and Hebrew literature; their studies contain very limited exposure to their own content areas, such as the Koran. The testing policy is in line with this. The final secondary school examination includes these content areas, and passing the test is a condition for entrance into higher education institutions. Interestingly, Jewish students are not required to study Arab content in school, and even the study of Arabic is not totally compulsory, although Arabic is an official language in Israel.

The above case indicates that some knowledge of minority groups can be recognized as important, such as the language, but not the content. Regarding content, Arabs are required to study the dominant knowledge of the Jewish population. This is perpetuated even more through the tests that are a condition for entrance into higher education institutions. Here, as well, the tests serve as gatekeeping devices, since those Arabs who do not master the knowledge of the dominant group cannot be accepted to higher education institutions.

Scenario 4: Majority languages are enforced through testing practices

The Latvian language policy recognizes the existence of both the Latvian and Russian languages as part of their language policy, yet in order to obtain jobs as well as citizenship, Russians have to pass tests in the Latvian language.

In the above example, while there is recognition of the Russian language in policy documents, it is testing that creates the de facto policy of limiting opportunities for minority groups, in this case Russian speakers in Latvia. Here, the testing policy is in contradiction to the official policy. While the language policy seems to be that of recognition, the testing policy is that of assimilation.

Scenario 5: One size fits all

Arab students learn three languages in school: Arabic, Hebrew and English. Jewish students learn two languages: Hebrew and English. Clearly, the proficiency of the Arab students in English is not as high as those of the Jews, yet the Arabs are being measured with the same tests and are evaluated by the same criteria. Not surprisingly, their scores in English are consistently lower than those of the Jews.

In the above case, which is norm-referenced, all groups are being compared to the dominant group, and success is measured by the same tools for all, although the conditions and learning experiences are entirely different. There is no recognition that English is a third language for Arabs, but a second language for Jews. Using the same test means using the same criteria for both groups, which is bound to result in a situation in which the Arabs will generally get lower scores. In most societies that apply assimilative models, the same tests are used for all groups regardless of different backgrounds and experiences, guaranteeing the superiority of the dominant group. Thus, by using a norm-referenced approach, various groups are compared to the dominant group. By applying criterion-referenced approaches, language proficiency is measured according to the experiences of each group.

The above scenarios describe how the linguistic and cultural knowledge of minority groups is often not recognized by majority groups, and how tests are used as tools to perpetuate inequality. Furthermore, even in situations where knowledge is recognized as part of multiculturalism, tests serve as tools to contradict such policies and thus to homogenize knowledge so that assimilative models are carried out. Clearly, testing is the de facto educational policy, and standardized tests that are based on homogeneous knowledge serve as tools to standardize knowledge and negate existing differences. These tests serve as tools to exclude and eliminate knowledge in covert ways, thus undermining multicultural practices that, in theory, recognize the voices of diverse groups as partners in multicultural societies. As Taylor (1998, p. 143) would argue, liberal democracies should apply philosophies of inclusion in which reference to "the people" is taken to mean everybody, without unspoken restrictions. Oller (1998; in Shohamy, 2001) wonders whether it is possible to introduce language tests that follow more democratic practices and asks whether it is not possible "to have testing of the people, for the people, and by the people".

If, as discussed in Chapter 1, ideas of crossing within and among languages were introduced, allowing freedom of expression using a number of codes simultaneously and crossing the language borders, tests work against these notions. Tests use very homogenous criteria for correction that do not allow any diversity, let alone the use of multilingual and multi-literacy codes.

The sources of power of language tests

Tests offer great temptation for decision makers to use them as mechanisms of language manipulations. They are viewed by the public, especially parents, as authoritative. They guarantee easy policy implementation, are effective for "proving" and are instrumental in redefining knowledge. Tests allow flexible cutting scores, which means that those in authority can determine what is considered good or bad knowledge of the language. In relation to other changes in the society, they are instrumental in creating changes in a cost-effective way, that is not to say that they are also effective from a quality perspective. Thus, tests offer great temptations for those in authority to use as policy tools.

This is so also because tests inspire confidence in people and can serve as tools to maintain social order (Bourdieu, 1991). The power of tests is derived from the trust that those who are affected by tests place in them as there is an unwritten contract between those in political and those who are affected by tests, by those who want to dominate and those who want to be dominated and grant tests their power and authority so they can perpetuate and maintain social order.

The power of tests as a language policy mechanism is obtained from the special features that they have. They are administered by powerful organizations such as government and testing agencies. In addition, they make use of the language of science and numbers, which is most influential and impressive for the public at large; they use written forms and documents, which, according to Foucault (1979), are very powerful tools of domination. And they make use of "objective" formats that make the tests seem reliable and trustworthy.

The impact of tests as a mechanism of control is enormous, as they have the strongest effects on the lives of individuals. They determine rites of passage, they create dependence, they grant test scores economic value, and it is the combination of the power of tests with the power of language, especially the English language, that makes them even more powerful. Moreover, tests are fed by propaganda and ideology; most people trust tests and believe that they are good and effective tools. As Spolsky writes, "For much of this century, the general public has been brain-washed to believe in the infallibility, fairness and meaningfulness of the results of tests and examinations" (Spolsky, 1998a, p. 1).

Moreover, tests lead to high-stakes decisions for individuals (or for society as a whole); they create winners and losers; successes and failures, rejections and acceptances. Moreover, test scores are sole indicators for placing people in class levels, granting certificates and prizes, determining whether persons will be allowed to continue in future studies, deciding on professions, entering special education classes, participating in honour classes, continuing to higher education and obtaining jobs.

Further, tests are used as disciplinary tools to impose behaviors on test-takers (e.g. in school systems) who are affected by their results. Test-takers develop a fear of tests, as they feel that they have no control over their behavior as they are in the hands of the tests and testers. Tests are capable of dictating what will be studied, learned and taught by students and teachers. In return, test-takers and teachers comply with the demands of the tests and change their behavior accordingly, in order to maximize their scores, given the detrimental effects of the tests.

Research on the use of tests demonstrates this in terms of *intentions* and *effects*. With regard to *intentions*, they specifically declare that the rationale, purposes and expectations for introducing tests is to affect learning and teaching. In terms of *effects*, there is ample evidence that tests have an effect on curriculum change, teaching and testing methods, redefinition of language knowledge, motivation to teach "test language", narrowing the linguistic knowledge. Furthermore, even in these very situations where intentions are not explicitly stated, tests do result in major effects on individuals and meaningful impacts beyond any expectations of education and society.

In terms of the quality of the effect, it has been shown that tests have negative effects on the quality of knowledge; for example, the teaching of a "test language", as a result of introducing tests, creates parallel forms of education and the "tested knowledge" becomes the "de facto" knowledge. It also leads to unethical and undemocratic ways of making policy, in other words a covert means of controlling education and in this case language education policies. Yet, it is also shown that patterns of effect depend on whether the test is of high or low stakes. The effects of tests in English are high, as the subject has high status in the society. The effect of tests of Arabic on teaching are low, as the subject has low status in society (Shohamy, Donitsa-Schmidt, Ferman, 1996).

The role of teachers in language testing

As was noted in Chapter 5, teachers play a major role in creating de facto language education policies by implementing those policies. A similar situation happens with carrying out "testing" orders. Here, too, teachers and testers are treated as bureaucrats and not as professionals. Thus, while teachers are rarely involved in making language testing policies, they are expected to carry out the testing orders of "teaching for the tests" and change their pedagogical strategies accordingly. Thus, teachers become the agents through whom such power and control agendas are being exercised, as teachers are often responsible for implementing the testing policies of central agencies with no power and authority to resist. This phenomenon is especially noticed in contexts in which national and state-wide tests are used (Shohamy, 2004).

There are currently two views with regard to teachers in testing. There are those who view teachers as bureaucrats and others who view them as professionals. In most cases, teachers are viewed as bureaucrats; they are being used by those in authority to carry out testing policies and thus become servants of the system. In other situations, teachers are viewed as professionals when they take an active role in creating testing policies and initiate meaningful dialogues about tests and their uses and effects.

In situations where teachers are viewed as bureaucrats, they are being forced to comply with the demands of the tests as declared by central agencies. Those in authority have the tools to force and control teachers to do it and they are capable of dictating to teachers what to teach and what test-takers will study, as teachers have no choice but to comply with the demands of the tests. They do it by changing their behaviors to maximize the scores of their students, given the detrimental effects of tests on their students' lives and their own reputation. This is especially relevant in final high school tests, university entrance tests and multinational tests such as the TOEFL, mentioned earlier. Teachers carry out the "testing orders" even in situations that contradict their own beliefs.

In most cases, teachers are not involved in decisions to introduce national and/or state-wide tests. Yet, at the same time they are expected to carry out the order of "teaching to the tests" and to change their pedagogical strategies accordingly. Even in situations when it is not explicitly stated, teachers view tests not only as testing the language performance and proficiency levels of their own students but also as assessing or "testing" their own performance. Those who introduce the tests know very well that teachers and students will change their behavior in order to succeed on the high-stakes tests and this is often, as noted earlier, the rationale for introducing such tests. Thus, centralized tests are capable of dictating to teachers what to teach and what test-takers will study, as teachers, and test-takers, comply with the demands of the tests by changing their behavior so as to maximize the scores, given the detrimental effects of the tests. Broadfoot (1996) demonstrates how teachers become the new servants of the central systems, which she refers to as "a new order of domination" (p. 87).

Tests as a mechanism for de facto policies

In conclusion, a very widely used mechanism employed by central authorities to control language is the device of language tests. It is used to create,
perpetuate and manipulate language education policy. While language
education policy that is expressed in official documents provides relatively
transparent information about specific decisions regarding languages,
much of language educational policy is actually realized through tests as
the indirect action and practice that serves as de facto language education
policy. These new de facto language education policies override and
contradict existing policies and create alternative language policy
realities. In nation-states, therefore, language tests serve as a significant
main mechanism affecting the linguistic repertoire, teaching material
and language standards and also affecting the population in terms of
admission criteria. Given the power of tests, language education policy
documents often become no more than declarations of intent that can easily
be manipulated, even in ways that contradict the official language education
policy.

To demonstrate that point, one can examine a situation where the language education policy declares a specific language as significant and of
priority for the educational system. At the same time, by establishing
entrance criteria that include a test of another language, a new de facto
policy is created, the implication of which is that the "tested language"
becomes the only important language. Indeed, as noted, since tests are
often more powerful than any written policy document, they lead to the
elimination and suppression of certain languages in societies. Tests can
also be used as tools to privilege certain forms and levels of knowledge of
languages. Language education policy may state that correct grammar
or "native-like" accents are not essential for acceptable proficiency; yet
language tests that demand correct grammar and accent (mostly adhering
to the native) create different de facto criteria that can at the same time
become barriers for keeping unwanted groups, such as immigrants, from
entering educational institutions and/or the workplace.

In conclusion, language tests are considered powerful because they are
used by central authorities as tools for imposing what will be learned in
schools, how it will be learned, who is eligible to learn and to continue
learning and what the criteria for correctness will be. The choice of the
languages that are being tested in society determines their importance.
Those who make these decisions, ministries of education and other government agencies and groups in authority, are in control of knowledge and
of classes in society that determine the criteria for achievement and measures
of success, and all through language tests. Thus, language tests affect the
choice of languages, the methods and content studied as well as the criteria
for language standards and correctness.

In most political systems in the world today, tests drive the system and perpetuate its power and thus serve as an effective mechanism influencing de facto language policy.

Democratic processes and language rights

As is discussed in Chapter 9, such mechanisms violate democratic practices, contribute to the loss of languages and diminish "other" languages. They also act as a gatekeeper to prevent people from entering schools, universities and the workplace and expel them from countries that impose citizenship tests, thus contributing to the violation of democratic processes and language rights.

Given the power of the tests and their consequences, those tested tend to comply with every decision that is made through the tests, as their consequences are so crucial. Thus, when tests are given in national languages and violate language rights, even if those are granted in language policies, test-takers have no choice but to comply. The testing in these languages contains a direct message about language priorities and the marginalization of other languages, even those that are stated in the national LEP. Thus, testing in the powerful and prestigious language in schools contributes to the loss of languages, as it diminishes the status of all other languages, those which are not being tested. It further excludes people of other languages from education and from the workplace. Such testing clearly violates language rights. The study reported in Chapter 5 about the length of time it takes students to demonstrate their knowledge in certain subjects, compared to those born speaking the language of power, prevents students from participating effectively in schools and gaining academic knowledge. Such low achievements can have powerful ramifications, such as when they are prevented from graduating or from obtaining jobs as a result of low scores on tests that happened only because they were given in a language that they were in the process of acquiring. In contrast, when students obtain different types of language accommodations, they obtain higher scores.

In Figure 8, it can be seen how when immigrant students obtain bilingual accommodations in mathematics, that is, when the test in mathematics is given in two languages, Hebrew and Russian, compared with a control group that obtains the test in Hebrew only, those who receive the bilingual version perform significantly better.

Once such results as above are obtained, protecting and defending language rights means that it is the obligation of school boards and ministries of education to provide such accommodations. Not administering the tests in such a form therefore leads to a violation of personal rights. This is so, since they are not given the optimal conditions to demonstrate their knowledge and they are therefore discriminated against.

Testing has further manifestations in terms of language rights for adults in the context of immigration. Thus, when citizenship tests are administered,

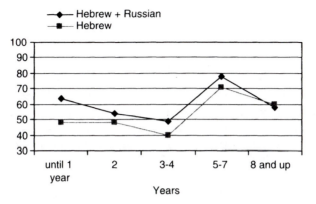

Figure 8 Bilingual test accommodations as enhancing achievement.
Source: Levin *et al.*, 2003.

and in many European countries, as was described in Chapter 4, immigrants need to demonstrate high levels of proficiency, which also represents a strong form of discrimination. This is because expelling and de-legitimizing people because of their not knowing the dominant language is again a form of violation of language rights: knowledge of a power language, or in fact of any language, should not be used as a condition "for living". It is a combination of tests, citizenship and language that creates a particularly strong mechanism of exclusion. Tests in this context also represent a strong form of violation of personal and language rights as well as of democratic practices, as it is difficult to prove a connection between proficiency in the local and power language and being a good human being.

Language tests are considered hidden mechanisms as they affect and create de facto policies, which are generally not known to the public. In fact, only rarely are these issues raised and openly discussed. Given the power of tests and their role in moving hidden agendas of manipulating language policies, there is a need to apply democratic principles and practices to language testing.

Tests that were originally developed for democratizing purposes have been utilized in acts that are not democratic in that they have become tools used by centralized authorities to exercise power and control, and to manipulate educational systems. Tests are central to a number of competing battles: between the need of central agencies for control and the desire for individual freedom; between the urge of groups for a common unifying knowledge and open, creative knowledge; between a monolingual "one language for all" policy and multilingual tolerance; between the public need for symbolic devices of social order and the need of individuals and groups for personal expression and freedom; between increased control in growing technological societies and fluid and relative knowledge; between resentment of control by centralized agencies and the need for control in order to maintain status and social order; between individual expression and group expression; between practical concerns and ideological forces.

A number of ways in which society can protect itself from undemocratic language testing are proposed. Specifically, it has recommended the inclusion of different voices in the assessment process; offered a number of ways in which test-takers can guard themselves from the misuses of tests; examined the uses of tests from a critical language-testing perspective; considered the development of shared and collaborative assessment models; and insisted on accountability from those who are engaged in test development. The message of this chapter is not a call for the abolition of tests, but rather a call for practising democratic testing, which requires shared authority, collaboration, the involvement of different stakeholders (test-takers included), and the monitoring of test use. There is a need for continuous examination of the quality of tests, for in-depth insight into how they are used, for the public exposure of test misuse, and for the education of the public regarding the motivation, harmful effects, and consequences of tests. The price of such democratic approaches is high, as they take more time, involve more people, require greater resources, and involve compromise, as all democratic practices do. But if tests are so central, and they represent such strong potential for misuse, the price is worth paying. This is the challenge that language testers need to face.

Conclusions

In contrast to the lack of information about the effect of the other categories of mechanisms mentioned so far, there is research that has investigated the effects and consequences of the mechanism of language tests on de facto language policy. Some of these studies are reported and discussed in Chapter 6, demonstrating how language tests are capable of manipulating language realities, redefining language knowledge, determining prestige and status of languages, standardizing and perpetuating language correctness, diverting the focus of learning to the very languages that are considered important by those in authority, perpetuating the power of the English language and especially homogenizing and suppressing linguistic diversity.

Further, as has been demonstrated, language tests are often introduced in undemocratic and unethical ways, mostly for disciplinary purposes and for carrying out the policy agenda of those in power. Tests can change test-takers' behavior according to set agendas, impose the values and knowledge of those in authority with regard to national language, perpetuate unrealistic "native-like" criteria, and suppress multilingualism. It is also shown how tests are used as disciplinary tools in covert ways for manipulating educational systems. The consequences of using tests in such powerful ways is that they narrow the language knowledge and create contradictions with existing knowledge as expressed in official curricula, and that they lead to exclusion and violation of personal rights. Such misuses are possible given that tests are of high stakes and cause those who are affected by them (i.e., individuals and educational systems) to modify their behavior in accordance with the agendas of the tests.

Summary

- Language tests, as policy mechanisms, have been shown to be capable of manipulating language realities by redefining, standardizing and perpetuating language knowledge and correctness, maintaining and promoting the status of a particular (often national) language(s) while eliminating others and monitoring the prestige of that favored language.
- Language tests are often introduced with an ulterior motive connected with furthering the policy agendas of those in positions of influence, especially in the cases of national tests as well as language tests for citizenship. In this way such tests become a means of narrowing the curriculum, manipulating education systems, suppressing diversity and provides legitimacy for the nation to keep out those it wants to exclude.
- The considerable social value placed on language tests and the high stakes involved mean that those being tested often find themselves obliged to modify their language use in order to succeed at all.
- The language policies that result from the use of language tests as a policy mechanism are often in contradiction to declared policies and violate language rights, especially in schools when students are being tested on academic knowledge in an unfamiliar language and with no allowance for building upon the languages they already know.

7   Language in the public space

Overview

"Language in the public space" refers to all language items that are displayed in a variety of contexts in the environment. The first part of the chapter will address the linguistic items found in the public space, while the second part addresses issues related to language ideology, myths, propaganda and coercion. In terms of language displayed in the public space, it refers to actual language items that are found in streets, shopping centres, schools, markets, offices, hospitals and any other public space (and often private ones, such as homes), for example names of streets, public signs, names of shops, advertisements, documents, newspapers, billboards, verbal as well as non-verbal items such as pictures and images. It is also referred to as language ecology. It is argued here that the presence (or absence) of language displays in the public space communicates a message, intentional or not, conscious or not, that affects, manipulates or imposes de facto language policy and practice. Thus, the presence (or absence) of specific language items, displayed in specific languages, in a specific manner, sends direct and indirect messages with regard to the centrality versus the marginality of certain languages in society. The display of language transmits symbolic messages as to the legitimacy, relevance, priority and standards of languages and the people and groups they represent. The public space is therefore a most relevant arena to serve as a mechanism for creating de facto language policy so that the ideological battles that are taking place in the new nation-state can be turned into practice.

In general, those in authority use language in the public space to deliver symbolic messages about the importance, power, significance and relevance of certain languages or the irrelevance of others. On the other hand, it is also the case that groups and individuals in the private domain feel manipulated by symbolic displays of language in the public space and protest against it, either by displaying items in "other languages" that provide different and contradictory symbols or by preventing the display of any verbal languages in the public space, as they perceive it as an imposition on their personal freedom and/or ideologies. Such phenomena are often observed in protests against globalization, as the use of the English language on billboards symbolizes and represents for these groups aspects of globalization, colonialism and further evidence of domination. Similarly, groups that strive to revive or obtain recognition for their perceived neglected identities will use the public space to present their language publicly on billboards, road signs, public advertisements, names of buildings, streets and so on.

Governments, municipalities, NGOs, global and smaller companies, all use the public space as an arena for conducting their battles for power, control, national identity, recognition and self-expression. They will use the public space to send different ideological messages, and to turn them in to practice. Thus language in the public space needs to be recognized as one of the major mechanisms affecting de facto policies. The appearance of language in the public space serves as an important mechanism through which language battles among various interested groups, as discussed in Chapter 2, take place. Thus, the public space serves as a tool in the hands of different groups for the transmission of messages as to the place of different languages in the geographical and political entities and for influencing and creating de facto language realities.

The public space as a focus of attention in language policy as well as in language use is a relatively new area of attention, as most research on language use tends to focus primarily on speakers and not on their environments. Yet, recently language ecology has been getting attention in the literature of cultural geography, urban studies, semiotics, social psychology and applied linguistics (Scollon, 2001, 2003; Landry and Bourhis, 1997; Spolsky and Cooper, 1991; Romaine, 2002).

Relying on the work of Lefebvre (1991), in environmental studies, language in the public space focuses on language in the "spatial practice", referring to the moulding of the physical-geographical areas, that is, the "spaces". According to Lefebvre, space is socially produced by "spatial practice", which consists of coordinated and uncoordinated human actions in the physical space. The analysis of these spatial practices identifies their constituent elements, and subsequently, in each particular space, it is possible to pinpoint integrative principles or alternatively disordered, mutually unrelated practices. Lefebvre also differentiates between institutional agencies that act under the control of central policies and individuals, associations or entrepreneurs – who enjoy some autonomy of action within legal limits. This will be referred here as top-down vs. bottom-up and will be defined later in the chapter.

The focus on language in the public space in this book originates from the view that it serves as a mechanism to affect, manipulate and impose de facto language practices in hidden and covert ways. In that respect, it is similar to other mechanisms discussed throughout Part II, such as language tests and education policies, where the argument is that these mechanisms can turn ideologies into practice and are therefore part of the broader view of language policy. Yet, as with the other mechanisms, this one can also serve as an arena for protest and negotiations.

Of the endless and unlimited number of language items to be found in the public space (e.g., labels, the Internet, signs, instructions, directions, titles of books, the language of the Internet, names of buildings), the following section will focus on one type of mechanism displayed in the public space, that is, *linguistic landscape* (Landry and Bourhis, 1997). The focus on linguistic landscape originates from the relatively large number of studies that have been conducted on the topic in the past few years that document its presence and roles in shaping the public space. These studies provide some insight and understanding as to the patterns and functions of linguistic landscape as a mechanism of language policy.

Linguistic landscape

Linguistic landscape (LL) can be viewed as one domain within language in the public space; it refers to specific language objects that mark the public sphere and is used here as one case. Examples of LL are road signs, names of sites, streets, names of buildings, places and institutions, advertising bill-boards, commercials and personal visiting cards as well as labels, instructions and public forms, names of shops and public signs. Plates 1 and 2 show examples of LL items representing names of a streets in a suburban town north of Tel Aviv. As can be seen, the names of each sign are displayed in two languages, Hebrew and English. The first sign reads in Hebrew *Medinat Hayehudim*, which means "The Jewish State"; the English words are not the translation but rather the transliteration into the Hebrew. The second sign reads *Kdoshei Hashoaa*, meaning "the holy victims of the holocaust"; again, the English is an exact transliteration of the Hebrew. There is no need to elaborate here on the ideological message transmitted through these two signs; this is even before any comment is made with regard to the choice of languages. These types of signs are commonly found as road signs in most cities in Israel. They often vary from street names that symbolize ideological messages of unity, solidarity and patriotism to names of important figures in Zionist and Jewish history, to names of battles and wars. A few examples of these names are *Zahal* (the Israeli Defence Army), *Komemiyut* (the revival of the state of Israel), and *Palmach* (the early defence units before the establishment of Israel).

Landry and Bourhis (1997) elaborate on the notion of LL, referring to the visibility of languages as objects that mark the public space in a given territory. An important characteristic of LL, according to them, is that it is shaped by public authorities (e.g., government signs) as well as by individuals, associations or firms. Accordingly, the LL of a country, region or urban setting may function as an informational and symbolic marker of the relative power and status of the linguistic communities inhabiting the territory. Items 1 and 2 function as symbolic markers of the territory and clearly communicate the message of who is in power in that territory. It should not be too difficult to imagine the perceptions or feelings of any Muslim or

Plate 1

Plate 2

Christian pedestrians walking by these two signs and noticing their meaning. Interestingly, such patriotic and ideological signs are also found in the mixed town of Tel Aviv-Jaffa, and even in neighborhoods that are inhabited only by Arabs.

In their study, Landry and Bourhis (1997) examined LL in Canada from the point of view of language maintenance, using the framework of ethnolinguistic vitality (Giles, 1977). They found that LL affects the perception of members of the groups and their relative status and concluded that LL plays an important role as it contributes to language maintenance or shift in bilingual settings.

The displays of the particular languages of LL items also have symbolic value for the places and the inhabitants. Thus, when a street name appears in three languages – Hebrew, Arabic and English – it may provide some recognition that Arabs or Arabic speakers reside in the area; it therefore indicates their visibility and presence. Similarly, in a situation in which there is no Arabic, even in Arab neighbourhoods and towns, this may imply that this group is being overlooked and ignored and thus the LL items transmit a direct message as to their status, prestige and presence in given territories in society. In similar ways, the presence of English in certain places also provides symbolic messages of global, Western and possibly some universal/world values. These issues will be further discussed below through the example of the LL study.

While research on LL is relatively new, a number of studies have emerged in the past few years that examined LL in the public space. Spolsky and Cooper (1991) studied the LL in Jerusalem. Huebner (2006) examined linguistic landscape in areas of Bangkok, Cenoz and Gorter (2006) studied the LL in the Basque country and in Friesland and compared language representations in territories with regard to minority languages and de Bot studied the LL of Amsterdam and Madrid.

In the study that will be described next (Ben Rafael *et al.*, (2004), representations of LL, with special focus on Hebrew and Arabic, were examined and will be described next pointing to the use of LL as a mechanism in the midst of language negotiations and battles.

A linguistic landscape study

Background

The LL study (Ben Rafael *et al.*, 2004) examined and compared aspects of multiculturalism as reflected in the LL of Israeli settings and specifically the extent to which LL expresses Jewish-Arab bilingualism in Israel and East Jerusalem. The LL items were collected as a representative sample of six cities where Arabs and Jews reside. The data were collected via digital cameras and then analysed according to a defined list of criteria, mostly focusing on language representation.

The aspect that is most relevant to the LL as a mechanism affecting de facto language policy in the midst of the battles described in Chapter 2, is that of LL items as representing "top-down" vs. "bottom-up". Top-down LL items represent items that are issued by the state and/or central bureaucracies, while bottom-up refers to items that are issued by autonomous social actors selected by individuals and representing a number of domains, names of shops, private announcements, businesses, etc.

In the case of Israel until recently, there were no specific laws requiring the use of signs and other items in the public space that stipulated the need for certain languages, as in Quebec, Catalonia or the Basque Country as well as in the territories of the Baltic States after the fall of communism, and being engaged in the process of language revival.

The background to the language situation of Israel was presented in Chapter 4 (for more details about the language demography of Israel, see Spolsky and Shohamy, 1999 and Ben Rafael, 1994).

The study

The research consisted of the collection of approximately 1000 LL pictures in Jewish and Arab areas in Israel as well as in East Jerusalem, where mostly Arabs reside. All data were collected in August 2000, one month before the beginning of the Palestinian Intifada (the uprising). The items were collected in six towns, some of which were populated by Arabs only, others by Jews, and some were mixed. The items were then analysed according to defined criteria, such as the presence of specific languages, the order of appearance, size of letters, etc. Plates 3–11 shows examples of LL items taken from the corpus collected in the study. Each picture is accompanied by an explanation of the context and meaning below.

Results

The analysis of the data that documented the representation of the different LL items both top-down and bottom-up in the private and the public signs revealed the existence of differential LL patterns in each of these areas, reflecting the diverse ethnolinguistic settings of Israeli society. As can be seen in Figure 9, which describes the pattern of the LL representation, different patterns were found in the Jewish and Arab communities. Specifically, the pattern of Hebrew/English was found in the Jewish communities, Arabic/Hebrew in the Arab communities, while Arabic/English was the dominant pattern in East Jerusalem. In specific terms, with regard to each of the languages, Hebrew emerges as the language with highest visibility in both Jewish and Arab communities. While this is expected for the Jewish areas, it is surprising for the Arab area. Yet, Hebrew is nearly non-existent in East Jerusalem, apart from a few top-down trilingual signs in Arabic, English and Hebrew. Thus, the de facto language practice is that the officiality

Plate 3

Plate 4

Plate 5

Plate 6

Plate 7

Plate 8

Plate 9

Plate 10

Plate 11

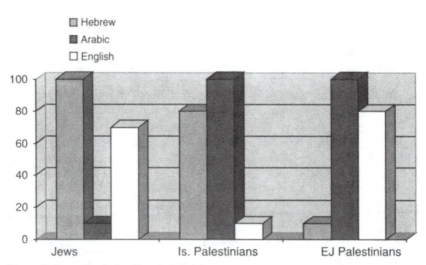

Figure 9 Patterns of plurilinguistic landscape.
Source: Ben Rafael *et al.*, 2004.

of Hebrew and Arabic is not represented in the public space as the graph in Figure 9 indicates.

The other dimension that was relevant to the study was the examination of the differences between top-down and bottom-up, as explained above.

These results are displayed in the three tables. The results show the large difference that exists between groups in this respect. In the Jewish population, there is no systematic difference between the bottom-up and the top-down, though the top-down is more trilingual than the bottom-up. Yet, in the Arab population, there is a stronger presence of Hebrew items in the bottom-up than in the top-down. Thus, there is a much stronger simultaneous presence of the two official languages, Hebrew and Arabic, in LL items than in the Jewish population. The presence of English is stronger in the bottom-up than the top-down. With regard to East Jerusalem, a trilingual pattern – Arabic, English, Hebrew – is most dominant in the top-down; the bottom-up is mostly bilingual, Arabic-English.

Table 1 LL items in "top-down" vs. "bottom-up" in the Jewish population

LL languages	Top-down	Bottom-up
Hebrew only	42.4 (n = 72)	46.9 (n = 265)
Hebrew/English	35.3 (n = 60)	43.0 (n = 243)
Russian – only or with other languages	3.5 (n = 6)	9.9 (n = 56)
Hebrew/Arabic/English	18.8 (n = 32)	0.2 (n = 1)
Total	100.0 (n = 170)	100.0 (n = 565)

Source: Ben Rafael *et al.* (2004)

Note: γ^2 (3df) = 109.98; p < .0001

Table 2 LL items in "top-down" vs. "bottom-up" in the Israeli Palestinian areas

LL language	Top-down	Bottom-up
Hebrew only	3.9 (n = 3)	40.7 (n = 55)
Hebrew/Arabic	59.2 (n = 45)	37.0 (n = 50)
Hebrew/Arabic/English	36.8 (n = 28)	22.2 (n = 30)
Total	100.0 (n = 76)	100.0 (n = 135)

Source: Ben Rafael *et al.* (2004)

Note: γ^2 (2df) = 33.04; p < .0001

Table 3 LL items in "top-down" vs. "bottom-up" in the Arab population in East Jerusalem

LL languages	Top-down	Bottom-up
Arabic only	15.4 (n = 4)	20.0 (n = 14)
Arabic/English	19.2 (n = 5)	75.7 (n = 53)
Hebrew/Arabic/English	65.4 (n = 17)	4.3 (n = 3)
Total	100.0 (n = 26)	100.0 (n = 70)

Source: Ben Rafael *et al.* (2004)

With regard to Arabic, the results showed that despite its official status as the second official language, it appears in less than 6 per cent of LL items in Jewish localities. Unlike the situation typical of Jewish localities, Arabic is much better represented in Israeli-Palestinian localities; still it appears *only* in 70 per cent of LL items.

In East Jerusalem, Arabic was found to be the dominant language appearing in all LL items. Arabic, the second official language of Israel, has a very low presence in Jewish localities in general. For example, in Tel Aviv-Jaffa, the largest metropolis, Arabic appears in only 2 per cent of the LL items, and in Jerusalem, the capital city and mixed metropolis since 1967, Arabic has a rather low representation (about 11 per cent) in the Jewish areas of the city. "Arabic only" LL items were found in 21 per cent of the cases in East Jerusalem, whereas in Israeli-Palestinian localities, such as Nazareth and Tira, "Arabic only" signs are found much more rarely (9 per cent and 3 per cent respectively). Thus, there is a noticeable difference between the LL patterns of East Jerusalem and that of Israeli-Palestinian localities.

With regard to English, its visibility and presence were strong in all domains, but especially among Jews in Israel and Arabs in East Jerusalem. It appears mainly in Hebrew-English and Arabic-English patterns, respectively. It was especially strong also in "bottom-up" branches in the Jewish population, such as clothing and leisure, and in middle- and upper-middle-class areas. In the Jewish population, it is where the middle-class and upper-middle-class people reside or shop that English is far more salient than in other layers of society.

In terms of Russian, it rarely appears in the "top-down" areas and is moderately represented in the "bottom-up" areas, even in neighbourhoods where Russians reside and in commercial areas frequently visited. In some branches, such as leisure (books and music) and offices (real estate, manpower and travel agencies), there is more presence of Russian. With regard to the bilingual patterns, the following patterns emerged. In the Jewish areas, Arabic appears mostly in the "top-down", as an expression of official policy reflecting the status of Arabic as an official language, and not in the "bottom-up". In Arab areas of Israel, the Arabic-Hebrew pattern emerged whereby there was more Hebrew in the "bottom-up". In East Jerusalem the pattern that emerged was that of Arabic-English, as there was Hebrew only in the top-down flow, mostly reflecting the officiality status and possibly some opposition to Israeli politics.

Conclusions

The study on the linguistics landscape reported above confirmed the multilingual reality of four dominant languages – Hebrew, English, Arabic and Russian – and the connection of language and social, political and economic realities. LL in the top-down flow reflected the official status of Hebrew, the main national language, as well as that of Arabic, which is an official language in Israel. We claimed that the bottom-up flow responded to rationale calculations where the primary drive is the market principle, on one hand, and ideological or political considerations, on the other. The market principle, we believe, explains the importance of English wherever this language is deemed a status symbol. For the Arabs in Israel, Arabic strengthens their Palestinian identity. However, this was in opposition to commercial interests. Thus, it created a situation in which Arabic gave way to Hebrew in the LL in the Arab community. The strong presence of English, we argued, indicated that it is *not* a *foreign* language but more a *second* language. English can therefore be considered as a *third* language in the Arab population. We argued that the outcome of the study was a mass of symbols that structured the public space and we viewed LL items mostly as a text, in which we could read the power, specific areas of influence and implications of processes such as globalization, the assertion of the national spirit or ideological as well as political venalities.

LL as a language policy mechanism

It is in the difference between the "top-down" and the "bottom-up" in the use of the different languages that one can see how the public space serves as an arena where language battles are taking place. LL, then, can be considered a major mechanism of language manipulation, as it determines not only the ideological message, but also the choice of languages. There is, therefore, a clear message with regard to "who is in charge" from the fact that all street names in Arab areas are in "Hebrew only" and not in Arabic. In that case, LL street names can be viewed as a form of colonialism, as it is through these LL items, as represented by the choice of languages and the message transmitted by them, that domination of the space is established. Thus, LL serve as a covert means of affecting and creating language realities, as was demonstrated so clearly in Plates 1 and 2.

It is clear that the messages are transmitted through LL items not only in terms of presence or absence of specific languages but with regard to its content as well. It is through the choice of names that LL promotes, perpetuates and establishes certain language policies and where ideologies may turn into practice. Clearly, the language of names of streets can be considered as a language policy mechanism that is used by those in authority who are often associated with majority power groups and serve as members of committees that assign street names.

Thus, it is through LL items appearing in the public space, in this case names of streets, that LL items are used as language policy mechanisms that exercise control over the public space and perpetuate certain wishful ideologies as well as the status of specific languages.

Negotiating policies through the public space

It is no wonder, therefore, that the importance of LL has been realized by groups of authority such as central governments. The most typical case is that of the government of Quebec, in Canada, which, as part of its effort to reverse the language shift of French while downgrading the status of English, established a law that stipulated that all public signs must be written in French and any sign in English must be displayed in smaller letters than the French ones.

While LL is capable of creating language policy that upgrades the status of one language, it is also capable of downgrading other languages. In the case of Quebec, the public display in French clearly downgrades English. In the case of Israel, it is the Arabic language that gets downgraded. This use of LL as a policy mechanism is a subtle and covert way to subtract and often eliminate the status of the Arabic language, in spite of its official status, which is clearly not much more than a declaration on paper only and, as has been noted earlier, one wonders about the status of officiality and its interpretation in practice. Clearly, one suspects whether the elimination of Arabic from the public space is a covert way of establishing a new de facto language policy and what this represents in the complex situation of the Israeli political milieu.

Yet, it is important to note that the use of LL items as mechanisms for manipulating languages is not unique to those in authorities, governments or municipalities; rather, it is used by bottom-up groups as well, referring to local communities, firms, associations as well as private individuals as has been shown in the LL study with regard to the selection of names of stores and shops in what was termed "bottom-up".

While the top-down flow is derived from governmental decisions and public policies, the bottom-up flow responds to market forces operating differentially in different areas, as well as to self-presentation velleities. The study concludes that representation of symbolic reality may constitute a power resource in itself and that through LL it is possible to observe both the extrinsic and intrinsic factors of power, material interests and other influences. This is how individual actors – store owners, car dealers or supermarket owners – participate in the moulding of LL, but indirectly, through their own strategies vis-à-vis their potential clients. These actors contribute to the creation of a whole area that shapes the public space. It is through the LL items that language negotiations between and among the various interest groups take place.

The consequence of using LL in the public space is that it reaffirms power relations; as a language manipulation mechanism, it clearly marks who is dominant and who is not. But as could be learned from the above study, LL also acts as an arena for making language policy; it is used by both top-down and bottom-up. By using the powerful languages, those of high status, LL has the potential to reaffirm the languages and groups in power while marginalizing the groups that are not. But at the same time, the use of LL is instrumental in upgrading the status of certain language groups, such as in the case of French in Quebec or in the case of the Supreme Court decision in Israel for the use of Arabic on main freeways in Israel. The discrepancies that might appear between LL items as shaped by public agencies on one hand, and as shaped by individuals, associations or entrepreneurs on the other, can illustrate the divergent interests that exist between institutional and autonomous actors. LL, then, is a powerful policy mechanism and an arena where language battles and negotiations and reaffirmations can take place. Below are a number of such cases.

Language in the public space is used as a battlefield and is the subject of negotiations between different groups. Thus, different groups and individuals often use the public space as a place where they can reject, protest against and negotiate the status and roles of languages, as will be shown in the examples below. For example, anti-globalization groups have on their agendas the resistance to the use of certain languages in the public space, specifically languages that symbolize power such as English. The main argument is that the public space belongs to all and therefore dominating it through public signs can be considered some type of colonialization or imperialism. They therefore protest against the way that some powerful groups, especially large corporations, use the public space without obtaining consent and permission from the public.

An article in the newspaper *Haaretz* (p. D-9, March 12, 2004) reports on an activist group that was formed to resist the domination of English in the public space. They want to return the public space back to the public. Specifically, they resent the overuse of English in the public space, which they claim represents big corporations and is a way of invading the public place and thus controlling it. The items that are encountered in the public space include graffiti, and they want to oppose it by inserting their own signs, so that people become more aware of the role that the public space plays in people's lives and become more involved in its furnishing. They should not allow only corporations or others in authority to control it. In addition to public signs and billboards, they note subtle items such as the delivery boy or girl who rides on a scooter that has the sign "Domino Pizza". They therefore claim that the public needs to reclaim the public space, not allow big corporations to control it and beautify it with pictures. Their activities consist of spraying over existing signs with pictures and other items that they view as more decorative.

Graffiti has been a very important language mechanism through which the battle for representation and visibility is taking place in the public space. Thus, the *Herald Tribune* (March 14, 2004) reports on the war that is taking place over the graffiti in the Paris Métro and at the same time on the different groups around Europe that are trying to "clean" the public space. It is claimed that the street movements are shifting from guerrilla graffiti raids to organized attacks; for example, several dozen Métro stations were hit simultaneously by hundreds of activists wielding spray guns and paint. The paper also reports that in response the authorities decided to fight back. The Paris rapid transit agency that sells advertising space in the Métro took legal action against 62 of the activists who had been rounded up by the police. They are now being sued for 1.2. million euros, "the amount they lost in direct damages and compensation to advertising clients". "We live in a democracy. They can organize demonstrations, but they cannot destroy property."

Zohar Shavit, a council member of the city of Tel Aviv, claimed that since shop names in Tel Aviv are not in Hebrew, the city is losing its Hebrew character and it gives the impression that Hebrew is not the first language, since the names of shops give the city its identity and cultural uniqueness. According to her, this is an indication of low culture and she therefore was successful in demanding that all signs should be in Hebrew, or that Hebrew should appear on the sign, over half the area of the sign. She also proposed assembling a committee to suggest Hebrew names and that the municipality should subsidize businesses that prefer Hebrew names over other names. In August 2004, she managed to get the proposition accepted by the council of the city of Tel Aviv (this is in spite of the fact that Tel Aviv-Jaffa is a mixed city of Jews *and* Arabs) (*Ynet News*, July 23, 2004).

Additional devices in the public space

While the discussion in this chapter focused on public and private signs, language exists in a variety of other places in the public sphere; for example, the names of food products, clothing companies and instructions for laundry, forms to be filled out for bureaucratic purposes, as well as medications. In all these products and others, language is displayed in different shapes and forms.

Thus, additional mechanisms which are used to define the public space are available as well; these include a variety of items through which ideologies are transmitted. A few of these items will be mentioned here but in fact once the object of the observation is the space, there are endless items of this sort. Below are just a few more examples of items in the public space that can be used as indirect devices to construct the public space and thereby affect people's de facto language behavior.

Labels of products and instructions

It is very common today for all products to come with labels and often with instructions. The languages of the labels can also be viewed as a mechanism for making statements about hierarchy and choices of languages.

Instructions for use on medication are considered to be high-stakes, as misuse of these products could be dangerous. In some places, these instructions are displayed in the official language only; in other contexts, they are displayed in a number of languages, including those of immigrants. Such displays of language can be influential in creating and affecting language practices in similar ways to how LL items are considered mechanisms of language policy impositions.

In a small study that examined the languages represented on products in Israel we found that Russian was rarely displayed on medication or on food products; Arabic on the other hand was represented on almost all medical products due to regulations of the Ministry of Health. Yet, Arabic was not included in any of the other products.

Other such mechanisms in the public space are *names of streets, names of people, names of places,* the language of *the Internet,* languages of *advertisements, newspapers* and *the cell phone.*

The cell phone

One example which represents a whole set of media instruments in cyber-space is the cell phone, such a commonly used device of using language in the public space that it is actually exposing oral (and often/private) language to the public space. As the article below shows, there are fierce battles with regard to the use of the cell phone in the public domain and especially about the right to use language in the public domain.

The article in the *International Herald Tribune* (February 16, 2004, p. 16) entitled "Challenge of the day: silencing the phone" reports on the discussion relating to the right of people to speak publicly on cell phones, given the ecological and environmental intrusion. If speaking is part of personal rights, why should it be a problem to talk publicly on the cell phones? What is considered an intrusion? ". . . the civility of daily life is evaporating in the grating, one-sided cell chatter", why is "one-sided chatter" considered an intrusion while a two-sided (i.e., regular) conversation is not? Is this an intrusion into privacy and personal freedom? Is it that talking on the phone requires "shouting" and therefore it poses an intrusion? To quote a person who travels regularly on the train to Washington from Philadelphia: "The obliviousness of a few to the fact that they are the only ones within shouting distance who are shouting the details of their meeting, commute, children's homework and other fascinating personal minutiae never ceases to amaze." "Around the world, museums and theaters are telling visitors to turn their phones off, and 'quiet cars' are catching on in train travel." The article continues to report on a study by the Lemeson–MIT Program, that "nearly a third of adults call the cell-phone the invention that they most hate but cannot live without". It continues to report on an incident when rules are enforced tyrannically, where a passenger on an Amtrak train grabbed another passenger's cell phone and smashed it to pieces and on airplanes, the article reports, laws and regulations of not speaking on the plane are often ignored. "disregarding the announcement".

The Internet is a domineering mechanism that serves as a powerful arena for language negotiations and that has a strong effect on language behavior and practice. The fact that so far cyberspace has been a free arena makes it a mechanism in which language negotiations take place. Relative to the other mechanisms mentioned in this book, cyberspace is still open and free, implying that different contents, languages and language practices are displayed and used. It can therefore be considered as a powerful mechanism nowadays, given its wide access in the world, and in perpetuating the English language. Below are some examples.

There is often strong resentment on behalf of a number of countries to the domination of the USA over the Internet, as expressed at the Geneva meeting. Twomey, a president of the Internet Corporation for Assigned Names and Numbers, protests that a group of diplomats – most of whom know little about the technical aspects – are deciding in a closed forum how 750 million people should reach the Internet, and that representatives of the news media and anyone who was not a government official had been evicted from the meeting that was making these decisions. The main item on the agenda of the meeting was to decide whether the Internet should be overseen by the United Nations instead of American groups like Icann.

In the past few years, there has been a growing number of sites presented in a number of national languages. Nowadays, many sites ask the user "the language question", that is, the preferred language that one would like to use. Thus, there is growing use of a variety of multiple languages on the Internet.

Further, some of the changes relate to allowing different languages and characters to be used within Internet addresses. Since October 2003 countries have been able to register domain names using Chinese (both simplified and traditional), Japanese and Korean, with Vietnamese and others to follow soon.

Effects on de facto LP

This type of mechanism, as noted in this chapter, is relatively new and there are no empirical studies that examined the effect of language in the public space on actual language behavior and on de facto language practice; it is therefore not known how successful it is in manipulating languages. From the study on linguistic landscape, reported in this chapter, where gaps were found between top-down and bottom-up linguistic landscape items, one can conclude that this mechanism is successful mostly on the level of top-down; in most cases there are strict laws and regulations that enforce the use of certain languages in the public space. Whether such impositions are meaningful or not in changing language behavior is another question that needs to be explored. Another question is the extent to which those who are exposed to language in the public space are consciously aware of it and how it affects their perceptions and views about language.

The following case shows how street names can be very meaningful to the people who pass through them. The distinguished judge Mr. Salim Jabrin was certainly not apathetic to language in the public space, in this case as exemplified through street names. Mr. Jabrin is an Arab from Haifa who is about to become the first Arab member of the Israeli Supreme Court. Residing in Haifa, a city with mostly Jews but also with a relatively large Arab population, still many of the street names (similar to those in Plates 1 and 2) are of the names of leading events associated with Zionist Jewish ideology. Being surrounded by Zionist names in the public space, as street names, did not leave him apathetic, as he told the correspondent in the *Haaretz* newspaper of April 11, 2004. He claims that by being surrounded by names that symbolize Zionism, he is well connected, by choice or otherwise, to Zionist ideology. He lives in a street named "the 2nd of November" (i.e., the date of the Balfour Declaration announcing the right of Jews to return to their homeland); on his way to his office, he drives through "the Zionism Boulevard"; from there he continues to Hertzeliya Street (a street named after Hertzel, the founder of the Jewish state); and from there to the "Prophet Street", in order to arrive at his workplace. Yet, he notes that in order to create a balance he would intentionally drive through a few streets that had Arabic names, such as Hassan Shukri, Omar, and then Omar Khayyám and Ab Sina. In this way, he claimed, he was practising co-existence between Jews and Arabs in the city of Haifa.

At the same time, language in the public space has a very good case for showing how it can also serve as a mechanism for resisting, protesting against and negotiating de facto language policies. As can be observed through the data from the LL study, de facto language practices are actually created in the public space in very different patterns from what official policies dictate. Thus, the public space, whether through signs, forms, instructions or cyberspace, is a very important arena where language battles are negotiated and crafted.

Violations of language rights?

Violation of language rights in terms of language in the public space has a number of manifestations. Thus, an inability to read and comprehend instructions regarding the ingredients and uses of medication, the ingredients of food products or travel instructions all imply a serious violation of language rights. It also leads to the marginalization of people, as names of their streets, towns and ideologies are often not represented and those displayed do not represent their ideologies especially in specific areas where they reside as full members of the community, as is the case with names of streets in Israel. Posting the names of streets that represent and symbolize national ideology and overlooks ideology of other groups in society is another form of violation of language rights, especially when they are posted in areas where "other groups reside". A powerful violation of language rights occurs in courts where only the national and prestigious language is used, and in most situations, no translators are provided.

Ideology, propaganda, myths and coercion

Language being in the midst of battles relating to ideology and practice implies also that various means are used to promote these ideologies. This book focuses on the use of language policy and a variety of mechanisms to promote these ideologies, but there is a need to notice the important role that other forms of influence have in the process of promoting certain ideologies. Specifically, it is language ideologies, propagandas, myths and types of coercion that often play such roles. These major strategies that are used in most societies with regard to language will only be mentioned briefly in this book, and they deserve more extensive treatment in other publications, given their powerful effects on language behaviors.

Ideology in this context refers to beliefs about languages, clearly not divorced from the political ideology of the nation-state, believing that languages and nations are identical, given that languages are the main markers of national identity. Language ideology, for example, refers to the beliefs that knowledge of certain languages are indications of belonging to certain groups, to hierarchy and status of certain languages within given societies, to "how" languages should be used as well as to how languages need to be learned and taught. The best-known language ideologies are those identifying language with people and where languages are markers of groups, so that knowing certain powerful languages implies loyalty, patriotism and inclusion while knowledge of "other" languages has the opposite values. It also refers to the notion that languages are viewed as a threat to the nation as these groups might strive for territorial independence and fight against the nation causing the speakers to be viewed as traitors. This is the case with Hispanics in the USA, who are suspected of hiding their resentment of and disloyalty to the nation and of being eager to seize pieces of territory. A monolingual ideology is not tolerant of "other" languages, often requiring full hegemony.

Myths originate from ideologies and refer to statements and slogans made about languages that are not substantiated, yet they tend to influence language behavior. Myths fall somewhere between ideologies and propaganda and refer also to the shared knowledge and beliefs that people have about languages. Since most people use languages, and many have learned additional ones, there are folk theories about the importance of languages, how they should be spoken and how they should be learned. For example, there are myths about the importance of grammar rules, language correctness, the importance of certain languages, the effect of age on language learning and subtractive approaches to language learning. One common myth about language concerns the correct way of using it (Milroy and Milroy, 1999; Lippi-Green, 1997; 2000). Hopper (1998) elaborates at length about "good" language being "correct", "native", "grammatical" and "accent-less", claiming that in multilingual societies this myth causes strong discrimination against those who do not use the languages in these ways. These types of myth are very influential in making people use certain languages, at home, at the workplace and in the public space. Takuhama-Espinosa (2003) provides a long list of myths about second language learning, many of which are driven by ideological national motivations. One of these myths is that in learning more than one language children can suffer "brain overload", or that multilingualism can cause language problems such as stuttering or dyslexia, or that adults cannot learn to speak a foreign language without an accent, or that the ability to speak many languages is a type of intelligence or that most of the world is monolingual. Takuhama-Espinosa claims that while such myths about multilingualism have existed for many years, it is only recently that definite refutations have been offered and that the myths about multilinguals that are being dispelled put a very positive face on polyglotism in the twenty-first century. Such myths, she claims, may originate because the phenomenon of thousands of new multilinguals is a relatively new one, and the research has a hard time reflecting reality. But they also may be a result of the feeling that "bilingual education" still sounds suspicious to many. Yet, since multilinguals nowadays account for a majority of the world's population, accurate information about the phenomenon must be documented. In school, the subtractive myth leads to situations in which student immigrants are often discouraged from using home languages at school as it will result in difficulties in learning the new language.

Propaganda is yet another strategy used in these language battles. Clearly, myths about languages can also be viewed as propaganda. It therefore refers to a more aggressive means of spreading ideologies and myths, which are often subtle. One example of such covert propaganda can be found in the *New York Times* (May 2004) and can illustrate how citizenship, language and terror can be interpreted as propaganda. In an article on the radical Islamic groups in France it was written: "Only about 10 percent of the imams preaching in France's mosques and prayer rooms are citizens, as half do not speak French, according to the Interior Ministry" (p. 4). This may suggest that those who are radical are so because they do not speak the language, and that citizenship, like language, is a tool; as if had they been citizens or known the French language, they would have been less radical. Thus political affiliations are directly correlated with knowledge of French and being part of the system. Other examples can be seen in the media after 9/11 with reference to Arabic, "the language of terror", as is found in the *Herald Tribune International* (March 29, 2004): "there are no common things among all terror organizations, except – they all speak Arabic".

Language in the public space, as is demonstrated in this chapter, provide examples of using language propaganda when specific languages of specific groups are displayed or are not displayed on public signs and thus influence views of which languages have legitimacy and which do not. Pavlenko (2003) provides numerous examples of the effects of various types of propaganda in promoting and suppressing language use over a long period of time.

Coercion is an aggressive strategy that actually involved persecution for exercising influences for using certain languages and not others, and forcing people to disrupt their regular language habits and free, personal and open use, in favor of using the languages according to specific language ideologies. Persecution can range from methods of creating stereotypes and bad-mouthing those who do not use the language according to the given ideology to actually using acts of violence. These include referring to some unwanted languages as "bad" or incorrect languages (Spolsky, 2004), to the language users as ignorant, unintelligent, or in the way used by General Franco in France, referring to the other languages as "languages of the dogs". Persecution and coercion can also take the shape of laws, declaring certain languages as official and thus persecuting those not using the languages according to set rules, forcing names, creating language police (Segev, 1999). Persecution often implies making people outcasts on the basis of language, denying them employment opportunities, citizenship, schooling opportunities or fining or even imprisoning them. As part of the revival of Hebrew such a language police was created, *Gdud Maginei Hasafa* (Unit for the Defense of the Language), whose role was to force people to use Hebrew and outlaw Yiddish. The unit engaged in organized intrusions of public events not held in Hebrew, as documented in Segev (1999). Some of the methods used were sending threatening letters to those using Yiddish, forcing shopkeepers and school principals to use only Hebrew in names of signs of buildings and shops, as well as stopping people in the middle of private conversations in public places to demand aggressively that they switch to Hebrew. They would interrupt public lectures not held in Hebrew and demand a switch to Hebrew and even, as reported, throw bottles of ink and stinky eggs at participants during the screening of a Yiddish movies. They organized violent demonstrations opposing the establishment of a Yiddish department at the Hebrew University in Jerusalem and threatening to break windows. Aggressive persecutions occur in other places with regard to Basque, Catalan and Galician, and in France with Alsatian, Basque, Breton and in many other parts of the world. Anecdotes of persecution and coercion report of beatings, washing mouths with soap, firing from work, as well as making people report others to the authorities when they overhear other languages. Stories of language persecution have not been widely recorded yet and they deserve more attention in the field of language studies. It is clear that different types of language persecutions and coercion are widespread today, with people being denied employment and higher education, as they are forced to take school tests in unfamiliar languages.

Conclusions

Language in the public space is clearly an important and possibly effective mechanism for creating de facto language policy. At times it is part of the official language when strict rules and regulations stipulate the use of certain languages in the environment, especially concerning official and state languages. In other situations, especially with regard to "bottom-up" items LL is a more subtle or covert mechanism that is being demanded by groups to obtain recognition, voice, rights and often control. Its main significance is in enlarging the scope of what is considered language policy, not only as a LP device but more so by giving attention to the notion that language practices and policies do not only arise from what people use but also in expanding the linguistic repertoire that needs to be studied, observed and interpreted, extending from what people say to the surrounding language symbols. Clearly, questions still need to be raised, as with the other mechanisms, regarding the effect of these linguistic visuals, as well as their absence, on de facto language use.

Summary

- Language policy manifests itself not only through such items as policy documents and test materials but also through the language used in the public space. The choice of language employed on a country's road signs, street and shop names serves as a powerful mechanism for creating actual language policy. At times these policies are overt; at others they are more covert and subtle.
- Focusing on the public space as a further arena for the display of language policy will enable us to gain a deeper understanding of the conflicts between declared policies and the demands of groups for representation, as manifested in top-down vs. bottom-up displays. LP is not only about how people speak but also about how they choose to use language as a symbol for constructing identities.
- Studying LP through language in public places can also be viewed through advertising, product labelling, instructions on medication and the internet, as well as through language ideologies, propaganda, myth and coercion.

Part III

Consequences and reactions

Part II introduced an expanded view of LP, beyond formal policies, that incorporates the different LP mechanisms that can be considered as policy devices as they are influential in creating de facto policies. It was shown how official policies become no more than declarations of intent that can easily be manipulated in different ways through a variety of mechanisms. LP was thus observed in broader ways as the mechanisms create de facto LP.

These mechanisms take place in a variety of contexts. While in the past LP referred mostly to top-down mechanisms, nowadays, democracy implies that these mechanisms or policy devices can be used by all groups in the negotiations, dialogues and battles as part of democratic practices. Thus, it is essential that the effects of these mechanisms on language policy should be open and exposed so all groups can make use of them for their benefit as part of the negotiations of democratic practices and personal rights. Democracy in practice means that all groups are entitled to employ a variety of civic devices for promoting their causes. Using these procedures also means that while it is expected that policy affects practice, it is also understood that practice has the power to affect policy. Thus, Part III of the book discusses the role that the mechanisms play in democratic societies, in terms of participation, representation and personal rights (Chapter 8). This leads to Chapter 9, which proposes strategies for change in the form of critical language policy, language awareness and activism. Given the violations of democratic processes and rights, the concluding chapter (Chapter 9) offers a number of proposals for minimizing violation of democratic principles. These include principles of democracy of inclusion, protection of personal rights associated with language, developing critical awareness of an expanded view to language and language policy and language activism. Each of these proposals will be discussed next.

8 Consequences

As long as it is a matter of demonstrating the ills of society and the abuses of those who abuse, he has no hesitations (except the fear that, if they are talked about too much, even the most just propositions can sound repetitive, obvious, tired). He finds it more difficult to say something about the remedies, because first he would like to make sure that they do not cause worse ills and abuses, and that wisely planned by enlightened reformers, they can be put into practice without harm by their successors.

(Calvino, 1985, p. 111)

Democratic principles

The methods of creating LP via the different mechanisms may be viewed as part of the process of decision making in democratic societies. In fact, as already noted, all groups, not just those in authority, use these mechanisms to influence language behavior and to ensure that their own ideologies turn into practice. Yet, it is often those in authority, government agencies and big corporations that are more influential as they are more powerful. After all, they have access to sources of power, such as judiciary systems, parliaments, education authorities, testing organizations, propaganda and sanctions, and can therefore enforce and promote their ideologies more easily and be more influential in affecting de facto language policies. Decisions about language are generally imposed on residents of the nation in an area (i.e., language) that they know little about, where, as was noted, a large number of myths exist and where people have no choice, but to comply. In fact, as stated by Tollefson (1995, 2002), May (2001), Pennycook (2001) and Cameron (1995), LP has been uncritically developed and implemented to avoid addressing issues of social and political matters in which languages are embedded. Careful examination is required to discover whether these decisions follow democratic principles, protect the rights of individuals and groups and include groups in the multilingual and multicultural societies.

Violations of democratic principles

Various definitions of democracy have been proposed over the years. Yet, many of the features of democracy outlined by the Greeks in the oldest democracy still remain today. These include representation and participation, equality, liberty, respect for the law and justice, viewing human beings as individuals with rights, participation in public affairs and resistance of tyranny. The assumption is that individuals are not just interested in their own affairs but in the affairs of the state as well. Individuals, then, need to be informed; they should have the right to know; they should be equal before the law; they should have equality for participation in decision making; and these are the basis for intensive debates. In examining LP in its expanded view, via the mechanisms, it will be shown how they violate some of these basic democratic principles.

Imposition

The use of the mechanisms at times violate principles of openness and participation, regardless of who they are used by. This is so since it is often the case that LP represents a form of imposition as those affected by it have no choice but to comply and change their language behaviors accordingly. While LP should be visible to the public as is the case with official documents, the fact is that de facto policies are created in covert and indirect ways. Thus, the mechanisms can often serve as tools for creating covert and hidden policies. This is because the de facto policies, via the mechanisms, are most often initiated by central authorities, often in contradiction to the declared policies and thus circumvent official policies and create new ones.

As was noted, language tests, entrance criteria, teaching materials and language standards, are all examples of devices that perpetuate de facto language policies. While educational policies may declare specific languages as significant for the educational system from a liberal point of view, educational institutions may decide to include tests in specific languages as entrance criteria and thus create different de facto policies, as people will learn the tested languages, and not others, given their high stakes. Thus, new de facto policies are created. The use of tests as mechanisms can perpetuate different levels of knowledge. Similarly, while LEP may state that correct grammar or "native-like" accents are not essential for the definition of high levels of language proficiency, once language tests put demands on correct grammar and a specific accent, these tests become definers of criteria of language and create de facto realities. As was shown in Chapter 6, this use of tests leads to exclusion of those who cannot attain these very criteria, as is often the case with immigrants. Similarly, some countries that do recognize the importance of English as a global language will ensure that tests in English will be used and receive more credits in graduation. As was shown, the introduction of tests in the USA as part of the No Child Left Behind law delivers a clear message as to the irrelevance of "other" languages. It is through the use of English as the language of instruction in schools and as a requirement for acceptance to institutions of higher education, that the power of that language and its speakers is perpetuated. Such oppressive policies are spread further through the process of colonialization as is the case with the establishment of universities in different parts of the world where the language of instruction is English, overlooking local languages, framing it as "the language of democracy", "the language of freedom and openness", thus enabling the imposition of English language policies while devaluing other languages.

Yet, LPs need to be open, overt and known to the public, which should not be manipulated via these mechanisms and their consequences by being unaware of their influences. Introducing policies without the awareness and knowledge of those who are affected by them means that they are not open to criticism and monitoring, and the public are not viewed as legitimate and equal partners and participants. Such a process of using mechanisms in covert ways violates basic democratic processes of inclusion, representation and participation. Those affected by the mechanisms have no choice but to abide by them, especially through not being aware of the effects and consequences. Thus, through the different mechanisms, groups of authority are capable of controlling language behavior in broader ways and of perpetuating agendas of power and ideologies more aggressively. At the state and national levels, officiality and citizenship, which are conditional on having knowledge of the power languages, are used throughout the judicial system. At the educational level, a major part of the central authorities, mechanisms are used to implement language policies through LEPs, and language tests. At the public level, the mechanisms are used through language in the public space, as a way of manipulating language by public signs and other linguistic landscape items as described in Chapter 7, and are used to deliver ideological and patriotic messages while marginalizing others.

A "top-down" approach

One important aspect in examining the extent to which LP follows democratic principles is the manner through which LPs are introduced. Most mechanisms, and the de facto policies they create, whether at national, state, municipal or local levels, are introduced by these groups in a top-down manner, without any input from the constituents who are supposed to follow the policies. Thus, language policies represent authoritarian ways of making policies. LPs, LEPs and LTs often serve as arms of central authorities carried out in a "top-down" manner by central authorities, whether at national, state or municipal levels, or by collective groups. These policies are then imposed on educational and political systems. This top-down method of imposition can be interpreted as an authoritarian way of making policies and as a form of social and political domination.

True, one can observe some bottom-up initiatives by various groups, especially those creating their own LEPs and practices often in contradiction to the declared and official language policies, as is demonstrated in a number of countries where parents demand early study of the English language, such as Hong Kong and other European countries, in opposition to the national LEP, or when immigrants form classes to learn language skills needed for the workplace. Yet, these acts represent a relatively small number of cases, while in most situations, central authorities introduce LPs in a top-down manner. Such decisions include the specific languages that should be declared "official" for the whole entity, languages that will be compulsory in schools and in the public domain, including the workplace, thus reinforcing the situation whereby certain individuals gain priority in the society as they also impose criteria for the specific levels of proficiency for exit and/or entry. This type of top-down approach also violates the principles of participation and representation.

Lack of representation and involvement of constituencies

Related to the above is the limited representation of broad sectors of the population in decisions and the implementation of sweeping mechanisms leading to policies, even though they are strongly affected by it. Most mechanisms are introduced by those in authority, usually government administrators and, at times, with the advice of academic experts. It is often the case that citizens, students, parents and ethnolinguistic groups are excluded from the process of making these decisions, which leads to the creation of policies without the input of the constituencies. This results in the imposition of these policies by those in authority. These policies represent the views of a few who may have specific interests in the public's learning specific languages and not others. Given the loaded agendas representing a variety of ideologies, as was discussed in Chapter 2, such an approach can be viewed as violating democratic principles, as there is no broad representation of groups if policies are to be accepted as fair, ethical and inclusive. It is therefore surprising that in the process of creating and introducing these mechanisms those who are affected by them are rarely asked to be involved.

It is also interesting to note that issues of languages are not viewed by decision makers to be of interest to the general public, as such matters are often determined by ministries of education and other central groups in internal meetings leading to policy documents that schools and the nation need to follow, with no input whatsoever from language teachers, principals, students and parents and the public at large. Such a lack of involvement of the constituencies can be considered undemocratic and unethical as it ignores public opinion, is neither inclusive nor representative and fails to consider the wishes, aspirations, interests and especially the realities of local educational groups who are affected by the policies. Further, teachers and principals become servants of the system; they have the responsibility of carrying out the policies but no authority to influence them.

A crucial component of a more democratic decision-making is the ready and timely availability of pertinent information for the diverse constituencies, in order to help them understand what is at stake and what is not at stake. While, as was noted, there are occasional independent initiatives by the local community or teachers, these are often of limited scale and scope.

Most language policies do not involve the public at large, including students, language learners and residents of the different geographical groups. Thus, the public normally lacks knowledge of language and its power in societies. Such lacunae in the public's knowledge lead to myths and misconceptions about language learning, a state of affairs that is most visible in pluralist, democratic societies. For example, the public may support language policies that perpetuate the learning of majority languages and reject the need for maintaining home or community languages, believing them to have no value. Such beliefs may even exist among immigrants and indigenous groups who are led to perceive their languages as liabilities for their children's acquisition of majority languages and for their success in schools and society. As a result, politicians can easily convince the public, majority and minority groups alike, to agree with their ideologies and constructs such assimilative and subtractive approaches to language learning. While some current initiatives require parents of children of speakers of other languages to choose the type of language program for their children, these parents are rarely informed and lack accurate information as the basis for sound decision-making and functioning in democratic societies. Thus, LPs that are made without the knowledge and involvement of citizens violate the democratic principle of inclusion.

Lack of involvement of language teachers

This violation is especially relevant to LEPs and language tests, but also to other de facto policies. The lack of representation of constituents is especially noticed with regard to teachers and the framing of language education policies. By framing policy decisions as political acts, their creators remove them from professional input and action, even though teachers are expected to implement the policies through their teaching practice in the classroom. It is also interesting to note how rarely the consequences of language education policies ever get examined. This shows that policies of this sort are mostly lip service and not meaningful. Such approaches reduce teachers to bureaucrats who are the agents of big government policies without having any say in their formation and delivery. These issue were discussed in Chapter 5 within the broader discussion of LEPs as mechanisms for creating and affecting de facto language practices.

Traditionally, language teachers have not been included and involved in language education policy decisions and their voices have not been heard. Excluding teachers also means that there is no input to the realities of schools and classrooms in language education policies. It further implies that teachers' roles are to carry out the order of "big government" policies without having a say in them. Surprisingly, language teachers themselves "buy" into this view and they are often unaware that the languages they teach are embedded in a variety of ideological and political agendas, as no language teaching is neutral. It is interesting to note that teacher education programmes do not include knowledge about language policy as part of teacher knowledge to be taught and discussed in such training programmes. The study of how to affect policies, especially in the educational domain, should be an integral part of the basic intellectual preparation of language teaching professionals. As educational goals are transformed to meet the evolving needs of an increasingly diverse student population, teachers can provide such input through active involvement in educational policies. Teachers should not view themselves as "just teaching languages" but rather become aware of and knowledgeable about the loaded agendas of the languages they teach. They should be listened to and thus have opportunities to influence and affect policies, as their input is crucial to success in addressing the realities of schools and students.

There is a special role for the inclusion of teachers when it comes the teaching English, as in most non-English-speaking countries, English language teachers have special status, given the power of the language they teach. While it is true that a knowledge of the English language is important for increasing opportunities in the global environment, it is also known that the English language represents a form of inequality, creating a world division between those who know it and those who do not, and it often becomes a threat to local languages (Phillipson, 2003; Skutnabb-Kangas, 1998, 2004; Pennycook, 2001; Tollefson, 2002). English language teachers need to become aware of these issues and not be used by systems to impose and perpetuate the language of power and ignore other languages. Rather, they need to become aware of the power of the language they teach and become involved with the political and social implications of the power of English in societies and its relationship with other languages. English language teachers should view themselves as belonging to a larger profession of "language teachers" who are concerned about languages in general and broadening their knowledge about language teaching beyond "just the English language". This also relates to current debates about native and non-native teachers (Davies, 2003) as well as to what are considered correct and accepted levels of English and the need to apply more realistic categories for the inclusion of "non-native" language teachers.

Organizing society in "language units"

For most people, the language they use represents only one aspect of their identity; at times it is more highlighted, at others it is less so. Languages should not be the only criterion that defines societies; rather they should be observed in more integrated ways. Linguists, especially, analyze and define the world in linguistic terms, often not realizing that languages represent only one aspect of identity. Using language as the sole indicator of identity can be considered a discriminatory act as not much can be done about it, especially when it comes to issues of accent and correctness. There is a need to reject definitions of groups based on these single factors and avoid using such markers. Language is only one factor in this context in terms of identity and cannot be viewed as the only one; religion, culture, history, gender and additional variables play important roles as well. At the same time, there are situations of underrepresentation, in which languages are being totally overlooked. In general, LEPs also organize education and societies according to linguistic units (i.e., number of languages, specific languages of priority, etc.); the use of language as the primary markers and organizing principles are very strict and narrow as well as imposing, especially in multilingual societies such as in Africa or India, where clear divisions among the different languages do not exist, since languages are embedded in one another and are not arranged in "clean" isolated categories. Such issues are also relevant in the context of the discussion in Chapters 1 and 2 of transnationalism, where mixtures and a variety of hybrids are created and used by different diaspora groups, who develop complex loyalties, complex identities and complex language varieties. In fact, using language as the main organizing unit in language policies is always bound to exclude a large section of the population.

LP and language learning

A crucial issue with regard to LPs as exercised through these mechanisms is the problematic connection with actual language learning. Not much research is available on this issue, but what seems to emerge is that language policies are considered separate entities from language learning. At times, even the languages that such policies stipulate that it is compulsory to learn have no basis in reality and they are therefore not implemented. Further, even when these languages are being taught in schools, this does not guarantee success for those learning the languages. Too often LEPs serve only as statements or declarations of intent that cannot be enacted. Such is the case when certain languages are imposed by policy makers on schools through different mechanisms, for a variety of political and social reasons, without attention being paid to the needs and wishes of those who are affected by the policy, without including those who are expected to carry it out and without examining whether it is feasible. Such policies may have little effect on students' actual language learning, especially when the public has negative attitudes towards the languages and their native speakers, to begin with; learning these particular languages may lead to increased negative attitudes and low achievement. At the same time, there are situations where there are no official policies stating publicly the languages that should be studied; yet, languages are taught and acquired successfully in spite of this. This phenomenon is typical of the learning of the English language in many countries in the world today, where countries may not include English as part of the policy for a variety of reasons. Yet, there is strong demand for and success in learning those languages in schools and in other venues, especially by young learners, and actual learning occurs, nevertheless.

Not only is there little knowledge about the connection between language policies and language learning, there are hardly any studies that follow up the implementation and practices of policies. While policy makers may believe that such a connection exists, there is no evidence to show that this is in fact true. Is it because of how policies are derived, often driven by ideology and overlooking the aspirations and needs of schools and societies? Is it that educational policies focus mostly on the very languages that should be taught and not on learning and teaching practices? Is it a question of how languages are taught and learned? Is it that most educational policies overlook knowledge about language acquisition? Is it a question of what constitutes success in learning languages (e.g., achievements or attitudes). Is it that teachers are not paying much attention to language education policies? Or, is it that language policy makers are failing to notice educational realities? These issues need to be pursued further.

Perpetuating class differentiation and exclusion

As may be observed in numerous examples in Part II, many of the mechanisms, especially those that have to do with knowledge of the power language, or the "mother tongue", perpetuate hegemonic groups whereby speakers of those languages can maintain and perpetuate their power, while speakers of other languages are marginalized. This is especially noticed in political entities that pass laws granting further power to majority languages that are already powerful, leading to major discrimination towards those who do not possess knowledge of the majority language, as is the case with the English Only movement in the USA.

In countries where English is not the major national language, it is knowledge of the powerful global language, English, that often serves as a class marker enabling entrance to power groups in terms of education and social class and others such as universities and the labor market – while excluding others. Local languages are considered parochial in a global environment; those who lack the knowledge become its new victims, the new underclass, and their participation and representation are minimized. This creates situations in which speakers of hegemonic languages are in power, while speakers of other languages are marginalized and excluded.

According to Bourdieu (1991), language is a linguistic capital that can be negotiated on the linguistic market and it reflects power relations in society. Those who master the norm have the largest linguistic capital and are eager to keep it. "Petit bourgeois" is how he refers to the group possessing and controlling the norm. This differentiates between those who have access to power and language and those who have not; it is those who have the access who are responsible for manipulating it. For example, they can decide on issues like language reform, on language correctness, such as spelling reform, and other aspects that determine language norms and uses as to what is considered good language and what is not, "good language" vs. "bad", "correct" language vs. "incorrect", while those who are not in power are constantly viewed as those whose language is deteriorating. It is these people who always have to comply and follow the reforms set by those who are in power, as they are always considered to be violating the language norms, although this is their "normal", "unmarked" way of using language. Thus, the introduction of LP violates the principle of participation, as it creates class differentiation.

Mechanisms of power

According to Fairclough (1989), dominant classes exercise power in two basic ways, through coercion and consent, either by forcing others to go along with them or by convincing them that it is in their best interests. Consent is not necessarily the result of conscious choice, but rather an unconscious acceptance of institutional practices, which people follow without thinking. These often embody assumptions that directly or indirectly legitimize existing power relations. In other words, practices that are unconsciously accepted as the natural and inevitable ways of doing things may in fact be inherently political, serving to maintain the relative position of participants vis-à-vis each other. The everyday "taken for granted" practices constitute what Fairclough calls "ideological power", one of the central mechanisms of ensuring control by consent. He argues that discourse plays a particularly important role in exercising this control: authority and power manifested in and perpetuated by institutional practices around the ways that language is used and the purposes for which it is used.

It is important in this context also to mention the power of the combination of a number of mechanisms that are used simultaneously to influence and to exercise power and control, as in the example of tests for citizenship, each resulting in exclusion; it is the combination of the power of tests as mechanisms, the power of citizenship and certainly of language, that leads to exclusion of a more powerful magnitude and acceptance. It is important, therefore, to view mechanisms as being the discourse forms through which language policies are perpetuated and accepted.

Violations of personal rights

In discussing the different mechanisms in Part II, it was shown how the use of these very mechanisms led to violations of personal rights associated with language in a number of specific examples. This happens particularly in situations where people (especially immigrants and indigenous groups) do not have command of the language(s) of power and so cannot participate fully as residents and/or citizens in the society (Skuthabb-Kangas, 2006).

Problems with personal rights as a result of language issues originate from the different situations in which languages are acquired. Languages are acquired in contexts such as the home, the workplace, in schools and in the public space. A common situation is when the languages one acquires in specific contexts are not the relevant ones needed to function in other contexts; for example, when immigrants are not proficient in the languages used in the new context where they reside and are faced with difficulties of functioning in the new societies, especially at work and school. Another case is in political entities consisting of different ethno-linguistic groups using languages different to those used by the prestigious group. It is often the case that these languages are not considered "official" or "national" and do not have the status of other language(s), again preventing their speakers from full participation. At times, even when languages are considered "official", there is no guarantee that this status is manifested in terms of real benefit. Alternatively, certain languages may not be declared official yet have power and visibility, and the speakers of these languages benefit from special privileges, as is the case with English in many countries nowadays. This gap between the language(s) known by individuals and those used in education and society poses major obstacles for proper functioning in education and society. Thus, when the language that is used as the medium of instruction differs from the known language, the implication is that it is more difficult for students to acquire academic knowledge.

Thus, when a complex linguistic context is embedded in a political conflict and there are expectations that immigrants will be assimilated, on the basis of language and political ideology, language becomes the main symbol of belonging, and thus violations of language rights are bound to occur. The main argument is that such policies prevent people from full participation in society, in terms of obligations and rights.

Rights, then, are embedded in the gap between the mastery of specific language(s) by individuals and groups and those needed for functioning in societies. Rights are rooted in situations where people are *prevented* from participation in societies because of lack of proficiency in a certain language. They are especially relevant in democratic societies where residents have both the obligation to actively participate in the public domain and the right to benefit from the services such societies provide. In this respect, such rights associated with languages are identical to any other "personal" and "civil" rights that human beings are entitled to; lacking these rights implies direct discrimination, while granting such rights implies obtaining help to overcome the barriers and address strategies needed to compensate for such inabilities, by providing special services (i.e., benefits) so that maximum participation in society is feasible.

Many of the violations of these rights occur in nation-states, since these tend to associate language with national identity; the violations occur with the various language-speaking groups residing there. In general, it can be said that in most nation-states, there is often acceptance that indigenous groups deserve language rights (i.e., gaining rights because of "birth"), yet such a consensus does not apply to immigrant groups and often not to those who are considered second (and third) generations. Thus, it is more common for indigenous groups to be recognized as having the right to maintain their languages (i.e., Māori speakers in New Zealand, Basque and Catalan in Spain and Arabic in Israel) than immigrants who are not granted such rights.

In countries where English is *not* the major national language, it is knowledge of the powerful global and world language, generally English or any other powerful regional language, that serves as a class marker for entrance into power groups in terms of education, society and others such as universities and the labor market. Local languages are considered parochial in a world that is global; those who lack the knowledge become its new victims, the new underclass, and their participation and representation are minimized. This creates situations in which speakers of hegemonic languages are in power, while speakers of other languages are marginalized and excluded.

Rights associated with language are still not viewed as legitimate human and personal rights and result in situations where those who do not possess knowledge of the power language cannot fully participate in the society, leading to a policy of exclusion. Issues of language rights as part of LP are underrepresented and often ignored. Most LPs are concerned with language orders, so sweeping and categorical decisions about languages are made about language groups with little attention being paid to the rights of individuals, especially given the unquestioned legitimacy of national languages. There is therefore a need to examine in depth what these rights mean in different contexts and how they can be protected within the framework of different types of LPs.

Various definitions and distinctions are offered regarding different types of civil rights, referring to the right to understand and participate fully in societies. Kloss (1971; 1977) distinguishes between two types of rights. "Tolerance oriented" rights refer to the protection that individuals have against government interference with their own private language choices in domains such as the right to choose home languages and to use them in their own institutions. "Promotion oriented" rights refer to the rights of individuals to use their language(s) in public institutions, in courts, in commerce and public education. Another distinction is made between the rights of individuals and those of collective groups.

One form of violation of personal rights consists of imposing on people the use of certain languages in certain ways, while not allowing them the freedom to choose the manner of expression that best matches their personal needs. Judging people by the way they speak, both in the public and in the private domains, whether it is the use of language as indication of patriotism or as indication of willingness to assimilate, represents a serious violation of personal rights. This is manifested in the choice of the specific languages they need to use in private and public domains as well as the specific ways they are required to use the language; for example, not to include "foreign" words. Denying people citizenship on the basis of a lack of language proficiency is another case of violation, as there is no indication that being proficient in the national language necessarily creates better citizens.

Related to that is the imposition to use certain forms of language such as "written vs. oral form", "formal vs. informal" or "native-like" pronunciation. It is often the case that vernaculars are not legitimized as "real language" (e.g., Cantonese, Yiddish, spoken Arabic varieties). Using the oral variety is often associated with low levels of education and is stigmatized, especially in educational contexts. The ramifications are that the use of these languages in schools is prohibited, for both students and teachers, as schools being powerful institutions for imposing language behaviors. Related to that are rights to use a language different from the dominant one(s) in public or the right to use a language with specific types of lexicon.

Summary

- Language policies created through different mechanisms frequently result in violations of democratic principles and personal rights.
- This happens in the areas of imposition, top-down approaches, the limited representation and involvement of constituencies, organizing of societies into "language units", a lack of consideration of language learning, the perpetuating of class differentiations, exclusion and the violation of personal rights. Chapter 9 proposes strategies in response to these violations in terms of a democracy of inclusion, critical awareness, personal rights and language activism.

9 Reactions

He has only to expound these fine thoughts in a systematic form, but a scruple restrains him: what if all this becomes a model? And so he prefers to keep his convictions in the fluid state, check them instance by instance, and make them implicit rules of his everyday behavior, in doing or not doing, in choosing or rejecting, in speaking or in remaining silent.

(Calvino, 1985, p. 112)

Democracy of inclusion

Why inclusion? Diversity, Waggoner (2000) states, characterizes the population of most countries in the world today. In the USA, for example, racial and ethnic groups are growing, both in size and in the number of different groups. Immigration is increasing, bringing people with diverse backgrounds and new languages. To some, diversity represents the fulfilment of the meaning of nations, yet to others it is a source of fear that somehow those who are different will fracture national unity. Waggoner writes:

> The response of the latter are draconian and contradictory. They want to limit the rights of immigrants, deprive immigrant children of access to public education, abolish affirmative action, and outlaw programs that help limited-English-proficiency children acquire English in the US. They want to legislate the check of English by movements such as the English Only and the Official English movements. But diversity is a fact.
>
> (Waggoner, 2000, p. 5)

The view of nations as being based on ethnic unity defined by markers of common language, culture and history is out of date. Nations today have to face the reality, which was always there, that groups living within a nation have collective identities, whether it is marked by religion, language, ideology, gender or sexuality. The state, therefore needs to undertake the difficult task of *including* these groups under a different formula and fight against the view of homogeneous "imagined" societies that were reluctant to concede citizenship to the outsiders.

Taylor (1998) states that in spite of democratic views and beliefs, there will always be those who want to exclude others they see as taking away control and perhaps seeking ways to exercise influence. Those in power will never be enthusiastic about receiving new people, not just because of discrimination, but also because they fear that those "others" will violate their system. Thus, they will exercise a variety of methods, mechanisms and procedures, some of which were described in this book, to ensure that these groups remain resident aliens as they are still so used to functioning politically only among themselves and find it difficult to adjust, and refer to "them" and "us". Taylor (1998) writes that: "there is a standing temptation to exclusion, arising from the fact that democracies work well when people know one another, trust one another, and feel a sense of commitment towards one another". (p. 146). "The entry of new kinds of people into the country, or into active citizenship, poses a real challenge. The exact content of the mutual understanding, the bases of the mutual trust, and the shape of the mutual commitment all have to be redefined and reinvented. This is not easy given the temptation to fall back to exclusion."

In LP, this means that the democratic state is compelling and forcing immigrants and those considered "the others" into a single mold, to reshape them so they speak the "same" dominant language in the same way as everyone else does in uncompromising ways. It is so rigorous that the state constantly monitors this process through language tests in schools and establishes language tests as conditions for residence through citizenship tests. In France, the state insists on rules for excluding those who do not dress in certain ways. Thus, the state penetrates into people's lives, forcing them to assimilate, forbidding them to deviate from the dominant formula of belonging to the state in schools and society, in the name of freedom; freedom "my way". The state does not approve of other ways of being as it demands "the others" to assimilate in its way, in the name of social cohesiveness and democracy. Why is it that language needs to function as a criterion for good citizenship, for belonging to the group? What is it in "the other language" that denies people legitimacy? Is it not enough for a person to participate by voting in elections, paying taxes, and performing all other civil duties? Should the school and the state be obliged to provide language services to its residents? Why should immigrants, or even "others" born in the territory, have to pay a price for having the choice of going to a new place? Or, for being "different"?

It is in the current nation-state that there is a trend of those "others" to resent and resist the old model of assimilation, of "giving into" the majority formula of assimilation. They demand that the reigning formula be modified to accommodate them rather than the other way around.

Applying democracy of inclusion is therefore a difficult task because of the need to apply notions of liberal democracies as inclusive units, which originate from the new form of the nation-state. Taylor views it as a built- in paradox whereby current democracies are in fact the most inclusive politics in human history, this very inclusive phenomenon, also pushes toward exclusion resulting from a need of self governing societies for a high degree of cohesion and a common identity. In other words:

> for people to be sovereign, they need to form an entity and have a personality. The people are supposed to rule: this means that its members make up decision making units, through a consensus or a majority. Yet, it is not enough to decide together, people need to deliberate together, as democratic states are constantly facing new questions and need to form a consensus of the different individual opinions which are based on discussion with others. These deliberations require that the members know one another, listen to one another and understand one another. This view is different than in hierarchical and authoritarian societies as modern democracy obliges its members to show much more solidarity and more commitment to one another in the joint political project. This is a very important condition as when subgroups cannot be bound together, they may begin to demand their own states, their own political identities. Thus, a high level of commitment, a high level of participation and a high degree of mutual trusts are basic conditions of free societies; different than authoritarian regimes whereby rulers make all the decisions for the people. Yet, this form of commitment and participation only happens if the citizens have a feeling of community and solidarity with their fellow citizens.
>
> (Taylor, 1998, p. 145)

Applying this to the domain of *language* means that that there will always be those who will want to use language for exclusion as it gives them more power and authority in society. Exclusion is especially tempting in the language domain since languages "of the others" present elements of mystery, secrecy and symbolize threat. Yet, adopting a democracy of inclusion implies complementary and mutual understanding where each group and individual learns about the languages of the other; it is the totality of differences, as argued by Taylor, that best contributes to the existence of the democratic states; this is what is meant by "inclusion", as groups need to bind with one another in order to become an efficient political unit. Since each life can only accomplish some small part of the human potential we can benefit from the full range of human achievement and capacity only if we live in close association with people who have taken other paths. To attempt to impose uniformity is to condemn ourselves to narrower and poorer lives.

It is therefore the multiplicity and totality of different languages and views of languages that contribute best to the wealth and existence of democratic states, originating from the very differences. This implies a complementary and mutual understanding where groups and individuals are entitled to keep their own languages and in the process also learn about the languages of the others. Appreciation of these differences in the language area implies the creation of realities consisting of tolerance of the differences. Multiple languages are constructive and congruent with an expanded view of language. These include infinite varieties, hybrids, fusions and endless ways of languaging, crossing language boundaries, beyond words and finite linguistic systems, incorporating multi-modal ways of representation, all of which not only have the legitimacy to exist and co-exist but together contribute to the wealth of the land. Making everybody adopt the same hegemonic language is not considered inclusion. A multiplicity of languages implies multiple routes and avenues of communication between and among people in diverse contexts. This is what brings respect and efficiency to personal choices.

Yet, these types of interactions require intensive negotiations and meaningful interactions in order to create something new that is tolerant, open and free and follows expanded views of languages and their uses. For these approaches of democracy of inclusion to take place there is a need to understand and appreciate expanded views of languages. At the same time, there is a need to become attentive to the diversity of language in the diverse societies. It requires an insight into how languages often become manipulative tools, how knowledge of certain languages is appreciated and respected while others are not, how language correctness and language purism are socially constructed with no basis in reality, how languages are used to perpetuate the status of certain groups while taking the status away from others, how languages of "the others" are used for exclusion, how people are excluded because of the languages they speak and the others which they do not and how when such exclusion occurs people should have the right to resist. Such approaches of resistance should also refer to those speaking any language in "different" styles which do not match the prescribed version that is viewed as "correct" and "pure", as these are all political and socially constructed. For that to happen there is a need for education so that the role of language within democracy will be understood as it is often the case that the role of language within democracy of inclusion is not well understood.

It also needs to be understood that most immigrants still want to assimilate substantively into the society they have entered and be accepted as full members, *but* they want to do it on their own terms, *in their own ways*, so "to reserve the right to alter the host society even as they assimilate to it" (Taylor, 1998, p. 149). Current immigrants often refuse to assume such roles as they would rather view themselves as transnationals operating in two or more states and assuming a different identity as diaspora members. They do not reject the new state, but want to exist there in different terms than in the past, rejecting the notion of *total* assimilation, as also is manifested in the type of language(s) they choose to use and learn, often developing hybrids and fusions rather than following the usual reductionist pattern of erasing past languages in favour of new ones.

This is the case of immigrants from Latin America in the USA and immigrants in Europe; they will eventually learn the dominant languages. In the USA they want to change the notion of what it means to be an American and likewise in Europe and other areas of immigration, and they are demanding to co-determine it, as a given territory does not belong only to those who were born in it, so there is no need to accept all its rules. Thus, many of the old conditions set by the state are open for discussion and negotiation as they are co-determining the future of the place by contributing to it significantly. They also feel that there is no "one way" of assimilation but rather multiple ways, especially since the culture they are joining is in a continual state of evolution, and *they* are instrumental in its change. Immigrants to the USA and foreign workers in Europe are continually changing these territories; such societies do not remain the same. There is also a view that immigrants are not a possession of a given territory but part of a global territory and that they have the right to determine its nature and identity and at the same time to continue to function in multiple places especially in a world that is not "country" bound, retaining multiple passports, multiple identities and multiple languages.

Critical awareness

Applying the democracy of inclusion to LP implies that a country is made richer with a variety of languages, options and paths for understanding. On the other hand, imposing uniformity, monolingualism, one way of speaking a language, one way of understanding, even within one language, is a poorer way of living while learning to live with differences within and among languages is a better way of living; diversity is a resource.

It further means that when democracy of inclusion is accepted, the very mechanisms described in Part II used as devices for creating de facto language policies can actually serve as devices for such negotiations. As was noted, the application of the mechanisms, as used in nation-states, have been used mostly for assimilation, perpetuating the domination of majority groups and exclusion of others, leading to the violation of democratic principles and individual rights. Yet, adopting democracy of inclusion implies the application of interactive strategies based on negotiations, representation and participation. Specifically, it is not only that everyone uses their own languages, but there is learning and study about "the others", following the complementary approaches of negotiation, representation and participation. For each of the mechanisms described in Part II there was also evidence of other voices, other discourses, often referred to as "bottom-up" voices – implying, negotiation, protest and resistance. These can be expressed through the exercise of lobbying power, courts, education and most of all awareness and activism, as will be described next.

The implication of democracy of inclusion with regard to LP is therefore the need to think differently about language, in ways which are open, dynamic, personal, free and fluid. This is different than the strict notions of purism and correctness and other myths about language with which people have been indoctrinated from early age, especially through schooling, where language is viewed as static and hegemonic, constantly judged as good/bad, accepted/rejected, and manifested through different mechanisms, especially in the context of nation-states. One way of minimizing and resisting such views of language is by promoting an awareness of language as a free entity with minimal prescriptions and boundaries that legitimizes the language of multilinguals which crosses fixed borders of languages, maneuvering among languages beyond linguistic markers. It is especially in the educational domain that such views are manifested by teachers, textbooks and tests and need to be understood and practiced. There is a need to understand that language boundaries are socially constructed while there are endless creative and natural ways of using languages which are promoted by the free expression of human beings; language is much more creative than any grammar book can describe, encompassing a variety of sources, words, combinations, synthesis, codes, images, pictures and multi-modal manifestations.

Language is a creative act that evolves and emerges freely and it is harassment to force people to use language as a closed system with rigid rules that result in categorizations and discriminations, exclusions and violations of language rights; these are based on hegemonic views of language which are associated with ethnicity, birth, nations or any other fixed categories. Further, these are rules that hardly anybody abides by and are especially problematic as they lead to what Milroy and Milroy (1999) claim is the legitimacy of written languages while de-legitimizing oral language and its multiple varieties. The new types of languages that are emerging today from the electronic media (i.e., text messages, email), provide further evidence of these creations in written form as well.

Further, there is a need to view language in broader contexts of other disciplines that are related to language, such as economics, politics, ideology, philosophy, sociology, history, law, public policy, ethnicity, gender studies and any domain where language is employed. Pennycook (2004) claims that it is time to relocate language differently, beyond the traditional disciplinary boundaries of applied linguistics, trying "to understand it within diverse contexts by drawing on other areas such as cultural studies, philosophy, literary theory, postcolonial studies, sociology, history, gender studies and more" (p. 3). Over the years, language had become the possession of a few, those who knew most about language and its rules. But there is a difference between studying how people use language and imposing on them how they *should* use it. Educationalists often adopt these descriptions and pre-scribe them as "the right way" for people to use language, especially for students in schools. Makoni and Pennycook (in press) argue that it is time "to disinvent language, to expand it, and to open it . . . to find ways of using linguistic knowledge within a broader paradigm of language studies" (p. 7).

It is often argued that language is not just the possession of linguists who have the right to impose ways of using it, but rather that language needs to be given back to the people. It is important for those who know *about* language not to force and impose laws and regulations and to allow people the liberty to use language in the best and most appropriate ways they wish. Even more important is the need to trust people that they can and will use language in ways that serve them best as it is in their interest to communicate efficiently or, at other times, to remain "vague". Whether this happens via their home languages, regional languages, national languages, global languages, transnational languages or any other hybrids, including non-verbal ones, it is their choice.

Given the arguments made earlier regarding violations of democratic principles and language rights, such views are important in the current world where nation-states consist of multilingual and diverse communities. Demanding that people use a specific homogenous, pure, "native-like" code with monolingual standards is bound to lead to violation of democratic principles and language rights. "Without strategies of dis-invention, most discussions of language rights, mother tongue education, code-switching, or language rights reproduce the same concept of language that underlies all mainstream linguistic thoughts" (Pennycook, 2004).

Lippi-Green (2000) claims that linguists know that the boundaries among languages are very vague, not only among nations but also within nations as different varieties of English exist within certain regions and territories and there is no way to wipe them out. Yet, she argues, "There is a general lack of awareness that there is a disagreement about an issue as basic as the definition of English." Specifically,

> Linguists, who are more willing to take on this topic, reject the idea of "standard" English outright and yet many of them ultimately consent to it, because while the definition is deficient in every factual way, it contains a powerful idea that most people subscribe to without thought: the belief that there is a homogenous, perfect language, a language stripped of ethnic, racial, economic, religious diversity – the one English that we should be teaching to our children, according to so many who take this as such a self evident truth that they do not even bother to articulate it.
>
> (Lippi-Green, 2000, p. 244)

Related to the conception of the expanded view of language is the learning *about* languages in schools. There are ample courses about "language correctness" and "grammar" in schools; yet there is hardly any learning about the uses and misuses of language in society, in politics, in the public space and the ways that language ideologies are used for propaganda, impositions and coercion. While students in schools do obtain instruction on racism, discrimination and stereotypes, little attention is given to issues of how languages contribute to such ideologies. Students in schools rarely receive any education about language awareness, language misuses and abuses, rights associated with language, language manipulations, and the myths surrounding the views of homogenous standards and language correctness. We applied linguists find the public are unaware of the nature of our discipline; this is still the most frequent question that we are asked: "How many languages do you speak?" Yet, upon explaining what we really do, the reactions are always deep interest and involvement. "I did not know that such a field even exists", to be followed by personal anecdotes from their own biographies about their own "language discrimination", or "language switch" or "language mixes" or "language correctness".

Reagan (2004) argues for the need to develop approaches of critical language awareness as a subset of language awareness. Such approaches are needed, given that language specialists, as well as the lay public, have generally viewed language from a perspective that is positivist in orientation.

> "When we engage in teaching languages, our goal is to move the student's linguistic behavior in the second language closer to the norms of the singular reality of that target language. What we do is to engage in the objectification of the construct of 'language', which then leads us to misunderstand the nature of language and to accept a technisist view of the teaching and learning of languages.
>
> (p. 41)

Such approaches have negatively affected language teaching as well as linguistic human rights. Critical language awareness can develop a non-objective perspective of language learning as a powerful way to promote social justice since language skills are valuable for pragmatic, social and cultural reasons as well as for political and ideological ones.

> We are required to reject the positivist objectification of language, in favor of a more complex, sophisticated, and nuanced view of language. English doesn't exist, but *Englishes* do – and understanding this distinction is the key to developing a more critical, and cogent, view of "language".
>
> (Reagan, 2004, p. 56)

Another direction of expanding the notion of language is expressed by May (2003) about the need to connect language with political theory especially since language is a contributing feature in many political conflicts in the world today. Similar criticism can be stated with regard to the lack of relevance of the historical contexts claiming the need to focus on the specific socio-historical and socio-political processes by which particular national languages have come to be created and accepted as dominant and legitimate.

It is important to become aware of the fact that many immigrants are willing to learn the dominant language(s). According to Zachary (2003), it is not a question of whether immigrants will adapt to the new society, "but to what segment of that society will they adapt?" (p. 251). He notes that assimilation "isn't an all-or-nothing gambit, or an instant transformation either. It is a long-term process . . ." and that "Nor does there exist any neat checklist of items that 'qualify' someone as a bona fide American." (p. 251).

Diversity, as noted earlier, can exist in different shapes and forms and as races, cultures and languages proliferate and flourish within a very diverse type of global context. Although the English language is flourishing as the world's lingua franca, an endless parade of new hybrid cultures and languages arise, clustered around communities of interest and practice and located in neighborhoods and cities, places and spaces. "This tendency – proliferating local identities within a global context – may get diluted over hundreds of years as future generations find their differences wearing down, like smooth rocks on an ocean beach, under the weight of close and steady contact. Yet even over a millennium, hybridity may overwhelm homogeneity". (Zachary, p. 267)

Applying critical awareness to the mechanisms

The application of critical awareness within the language policy mechanisms described in Part II is as follows.

In terms of *rules and regulations* such as officiality and declared policies, there is a need to ask questions such as: What are the intentions and motivations behind declaring certain languages as official and others not? What does it imply? It is often the case that when people realize that a certain language will become official, i.e., Spanish in the USA, they view it as a threat to their own existence rather than seeing that what it really means is that the group that does not know the power language will be entitled to comprehend and participate in the society with greater ease. It is an additive approach and not subtractive. Yet, there is a need to ask questions about the motivations of imposing requirements such as the need to take a language test to become a citizen. What are the implications? How can it hurt or help certain people in the society? Is it realistic? Similarly, questions need to be posed about the agendas behind certain rules and regulations. Will they lead to oppression or to democratization? Or to exclusion or inclusion? Who will be included or excluded? Who will benefit? When officiality is granted, does it really get implemented or is it only a declaration of intent?

With regard to *language education policies*, questions need to be asked about the assumptions these are based on. What will they do to students whose languages are not the same as the dominant ones? What are the ideologies that drove the LEP? How will they help or hurt certain students and with regard to which languages? Do they allow freedom of practice? Are these policies realistic and can they be implemented? Are they related to theories of language learning? Who was involved in arriving at these policies? Were teachers and the public at large involved in the policy decisions? Do they reflect language the way it is used by real people or only imagined intentions?

With regard to *language tests*, how are they connected to real learning? Do they reflect languages the way they are used by real people or just false criteria of language correctness? Do they encourage creative language use or do they impose and prescribe set ways of using languages and perpetuate them? Do they legitimize hybrids and natural and more free and creative ways of using languages? What are the motivations and agendas behind imposing these language tests? What will the results of the tests be in the short and long term? Will learners be able to demonstrate their knowledge in different ways? Do the tests reflect actual goals and policies or are they in contradiction to existing policies and dictate other agendas? Which languages are being tested? Which languages are not being tested? What message do they convey in terms of language use and language priorities, diversity, correctness, other languages? What use will be made of the results? Are parents aware of the power and influence of these tests, the hidden agendas and their effects on language use? Will they discriminate against certain students? Can the public resist the uses of tests? Are they open for negotiations? Will those having difficulties in performing on the tests obtain certain accommodations?

In terms of *language in the public space*, questions need to be raised as to the real influence of language in the public space on language perception, choice, status and language practice. Are people free to use their preferred languages in the public space? To what extent do the languages on public signs, consumer products, public forms discriminate against those with little or no proficiency in the dominant languages? Are signs and public announcements presented in codes that all residents of the group can understand and share? It is interesting to observe that language that is presented in a bottom-up flow is free, open, rational and expressive and legitimizes a wide variety of language options, multilingual versions, different fusions, and often does not follow strict rules of grammatical and lexical purity. It can provide an important source of legitimacy, "a different type of language" that is diverse and creative, as manifested in texts on documents, public and private signs, names of streets, people, the Internet, billboards, commercials, textual and visual images, and the wide spectrum of language displays via the Internet. These language icons can provide a significant input that can upgrade certain language varieties and downgrade others. As was noted in Chapter 7, the existence of certain languages in the public space and the absence of others has direct implications and sends a clear message about the relevance or irrelevance of certain languages as well as their speakers. Asking questions and interpreting the messages delivered from language in the public space is an important source of influence and struggle, in all directions. Protesting and resisting such domination as is done by some anti-globalization groups with regard to English is one step in the activism direction along with the understanding of rationale choice where people often choose to use power languages to obtain the benefits associated with it.

The different mechanisms, then, can provide an arena for raising questions about LP, for negotiations and for demanding inclusions, mutual interactions and resistance that can lead to the creation of new realities in multilingual societies.

Language activism

It is clear by now that LP is not neutral as it represents a significant tool for political power and manipulations. Yet, as Scollon (2004) so eloquently puts it: "I believe that only where the tools of power are openly known, openly critiqued, and accessible to everyone can anything like a true democracy work (p. 274). Linguistic activism refers to specific actions that can be taken by linguists, teachers and the public at large to open up the discussion of LP as a tool of power that should be examined and critiqued. These include taking action to protest against the uses and misuses of LP affecting language behaviors in schools and society, through political movements as well as through the judiciary systems to so protect rights and promote inclusion. Activism calls for language professionals to take an active role in leading such a discussion of an expanded view of language and by making the mechanisms and their consequences more open, less hidden and monitor their consequences and thus incorporate democracy of inclusion with regard to LP.

In fact, all the topics mentioned earlier in terms of awareness and critical views can provide arenas for such activism; these include following democratic principles, protecting rights, making people aware of language phenomena, critiquing language misuses, and opening up for discussion the hidden agendas behind certain LPs. They also include strategies for monitoring LPs and their misuses, protecting rights, encouragement of resistance, warning against misuses of language for ideological purposes and demanding participation and inclusion.

Crawford (2000) argues that language professionals have no choice but to become activists especially in the area of language minority rights: "It is understandable that researchers and practitioners would prefer to avoid political distractions. Yet, for professionals in language-minority education today, they are inescapable (p. 52)." Educators, he claims, need to increase participation in policy debate, especially in the political context which members of the public can understand and endorse.

Scovel (2000), as well, claims that in today's complex world, sociocultural pressures inevitably encourage the general populace to pursue myths, and he is not convinced that even serious efforts by applied linguists and language educators can convince people. "But, if we in the academy do not follow our consciousness and attempt to educate the public about our particular domain of inquiry, who will? For those of us who harbor special appreciation for competence in more than one language, it is all the more essential to continue to contribute our professional knowledge to raising public consciousness on these vital issues and policies" (p. 133).

Teachers, too, need to take an activist role, as they are the most important agents through which various language agendas are transmitted, since most of these changes can begin in schools. Teachers need to become active partners in LP making and not just those who carry out the policy orders and servants of the system. As was noted earlier, teachers are generally not involved in the decisions about LP and the particular languages they teach. They are also often not aware of how the languages they teach are embedded in a variety of ideological and political agendas of issues of language policies. One is inclined to see the fact that teacher education programs in many countries do not include LEP as part of teacher preparation as one reason why language teachers are not more involved. As noted earlier, the study of how to influence language education policy has not yet become an integral part of the basic intellectual preparation of language teaching professionals. As educational goals are being transformed to meet the evolving needs of increasingly diverse student populations in many countries, teachers should not view themselves as "just teaching languages", or as responsible for carrying out orders. Rather, they should view themselves as social actors who are aware of the loaded agendas that they are helping to realize through their teaching and who should, therefore, provide differentiated and well-informed input through active involvement in the creation of language education policies. It is therefore important to make teachers aware of this role by including courses of language policy and language education policies in teacher-training programs.

Roles of applied linguists

Regarding the involvement of applied linguistics, experts in the field of language continue to perpetuate criteria of language correctness and purity and rarely participate in re-educating the public about new concepts about language and about the broad repertoire of ways of using it. They are often detached from the social and political roles of the material they work with. They rarely talk about the legitimacy of language fusions and hybrids, or about languaging through other means and other linguistic markers. Language educationalists, teachers, curriculum experts, text writers and language testers, in particular, continue to perpetuate the notion of homogenous languages as they continue to use criteria that are based on language purity. Rarely do we find tests that allow mixed codes as "legitimate" and accepted ways of using languages.

There is also a need to become aware of how languages are being manipulated and the hidden agendas beyond declared language policies. This implies acquiring knowledge about the uses, misuses and manipulations of languages via the different LP mechanisms described here and elsewhere and their effects and consequences on people, education and society.

A handful of applied linguists aside, rarely do language experts come up with public statements against misuses and manipulations of languages. Rarely do language experts take part in and contribute to discussions about the social role that languages play in excluding people in violation of rights as a result of using "one hegemonic language" in the public space and by global corporations, forms of oppression and domination made *via* language, in very subtle ways. There is a need to become aware of such intentions and manipulations as well as the motivations behind language in the public space and to include it as part of the repertoire of their personal rights that people are entitled to in democratic societies.

People need to become aware of the fact that rules about using languages are driven by ideologies, by a need to control, to impose and to determine closed categories of group membership. It is the main purpose of this book to open up these issues for discussion and to reveal these hidden agendas. People should become aware of the fact that they can remain both Spanish-speaking and American, Catalan-speaking and Spanish, Arabic-speaking and Israeli as well as having a multiple of other identities, such as trans-national, global as well as a variety of multiple linguistic and national identities. Awareness of these issues can be the first step to resisting such impositions. Critical language awareness, Reagan (2004) claims, is in the final analysis, concerned with empowerment, while objectifying language means that we forget why we are teaching languages altogether.

As shown in this book, decisions about LPs are currently being challenged as questions are raised with regard to the political and ideological drives behind language policies, the legitimacy of making sweeping policy decisions for whole populations, the mechanisms by which language policy is introduced, the focus on languages as uni-dimensional units, the involvement, or lack thereof, of a more diverse constituency of citizens, the over-looking of basic democratic principles and especially the lack of involvement of the educational establishment (teachers and schools), and especially the violation of democratic principles and language rights. With so many issues, questions, criticisms, and dilemmas, one wonders whether central-ized language policies of different kinds are needed at all. For governments language is a political issue and it will always be so as long as schools are part of political structures. For speakers, however, languages are central to their individual and social identities. As was noted, decisions about languages that are imposed on whole populations, whether in schools or in society as a whole, can be viewed as contradicting the essence of individual and social freedom because languages are part of both private and social identity and group membership and not the possession of nations.

Yet, even if policies are practiced in more interactive, representational, inclusive and democratic ways that safeguard the rights of individuals, it is worth asking whether political systems or educational systems should be agencies that organize language issues through such defined and discrete categories as *number* of languages, *priority status* for languages and correct language for entire populations. Likewise we must address the fact that the different types of language policies suffer from a noticeable absence of research regarding the long-range effects and consequences of policy for different groups and individuals in different contexts, including for language learning. We know far too little about the links between LP and LEP and the broader educational, social, economic and political practices within civil societies that represent democratic pluralism. As was noted above, language scholars, particularly applied linguists, language policy experts, language teachers and language testers, must play a crucial role in addressing these issues. They are challenged to contribute to the fund of ideas regarding language in the political arena by asking themselves these hard questions: are policies needed, when, where, how and for whom and what are their consequences? Such reflections would result in proposals for flexible rather than fixed categories, would lead to policies that engage citizens rather than exclude them, would apply approaches of democratic inclusion and would position languages not as means of control, order, even oppression but as mediating tools for creating equality, sustaining rights, creating contacts, and fostering communication and mutual understanding in societies. Certainly, such reflections would have to be shaped towards society as a whole and not only within the academic community.

Activism needs to take the role of helping protect personal rights associated with language as discussed in the previous chapter. Kymlicka and Patten (2003) admit that it is not possible to avoid taking a stand on LP issues, as language rights are an integral part of other public services, such as public education. Thus, not providing such rights has major ramifications possibly preventing groups from being included and from participating in societies as was demonstrated in Chapter 5 with regard to immigrants in schools and provide help to prevent these types of failures. Granting personal rights implies that governments or others need to provide compensation for language limitations so as to maximize the social, political and educational obligations and contribution needed for proper functioning in societies. This means teaching languages, making public documents available in a variety of languages, teaching and/or testing in the other languages, various types of social and educational accommodations, public and private signs and the media. Language services need to be included for protection of personal rights of residents. Further rights include the right to use language, in private and in public spaces, the right to use language varieties that do not comply with standards, especially "vernaculars", the right to choose the language variety as well as the right to silence, the right to use language in ways that seem appropriate for users, specifically with regard to accents, hybrids, etc. Finally, the right to learn prestigious and powerful languages, whether national languages or English, which are needed for proper functioning and access in societies. These rights need to be granted to all residents, with no differentiation between those who were born in the country, those who were not and the majority groups.

Policy, practice, negotiations

This book did not solve the LP issues but it raised a variety of questions resulting from introducing a broader view of LP that incorporated mechanisms that indirectly affect de facto LP and practice. In the same way that we cannot see the de facto and real policies through declared policies, as these do not represent the real policies, any changes in policy towards a democracy of inclusion and personal rights need to take place in the broader view incorporating these mechanisms.

Policies provide a reflection, a mirror, of the complexities and power struggles of society and too often they serve as tools in these struggles. LP often falls in the midst of two forces, of those attempting to view policy as an oppressive tool for control and those viewing it as constructive tool that can allow freedom of expression and creativity in language. LPs do not stand alone; not only do they serve as manifestations of political, social and economic agendas, they also emerge from the view of the essence of language itself. The types of violations of democratic processes and language rights of current LP do not originate from nowhere but are a product and an agent of creating misconceptions of language itself. Linguists started describing how people speak, how they use language, but it is on that basis that politicians, educators and others started communicating to people how they *should* use language. From there it was a short way to indoctrinating language by various interested bodies as language turned into another form of political oppression. Yet, the main point made is the need to undo these concepts of language and LP in an expanded view. It was shown how the mechanisms provide tools to perpetuate oppressive LP that can lead to the violation of rights and democratic principles *but also* act as forms of negotiation. Thus, by accepting a view of language as open, free and fluid, the mechanisms can provide effective tools for redefining language and for establishing LPs that can be used for creating the broad variations of languages in societies and for protecting those who pay the price for closed and restricted views of LP.

The mechanisms need to be interpreted as providing a better insight into how LP is carried out, but also viewing them as legitimate tools of negotiating and battling with language ideologies and agendas as part of democratic practices. In other words, if LP is defined in broader terms, beyond the explicit conscious decisions about languages, and they need to be included in order to obtain a more accurate picture of policy, then what is the difference between policy and practice? In the case of language tests, designed explicitly to assess language, but along the way contributing to language policies that determine language hierarchies, language correctness and the suppression of certain languages while empowering others, what is the difference between LP and language practices? Is it possible that once LP is defined in that way, there is no real difference between the two, as one influences and affects the other? Similarly, with language in the public space, there are mutual discourses taking place at the same time and not always top-down vs. bottom-up; it seems to be much more chaotic, and dynamic, and in constant negotiation in different points in time, as can be closely observed in the use of electronic language, in different places by different agents with regard to text, styles, genres, correctness, etc.

It seems that at this point there is a close interaction between the mutual effects of policies and practices, with no clear differentiation. Language realities are at times part of explicit policies, as with declared and regulated documents or as with language education policies. Yet, at other times they are "side effects" of "non-intentional" language policies, as with language tests or with language in the public space. But it is in combination, through the mechanisms, as well as other devices that are not discussed in this book, that language practice and policies are created, via negotiations, discussions, propaganda, all introducing different discourse into the LP and language practice and creating language realities. Language policy, then, as a field is a much more complex phenomenon in which multiple discourses, multiple agendas are brought up, presented, discussed, negotiated and fought in complex and unpredictable ways. It seems, therefore, that there is a need to examine, study and understand LP in the more integrated context of the policies and practices of societies in a variety of entities and categories – individuals, groups, nations, transnationalism and everything in between. Within this complex reality, there are still major issues in language that need to be addressed, incorporating the different policies and practices.

The claim of this book was that LP is created via different mechanisms that affect language practices, then practices affect policies as well. English is taught at an early age, as a result of a certain understanding of the global map by people, this is done in a bottom-up way, creating de facto policies, that then affect other policies, or perhaps no declared policies are ever made about it. At this point, as well, a complex and sophisticated discourse is taking place between those who do it on a very local level ("for my own kids") and national declared policies ("to do it for all" or "it will destroy national unity"). It is policy at the local or individual level that affects declared policies, and these may affect or be affected by educational policies, by testing policies, by ideologies and rationale choices. Likewise, when certain languages cease to be used, whether as a conscious decisions or not, these practices may affect declared policies, the visibility of languages in the public space, testing policies, media policies, etc.; but together they make up a variety of language realities which are a product of constant negotiations and struggles. It is therefore important to have open dialogues and negotiations about this dynamic process of decisions and practices that are based on an educated view of languages, their impact, motivations and meaning.

A number of points need to be inferred from the discussion in this book. The first is the awareness of the variety of ways in which policies are made, focusing mostly on the implicit ones and the realization of their consequences in terms of the specific mechanisms, discussed here. The second, resulting from the first, is the phasing of boundaries between policy and practice. Policy is practice and practice is policy as languages are discussed, negotiated and battled for using a multiplicity of discourses in very complex ways and on a fluid and dynamic basis. The mechanism is one such discourse. Third, there is a need to constantly evaluate the effects and consequences of these and other mechanisms in terms of democratic processes and personal rights. Fourth, when the effects are known, there is a need to ask what can be done about it. In other words, the need of all those participating in societies to continually dialogue and negotiate as well as struggle about language issues. Fifth, there is a need for the public to become aware, familiar with and knowledgeable about languages as a significant component of existence and rights in democratic societies that must be discussed and negotiated. For that there is a need for the public to shed stereotypes and myths about languages, to become aware of the issues, and to open them up for discussion like any other issue in democratic societies. Finally, there is a need to understand the value of the mechanisms as policy devices that can be used by *all* agents in society for negotiation and policy making. Although, as was noted, those in authority often have more access to these mechanisms, there are ample opportunities and possibilities for exercising influence, for negotiation and protesting through language awareness and activism and continuous conversation. It is important to understand that a test is not "just a test" and that when its negative ramifications for certain people are known to be damaging personal rights or democracy of inclusion, it can lead to various types of protest, via the media, lobbying groups, etc. But at the same time, these tests can become tools for negotiation as well.

LP, then, is a dynamic process that must be observed in all its discourses and complexities and its full ramifications are still not known. There is great significance in discussing and arguing these issues so that languages can serve as tools for meaningful communication and interaction and at the same time be prevented from being harmful.

Summary

- Language policy is made in a number of ways, both implicit and explicit.
- Language policy and language practice influence each other in very complex and dynamic ways.
- Language policy mechanisms should be regularly monitored and evaluated in order to ensure that personal rights are protected.

- People need to be made aware of the centrality of language as a social and political issue.
- Individuals at all levels of society need to question language policy and seek ways of renegotiating it. Policy devices are mechanisms that should be open to negotiation by everyone.

Epilogue: Language as a free commodity

Language is like life. There is an aspiration for order, for control, for possession, driven by fear of the unknown, of the powers and sources of evil. But there is always the reality that language, like life, cannot be controlled. Language, like life, is bigger than any one of us. We can go through language, like life; we can be with language, like life; we can use it, but we cannot control it. We can try to create all kinds of controlling devices – rules, regulations, laws, correctness, categories, policies, impositions; in life we also create ceremonies, anniversaries, prayers, rituals, insurances and other devices, all through the desire to impose order; but it does not work.

The author Primo Levi wrote about two opposing philosophical views in *The Periodic Table* (1984). One is "the praise of purity, which protects from the evil like a coat of mail" and the second "the praise of impurity, which gives rise to changes, in other words to life". Levi rejected the first as being "disgustingly moralistic" and opted for the second, "which I found more congenial. In order for the wheel to turn, for life to be lived, impurities are needed, dissension, diversity, the grain of salt and mustard are needed" (p. 34).

This is the story of language as depicted in this book. Language is a living thing, an organism; terms such as "good", "bad", "correct", "incorrect", "clean", "dirty", "high", "low" just do not apply; they are totally irrelevant. Language flows, it goes in all directions, it is full of "salt" and "mustard", but these are essential ingredients for its creation, for its main trait, for its essence, a living organism; it is fluid and flowing and goes in all places, in all shapes and forms; it is a free commodity, subject to each person's interpretation.

Yet, there are constant efforts to capture it, to control it, to possess it, to colonialize it, as it is so closely integrated with people, their beings, their identities. It is a unique trait of language that it is so personal; it is so much a part of us, of our bodies, of our souls, of our mouths, of our brains, of our hearts. Controlling language is a way of controlling us. For people, though, the power of language is also the power to reshape, to protest, to denounce oppression and resist its domination.

The writer Salman Masalha, an Israeli Palestinian, describes his on going relationship with the Hebrew language as evolving over time, from a language he felt was imposed on him, to a situation of curiosity, to viewing it as a threat, to a language that he feels he now owns, possesses and often uses for writing his stories and poetry.

Salman Masalha was born in the Arab village of Maghar, in Israel, and defines himself as "the second generation of the Nakba" (the Palestinian catastrophe of 1948). Salman Masalha speaks Arabic and writes in both Arabic and Hebrew. In the film *Misafa Lesafa* (From Language to Language), he explains the complex relationship with both languages over time.

> For me, Literate Arabic (versus the vernacular) is like a foreign language, as it was acquired in school but it is not a language I use at home. Hebrew is the language that was "imposed" on me. With time it has special charm of something new I learned in school; it later turned into some "foreignness" especially when I realized that the new state imposed a new language and culture. But at a later point, I realized that the Hebrew language I acquired turns out to be my own possession; very different than what those who imposed it on me actually meant.

Hebrew, in fact does not belong any longer to the Jews alone, but to everyone who speaks it and everyone who writes in it. The Jews revived spoken Hebrew, and destroyed other languages along the way; but now it belongs to all those who want to possess it. The Jewish founders of the Hebrew language never intended that someone, like Salman Masalha, would take possession of their ideological tool and start owning it. Yet, he concludes: "By means of the Hebrew language . . . not only [do] I gain ownership, I also strengthen my own ownership of this place". The Hebrew language is repossessed.

This statement summarizes the main essence of this book. In comparison to all kinds of biological features and categories, such as colour, blood, looks and gender, language has a major advantage: it is a free and open commodity that can be moulded, used and shaped in different ways and forms, according to what the user wants it to become. Hebrew was the language that was moulded and shaped by the Zionist ideologues as the prime symbol of the collective identity of the Jewish people in their new homeland. Spoken Hebrew, for a long time, was nobody's language. Then, the Jews reacquired it, repossessed it, reshaped it and started using it as *their* symbol, as an ideological tool, taking it over and in this journey recaptured it. They fought against all other Jewish languages, which were considered enemies of spoken Hebrew, including vivid languages such as Yiddish, that have been used by Jews for generations.

It is ironic that Jews should use a language as a symbol of group identity having used no one spoken language anywhere they have lived. In fact, as Hutton (1999) argues, the trait of not sticking to a specific spoken language was held against the Jews by the Nazis as part of their anti-Semitic and racist ideology.

For Jews were held to lack a sense of loyalty to their mother-tongue, and were therefore regarded as having an "unnatural" relationship to language. Jews lived in many countries and spoke many tongues; they were rootless nomads with loyalty only to their race. The separation of mother-tongue and race meant that language for them was an instrument of communication only, and a means of entry into other cultures and countries. Furthermore, Judaism was built on veneration of a sacred language, and that sacred language was not the mother-tongue. Jews, given that their culture was based on a separation of the sacred and the vernacular, could maintain their identity across different cultures and language situations. In contrast, German identity was inextricably tied to the mother-tongue.

(Hutton, 1999, p. 5)

Through Salman Masalha's words, it is possible to observe the lack of boundaries among languages. For him, he notes both Hebrew and literate Arabic have the same status, they are both "acquired", foreign languages as they were both acquired in school, very different than the "home" language. Yet, these languages are both being viewed as Arabic. Both these languages are distant from his home language, which is the only language he feels close and attached to. Languages cannot be defined *for* us, but they are defined *by* us according to our relationship with the language and what it means or us.

Eva Hoffman, as well (1989, p. 120), writes about how individuals can use any language as a tool: "The more words I have, the more distinct, precise my perceptions become – and such lucidity is a form of joy." (pp. 28–29); yet, she shows how these words helped her give meaning to the new world. Hoffman positions her choice to write in English in contrast to the state of immigration, in which she had no choice. Language is a free choice we make according to different criteria that are relevant for us. Eva Hoffman chose to write in English, not only because of the language practice, but also because she felt that the English language was the language of the present and that the documentation in her personal diary was documentation of the present, while the language of her mother – Polish – was an indication of the past:

I open the diary and close it again. I can't decide. Writing in Polish at this point would be a little like restoring to Latin ancient Greek – an eccentric thing to do in a diary, in which you are supposed to set down your most immediate experience and unpremeditated thoughts in the most immediated language. Polish is becoming a dead language, the language of the untranslatable past.

(Hoffman, 1989, p. 120)

Although she chose to write in English in order to write about her present life, from an identity perspective she found it difficult to use "I" and used "you". The writing in the diary is about herself but also about others. "The diary is about me and not about me at all." English for her is termed "my public language". Thus, writing in English helps her get closer to her new acquired identity that was created due to the immigration. The use of English thus enables her to "invent another me" (p. 121). Therefore, the choice is not an easy one and often points to the multiple identities, whether they are immigrants or not.

It is Hebrew, then, that was moulded to become the language of choice for the new Jewish Zionist ideology, a symbol of belonging, of renewal, of revival, of creating a new identity. This is why it is ironic that Hebrew, a symbol of the Jewish revival, of the new collective identity of Jews from the end of the nineteenth century, is becoming now, over a hundred years later, a language of identity, as well as a form of ideology or communication also by other users, immigrants as well as those who have been in this land long before, of the Israeli Arabs living in Israel. Language is a free commodity; it can be used by anyone in any way they want, to shape it, and to reshape it; it is a free choice.

For now, it is Salman Masalha who claims that he owns Hebrew; it is *his* language and it cannot be taken away from him. He acquired it. He now uses the Hebrew language for his own agendas noting that it is through the knowledge of the Hebrew language, a language that was a strict symbol of inclusion and belonging to the Zionists in Israel, that he finds a sense of territorial ownership. Language, in contrast to other "things", such as land, territory and biological traits, that are constant and cannot be changed and are often used for all kinds of racist ideas, *is* a free commodity to be used in ways that anyone wishes to. Although the freedom of language should not always be taken for granted; the right to use language, to speak it, does not exist in totalitarian societies; freedom of language is not always "a given".

But once there is free choice about using language, it is clear that it is far superior, far better, and much less limiting than other traits, as it is free. Thus, Zionists captured Hebrew and manipulated it to *their* needs, as a symbol of ideology, of belonging, of patriotism, of loyalty. Along the way, they excluded all those who could not learn it, who dared to use other languages, those who resented the language ideology; they were all excluded, taken out, gatekept away by those who used it as the ideological symbol. Now they have succeeded: everybody is using Hebrew; it is a power language in Israel; it is considered "a national" language.

But knowing a language does not give you the privilege to exclude others; you thought that through the language you would be able to control others, to include only Jews and exclude non-Jews; to perpetuate this idea, you even "allowed" the Arabs to use their own language (Arabic) in schools, to keep them even farther away. Yet, language is a free commodity: anybody can use it; it belongs to all; it is a truly democratic commodity; almost everybody can have the right to use it.

So the Arabs learned Hebrew, in a similar way that the Jews learned and acquired perfect German in Germany. When a group identifies a power tool that will give them what they view as opportunities, hope, a way out of frustration, even if it turns out to be a fallacy, they make the effort to obtain it; it is still "hope". There are almost as many public signs nowadays in Arab towns in Hebrew as there are in Arabic. So the first generation of Arabs may speak the language with an accent, but by the time the second and third generations use Hebrew, there will not be any difference from the Jews who speak it. They will acquire it fully, they will speak it, and like Salman Masalha, they will be bilingual in Arabic *and* Hebrew, speaking and writing in both languages and in a variety of hybrids of the two languages. Language is free, can be moulded in different directions and possessed by all.

"Who owns English?" is a question frequently asked about the language that has become the "world" language, the main means of communication, with no exclusive ownership of anybody. English is a free commodity as well, it is free to be used, shaped and moulded by anybody in different ways, as is the case for its million users who construct and create endless types of "Englishes". English does not belong to anybody specific, not to a nation, not to a group, it belongs only to those who want to own it.

A similar statement is echoed in post-colonialist countries by those who were raised in the colonies, such as in India or Hong Kong. English is their language; the colonizer cannot simply leave and take everything back without leaving any traces.

Yet, at the same time, and as was shown in the book, language is probably the most manipulated tool. Politicians make use of language for their own sake, people use language to claim ownership, associations and disassociations. But, again, compared to other "markers" in society, language is milder and is more flexible; it can be acquired in one generation or less. It is a more powerful tool for resistance than any other markers and identifiers, such as race, color or looks.

Language, then, is free in comparison to other biological factors. Thus, language, vs. other commodities or other biological factors, can be acquired to an almost "native-like" level in one or two generations, in spite of such limitations as "native-like" or "non-accent" proficiency. This is the advantage of language over other biological features – it can be acquired and changed. Hitler noted it about the Jews. While Hitler originally did refer to the different German dialects as identifiers and markers of regions as described by Hutton (1999), once the Jews acquired German and spoke like natives, and could recite Goethe by heart, he realized that language could not serve as a race marker, it could not serve his racist agenda of the purity of the race. So he did not include language as part of the definition of race. Hutton writes: "The German Jew who could speak German perfectly was a talking proof that the boundary was insecure, that the bounds of language were weak, and that it was possible to pass promiscuously from one language to another; Jews were native speakers of German and were not considered German" (Hutton, 1999).

Given the above, those who speak other languages have major advantages compared to those who speak majority and power languages, as they are able to choose. They have the best of both worlds, providing that they have the opportunities.

Yet, in this situation as well, their own groups often feel threatened by them being bilinguals as betraying the loyalty to the group. One wonders how the peers of Salman Masalha react to his statement that he writes in Hebrew. At each phase, and by each group, regardless of size, there will always be those who will try to manipulate and control language, as betraying the language is viewed as betrayal of the group and its loyalty and solidarity. It is then that they will use the variety of mechanisms to perpetuate these agendas.

This is why education is so needed, to undo such views, to realize, to understand the freedom of language. If language is, in fact, a free commodity, it also means that the rights of those who do not want to acquire it, or cannot learn it, or do not have opportunities, are also respected and protected. They should not be "forced" to acquire it, not feel humiliated, excluded or discriminated against if they do not acquire it.

In many ways, language is like wealth, like happiness; it is good to have, but people should not be held responsible or discriminated against if they do not have it. We need to trust people and their willing or unwillingness to communicate in the way that best suits them and to leave them alone with regard to how they choose to do so, not to force them into using it in specific ways. Rather, people should be allowed the freedom to choose to use languages in the best way for their diverse needs.

Educational systems should not feel they need to mould children into using languages in "their" ways. Rather, children and adults should be given the opportunity and space to choose how to use language, to legitimize options, to offer communication repertoires, to offer acceptance and to encourage values of tolerance and justice and to denounce irrelevant language features. There is a need to democratize language, to free it of society's manipulations, of imposing policies. Languages are there to use and they can be used in different shapes and forms.

It is the duty and obligation of linguists to make language users aware of these misuses of language and resist manipulations. Manipulations occur all the time but it is the extent to which the public is aware of these manipulations that makes a difference. Once they are aware, they can protest and resist, as they have already done with advertisements and other propaganda. Big corporations and powerful governments will always make efforts to blind people so they will not be aware of manipulations, fearing that they may refuse to be manipulated and make "educated" choices and decisions regarding their actions, to buy or not to buy, to learn the language or not, to use it in their own personal ways. The public has been blind to language and its uses for a very long time. These are the hidden agendas this book has tried to reveal.

It is therefore necessary for people to cherish language and guard against its enemies, those who want to lock it in a closed box and manipulate it for their own needs, to encourage its use as a free commodity and to protect it from misuse. Language should be protected against those who want to destroy its free nature and its free spirit as this is the true value and strength of language.

Because language *is* like life:

> I am energy – changing, evolving, weak at times, potent and powerful at others – merging with experiences, transforming from these mergers and then detaching and taking on a new meaning and form due to those mergers. But the light, energy, matter, remains unique, connected by sequence of history, experiences in a chain that define me and give me this ever so subtle unique distinction.
>
> (Orlee Shohamy, n.d.)

Bibliography

Akinnaso, F. N. 1989: One nation, four hundred languages: Unity and diversity in Nigeria's language policy. *Language Problems and Language Planning* 13(2): 133–46.

Auerbach, E. 2000: When pedagogy meets politics: Challenging English Only in adult education. In R. Duenas Gonzalez and I. Melis (eds.), *Language ideologies: Critical perspectives on the official English movement.* Mahwah, NJ: Lawrence Erlbaum, 177–204.

Augé, M. 1995: *Non-places: Introduction to an anthropology of supermodernity.* Trans. J. Howe. London and New York: Verso.

Baldouf, R. 1994: "Unplanned" language policy and planning. *Annual Review of Applied Linguistics* 14: 82–9.

Barron-Hauwaert, S. 2003: Parental strategies in the trilingual family: Five case studies. Abstract included in the program of The Third International Conference on Third Language Acquisition and Trilingualism. Tralee, Ireland, September 4–6, 2003, p. 18.

Barron-Hauwaert, S. 2004: *Language strategies for bilingual families: the one-paren-one-language approach.* Clevedon: Multilingual Matters.

Barthes, R. 1985: *The responsibility of forms.* New York: Hill and Wang.

Bauman, R. and Briggs, C. 2003: *Voices of modernity: Language ideologies and the politics of inequality.* Cambridge: Cambridge University Press.

Ben Rafael, E. 1994: *Language, identity and social division: The case of Israel.* Oxford: Oxford University Press.

Ben Rafael, E., Shohamy, E., Amara, M. and Trumpe-Hecht, N. 2004: Linguistic landscape and multiculturalism: A Jewish-Arab comparative study. Tel Aviv: The Tami Steinmetz Center for Peace Research.

Ben Rafael, E., Shohamy, E., Amara, M. and Trumpe-Hecht, N., 2006: Linguistic landscape as a symbolic construction of the public space: The case of Israel, *International Journal of Multilingualism,* 3, 1, 7–31.

Bialystok, E. 2001: *Bilingualism in development.* Cambridge: Cambridge University Press.

Bourdieu, P. 1991: *Language and symbolic power.* Cambridge, MA: Harvard University Press.

Broadfoot, P. 1996: *Education, assessment and society: A sociological analysis.* Buckingham: Open University Press.

Brutt-Griffler, J. 2002: *World English.* Clevedon: Multilingual Matters.

Brutt-Griffler, J. 2004: Introduction. *International Journal of Bilingual Education and Bilingualism* 7(2): 93–101.

Brutt-Griffler, J. and Varghese, M. 2004: Introduction. *International Journal of Bilingual Education and Bilingualism* 7(2/3): 93–101.

Butler, J. 1997: *Excitable speech: A politics of the performative*. London: Routledge.

Butler, J. 1999: Performativity's social magic. In R. Shusterman (ed.), *Bourdieu: a critical reader*. Oxford: Blackwell, 113–28.

Byram, M. 1989: Intercultural education and foreign language teaching, *World Studies Journal* 7(2): 4–7.

Byram, M. and Guilherme, M. 2000: Human rights, cultures and language teaching. In A. Osler (ed.) *Citizenship and democracy in schools: Diversity, identity, equality*. Stoke-on-Trent: Trentham Books, 63–78.

Byram, M. and Risager, K. 1999: *Language teachers, politics and cultures*. Clevedon: Multilingual Matters.

Byrnes, H. 2005: Perspectives. No child left behind, *Modern Language Journal* 89: 2.

Calvino, I. 1985: *Mr. Palomar*. Orlando, FL: Harcourt Brace.

Cameron, D. 1995: *Verbal hygiene*. London: Routledge.

Cameron, D. 1998: *The feminist critique of language: A reader*. London: Routledge.

Cenoz, J. and Gorter, D. 2006: Linguistic landscape and minority language. *International Journal of Multilingualism* 3, 1, 71–85.

Crawford, J. 2000. Proposition 227: A new phase of the English Only movement. In R. Duenas Gonzalez and I. Melis (eds), *Language ideologies: Critical perspectives on the official English movement*. Mahwah, NJ: Lawrence Erlbaum, 114–37.

Crowley, T. 1996: Signs of belonging: Languages, nations and cultures in the old and new Europe. In C. Hoffman (ed.), *Language, culture, and communication in contemporary Europe*. Clevedon: Multilingual Matters, 47–60.

Crystal, D. 2000: *Language death*, Cambridge: Cambridge University Press.

Crystal, D. 2004: *The stories of English*. New York: Overlook Press.

Cummins, J. 1996: *Negotiating identities: Education for empowerment in a diverse society*. Ontario, CA: California Association for Bilingual Education.

Cummins, J. 2000: *Language, power, and pedagogy: Bilingual children in the crossfire*. Clevedon: Multilingual Matters.

Davies, A. 1997: Demands of being professional in language testing. *Language Testing* 14(3): 328–39.

Dawson, R. 2001: *The treaty of Waitangi and the control of language*, Institute Policy Studies, Victoria University.

de Swaan, A. 1998: A political sociology of the World Language System: The unequal exchange of texts. *Language Problems and Language Planning* 22(2): 109–28.

de Swaan, A. 2004: Endangered languages, sociolinguistics, and linguistic sentimentalism. *European Review* 12(4): 567–80.

Dewey, J. 1916/1985: *Democracy and Education*.

Doyé, P. 1992: "Fremdsprachenunterricht als Beitrag zu tertiärer Sozialisation." In D. Buttjes, W. Butzkamm and F. Klippel (eds), *Neue Brennpunkte des Englischunterrichts*. Frankfurt A.M.: Peter Lang, 280–95.

Edwards, J. D. 2004: The role of languages in the post-9/11 United States. *Modern Language Journal* 82: 268–71.

Errington, J. 2001: Colonial linguistics. *Annual Review of Anthropology* 30: 19–39.

European Commission 1996: *Teaching and learning. Towards the learning society*. Brussels: European Commission.

Fairclough, N. 1989: *Language and power.* London: Longman.

Fishman, J. 1998–9: The new linguistic order. *Foreign Policy,* 26–40.

Fishman, J. A. 1991: *Reversing language shift: Theoretical and empirical foundations of assistance to threatened languages.* Clevedon: Multilingual Matters.

Fishman, J. A. 2000: The status agenda in corpus planning. In Lambert, R. and Shohamy, E. (eds), *Language policy and pedagogy.* Philadelphia, PA: John Benjamins, 43–51.

Fishman, J. A. 2001: Can threatened languages be saved? *Reversing language shift, revisited: A 21st century perspective.* Clevedon: Multilingual Matters.

Foucault, M. 1979: *Discipline and punish.* New York: Vintage Books.

Garcia, E. 2000: Treating linguistic and cultural diversity as a resource: The research response to the challenges inherent in the improving America's Schools Act and California's Proposition 227. In Duenas Gonzalez, Roseann and Melis, Ildiko (eds), *Language ideologies: Critical perspectives on the official English movement.* Mahwah, NJ: Lawrence Erlbaum, 90–113.

Giles, H. 1977: *Language, ethnicity and intergroup relations.* London: Academic Press.

Glinert, L. 1996: Product safety information and Language policy in an advanced Third World economy. The case of Israel. *Journal of Consumer Policy* 19: 411–38.

Gubbins, P. and Holt, M. 2002: *Beyond boundaries: Language and identity in Contemporary Europe.* Clevedon: Multilingual Matters.

Handoko, F. 2003: Nine codes, three generations, one family: Types and functions of intergenerational code-switching in an ethnic Chinese family in Surabaya, Indonesia. Abstract included in the program of *The Third International Conference on Third Language Acquisition and Trilingualism.* Tralee, Ireland, September 4–6, 2003, p. 33.

Helot, C. 2003: Language policy and the ideology of bilingual education in France. *Language Policy* 2(3): 255–77.

Hoffman, E. 1989: *Lost in translation: A life in a new language.* London: Penguin Books.

Honey, J. 1989: *Does accent matter?* London: Faber and Faber.

Honey, J. 1997: *Language is power: The story of standard English and its enemies.* London: Faber and Faber.

Hopper, P. 1998: Emergent grammar. In M. Tomasello (ed.), *The new psychology of language.* Mahwah, NJ: Lawrence Erlbaum, 155–75.

Hornberger, N. 2002: Multilingual language policies and the continua of biliteracy: An ecological approach. *Language Policy* 1(1): 27–51.

Huebner, T. 2006: Bangkok's linguistic landscape: Environmental print, code mixing, and language change. *International Journal of Multilingualism,* 3, 1, 33–54.

Hutton, C. 1999: *Linguistics and the Third Reich.* London and New York: Routledge.

Kaplan, R. and Baldouf, B. 1997: *Language planning from practice to theory.* Clevedon: Multilingual Matters.

Kloss, H. 1971: Language rights of immigrant groups. *International Migration Review* 5(2): 250–68.

Kloss, H. 1977: *The American bilingual tradition.* Rowley, MA: Newbury House.

Kress, G. 2003: *Literacy in the new media age.* London: Routledge.

Kress, G. and van Leeuwen, T. 1996: *Reading images – the grammar of visual design.* London: Routledge.

Kubchandani, L. 2003: Defining mother tongue education in plurilingual contexts. *Language Policy* 2(3): 239–54.

Kubchandani, L. M., 1997: Language policy and education in the Indian subcontinent in Wodak, R. and Corson, D. (eds.) *Encyclopedia of Language and Education*, vol. 1, pp. 197–8. Dordrecht: Kluwer Academic Publishers.

Kymlicka, W. 1995: *Multicultural citizenship: A liberal theory of minority politics.* New York: Oxford University Press.

Kymlicka, W. and Patten, A. 2003: Language rights and political theory. *Annual Review of Applied Linguistics* 23: 3–21.

Lambert, R. 1995: Language policy: An Overview. Paper presented at the Language Policy conference, Bar Ilan University, Israel.

Landry, R. and Bourhis, R. Y. 1997: Linguistic landscape and ethnolinguistic vitality: An empirical study. *Journal of Language and Social Psychology* 16(1): 23–49.

Lantolf, J. and Thorne, S. (in press): *Sociocultural theory and the genesis of second language development.* Oxford: Oxford University Press.

Lefebvre, H. 1991: *The production of space.* Oxford: Blackwell.

Levi, P. 1984: *The periodic table.* New York: Schocken Books.

Levin, T., Shohamy, E. and Spolsky, B. 2003: *Academic achievements of immigrants in schools.* Report submitted to the Ministry of Education (in Hebrew).

Lippi-Green, R. 1997: *English with an accent.* London, Routledge.

Lippi-Green, R. 2000: That's not my language: The struggle to (re)define African American English. In R. Duenas Gonzalez and I. Melis (eds), *Language ideologies: Critical perspectives on the official English movement.* Mahwah, NJ: Lawrence Erlbaum, 230–47.

Luke, A. 2004: Two takes on the critical. In B. Norton and K. Toohey (eds), *Critical pedagogies and language learning.* Cambridge: Cambridge University Press, 21–9.

Makoni, S. 1998. African languages as European scripts: The shaping of communal memory. In S. Nuttall and C. Cotzee (eds), *Negotiating the past: The making of memory in South Africa.* Cape Town: Oxford University Press, 242–9.

Makoni, S. 2002: From misinvention to disinvention of language: Multilingualism and the South African Constitution. In S. Makoni *et al.* (eds), *Black linguistics: social and political problems of languages in Africa and the Americas.* London: Routledge, 132–53.

Makoni, S. and Pennycook, A. 2005: "Disinventing and (Re)Constituting, Languages". *Critical Inquiry in Language Studies: An International Journal*, vol. 2, no. 3, 137–56.

May, S. 2001: *Language and minority rights.* London: Pearson Longman.

May, S. 2003: Misconceiving minority language rights: Implications for liberal political theory. In W. Kymlicka and A. Patten (eds), *Language rights and political theory.* Oxford: Oxford University Press, 124–52.

Mesthrie, R., Swann, J., Deumert, A. and Leap, W. 2000: *Introducing sociolinguistics.* Amsterdam: John Benjamins.

Messick, S. 1981: Evidence and ethics in the evaluation of tests. *Educational Researcher* 10: 9–20.

Messick, S. 1994: The interplay of evidence and consequences in the validation of performance assessment. *Educational Researcher* 23: 13–23.

Messick, S. 1996: Validity and washback in language testing. *Language Testing* 13(4): 241–57.

Messick, S. 1998: Validity. In R. L. Linn (ed.), *Educational measurement* (3rd edn). Washington, DC: The American Council on Education and the National Council on Measurement in Education, 13–103.

Milroy, J. and Milroy, L. 1999: *Authority in language. Investigating standard English* (3rd edn). London: Routledge.

Moll, L. 1992: Funds of knowledge for teaching: Using a qualitative approach to connect home and classrooms. *Theory and Practice* 31(2): 132–41.

Mitchell, W. J. T. 1986: *Iconology*. Chicago, MI The University of Chicago Press.

Nafisi, A. 2003: *Reading Lolita in Teheran*. New York: Random House.

Pavlenko, A. 2003: Language of the enemy: Foreign language education and national identity. *International Journal of Bilingual Education and Bilingualism* 6(5): 313–31.

Pennycook, A. 1994: *The cultural politics of English as an international language*. Harlow: Pearson Education.

Pennycook, A. 2001: *Critical applied linguistics*. Mahwah, NJ: Lawrence Erlbaum.

Pennycook, A. 2004: Performativity and language studies. *Critical Inquiry in Language Studies: An International Journal* 1(1): 1–26.

Pennycook, A. 2005: Language policy and the ecological turn. *Language Policy* 3(2): 213–39.

Phillipson, R. 1992: *Linguistic imperialism*. Oxford: Oxford University Press.

Phillipson, R. 2003: *English-Only Europe? Challenging Language policy*. Routledge: London.

Reagan, T. 2004: Objectification, positivism and language studies: A reconsideration. *Critical Inquiry in Language Studies: An International Journal* 1(1): 41–60.

Ralston Saul, J. R. 2004: The collapse of globalism, *Harper's Magazine* March, 33–43.

Recommandation du Comité des Ministres aux États membres R(98) 6, issue du Projet "Apprentissage des langues et citoyenneté européenne", qui a été conduit au sein du Comité de l'Education de 1989 à 1996.

Recommandation 1383. 1998. de l'Assemblée parlementaire du Conseil de l'Europe, consacrée expressément à la "Diversification linguistique".

Ricento, T. (ed.) 2006: *An Introduction to Language Policy: Theory and Methods*. Oxford: Blackwell Publishing.

Romaine, S. 2005: "The impact of language policy on endangered languages". In M. Koenig and P. De Guchteneire (eds), *Democracy and Human Rights in Multicultural Societies*. Aldershot: Ashgate/UNESCO.

Romaine, S. 2002: "Signs of identity, signs of discord: glottal goofs and greengrocer's glottal in debates on Hawaiian orthography". *Journal of Linguistic Anthropology* 12(2): 189–224.

Safran, W. 1999: "Nationalism". In J. Fishman, *Handbook of Language and Ethnic Identity*. OUP Inc.

Schiffman, H. 1996: *Linguistic culture and language policy*. London: Routledge.

Schmidt, R. 2000: *Language policy and identity politics*. Philadelphia, PA: Temple University Press.

Scollon, R. 2001: *Mediated discourse: The nexus of practice*. London: Routledge.

Scollon, R. 2003: *Discourses in place: Language in the material world*. London: Routledge.

Scollon, R. 2004: Teaching language and culture as hegemonic practice. *Modern Language Journal* 82: 271–4.

Scovel, T. 2000: "The younger, the better" myth and bilingual education. In R. Duenas Gonzalez and I. Melis (eds), *Language ideologies: Critical perspectives on the official English movement*. Mahwah, NJ: Lawrence Erlbaum, 114–37.

Segev, T. 1999: *Palestine under the British*. Jerusalem: Keter Publishing House (in Hebrew).

Shain, Y. 1999: *Marketing the American creed abroad. Diasporas in the U.S. and their homelands*. Cambridge: Cambridge University Press.

Shain, Y. (in press): *Kinship and diasporas in international affairs*. Michigan University Press.

Shain, Y. and Barth, A. 2003: Diasporas and international relations theory. *International organization* 57: 449–79.

Shohamy, E. 1994: Issues of language planning in Israel: Language and ideology. In Lambert, R. (ed.), *Language planning around the world: Contexts and systemic change*. Washington, DC: National Foreign Language Center, 131–42.

Shohamy, E. 2001: *The power of tests: A critical perspective of the uses of language tests*. Singapore: Longman.

Shohamy, E. 2003: Implications of language education policies for language study in schools and universities. *The Modern Language Journal* 87: 278–86.

Shohamy, E. 2004: Assessment in multicultural societies: Applying democratic principles and practices to language testing. In B. Norton and K. Toohey (eds), *Critical pedagogies and language learning*. New York and London: Cambridge University Press, 72–93.

Shohamy, E. 2005: The power of tests over teachers: The power of teachers over tests. In D. J. Tedick (ed.), *Second language teacher education: International perspectives*. Mahwah, NJ: Lawrence Erlbaum Associates, Inc. 101–11.

Shohamy, E., Donitsa-Schmidt, S. and Ferman, I., 1996: Test impact revisited: washback effect over time, *Language Testing*, 13, 3, 298–317.

Shohamy, E. and Donitsa-Schmidt, S. 1998a: *Language proficiency of immigrants at the work place*. Sapir Center for Research, Tel Aviv University.

Shohamy, E. and Donitsa-Schmidt, S. 1998b: *Jews vs. Arabs: Language attitude and stereotypes*. The Tami Steinmetz Center for Peace Research, Tel Aviv University.

Shohamy, O. 2000–1: Collecting numbers. *Black Book*, 168.

Skutnabb-Kangas, T., 1995: *Multilingualism for all*. Lisse: Swets and Zeitlinger.

Skutnabb-Kangas, T., 2006: Language policy and linguistic human rights in Ricento, T. (ed.) *An Introduction to Language Policy: Theory and Methods*, pp. 273–91. India: Blackwell.

Spolsky, B. 1998a: What is the user's perspective in language testing? Paper presented at the colloquium, *The State of the Art in Language Testing: The Users' Perspective*, National Foreign Language Center, The Johns Hopkins University, Washington, DC, 15 June.

Spolsky, B. 1998b: The ethics of gatekeeping tests: What have we learned in a hundred years? *Language Testing* 14(3): 242–7.

Spolsky, B. 2004: *Language policy*. Cambridge: Cambridge University Press.

Spolsky, B. and Cooper, R. 1991: *The languages of Jerusalem*. Oxford: Clarendon Press.

Spolsky, B. and Shohamy, E. 1999: *The languages of Israel: Policy, ideology and practice*. Clevedon: Multilingual Matters.

Stein, P. 2004: Representation, rights, and resources: Multimodal pedagogies in the language and literacy classroom. In B. Norton and K. Toohey (eds), *Critical pedagogies and language learning*. Cambridge: Cambridge University Press, 95–115.

Steiner, G. 1975: *After Babel*. Oxford: Oxford University Press.

Steiner, G. 1998: *Errata: An examined life*. New Haven, CT and London: Yale University Press.

Sudjic, D. and Jones, H. 2001: *Architecture and democracy*. Glasgow: Laurence King Publishing.

Tankersley, D. 2001: Bombs or bilingual programmes: Dual-language immersion, transformative education and community building in Macedonia. *Bilingual Education and Bilingualism* 4(2): 107–24.

Tannenbaum, M. 2003: The multifaceted aspect of language maintenance: A new measure for its assessment in immigrant families. *Bilingual Education and Bilingualism* 6(5): 374–93.

Taylor, C. 1998: The dynamics of democratic exclusion. *Journal of Democracy* 9: 143–56.

Tokuhama-Espinosa, 2003: The multilingual mind: Issues discussed by, for and about people living with many languages. Praeger Pub. Text.

Tollefson, J. 1995: "Introduction" in Language policy, power, and inequality. In J. Tollefson (ed.), *Power and inequality in language education*. London: Cambridge University Press.

Tollefson, J. 2002: *Languages policies in education. Critical issues*. Mahwah, NJ: Lawrence Erlbaum.

Trim, R. 2002: The lexicon in European languages today: Unification or diversification? In Gubbins, P. and Holt, M. (eds), *Beyond boundaries*. Clevedon: Multilingual Matters.

Valdes, G. 2004: Between support and marginalisation: The development of academic language in linguistic minority children. *International Journal of Bilingual Education and Bilingualism* 7(2 & 3): 102–32.

Vygotsky, L. S. 1978: *Mind in society* (M. Cole, V. John-Steiner and E. Sauberman, eds and trans.). Cambridge, MA: Harvard University Press.

Vygotsky, L. S. 1981: The genesis of higher mental functions. In J. V. Wertsch (ed.), *The concept of activity in Soviet psychology*. Armonk, NY: Sharpe, 144–8.

Waggoner, D. 2000: The democratics of diversity in the United States. In R. Duenas Gonzalez and I. Melis (eds), *Language ideologies: Critical perspectives on the official English movement*. Mahwah, NJ: Lawrence Erlbaum, 5–27.

Yudovitch, D. 2004: Spring of strength, *Essence Magazine*, March–April 2004.

Zachary, P. 2003: *The Diverstiy Advantage*. Boulder, CO: Westview Press.

Zuckerman, G. 2003: *Language contact and lexical enrichment in Israeli Hebrew*. London and New York: Palgrave Macmillan.

Index

Lightning Source UK Ltd.
Milton Keynes UK
UKOW03f2213090813

215068UK00003B/77/P